SIXTH EDITION

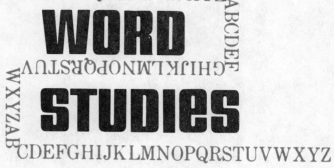

ABCDEFGHIJKLMNOPQRSTUVWXYZ

WORD
STUDIES

CDEFGHIJKLMNOPQRSTUVWXYZ

by

MARION M. LAMB

Sacramento State College
Sacramento, California

E59

Published By

SOUTH-WESTERN PUBLISHING CO.

Cincinnati   Chicago   Dallas   New Rochelle, N.Y.   Burlingame, Calif.   Brighton, England

Standard Book Number: 0-538-05590-1
Library of Congress Catalog Card Number: 73-132967

6 7 8 9 0 H 3 2 1 0 9

Printed in the United States of America

PREFACE

In this Sixth Edition of *Word Studies*, first emphasis is still upon correct spelling but with new emphasis on word structure and word histories (etymology). Word meanings have been made more precise and many words have been added to the book. Technological developments produced floods of new words during the 1960's and some of the most commonly used ones have been included in this volume.

Word Studies has been reorganized into four parts:

Part 1. Introduction to Words: Dictionary usage and an introduction to phonetics

Part 2. Word Structure: Prefixes, word roots, suffixes, compound words, syllabication, plurals, and possessives

Part 3. Basic Words: Homonyms, antonyms, synonyms, troublesome words, names of states and state capitals, abbreviations

Part 4. Enriching Your Vocabulary: Words relating to special areas of interest

Lessons have been grouped for easy learning, with every fifth lesson a review lesson and with spaced general reviews to provide additional challenge. Additional tests are available upon request.

The Third Edition of *Webster's New International Dictionary of the English Language* and its portable companion volume, *Webster's Seventh New Collegiate Dictionary,* are the basic authorities for the definition and spelling of vocabulary words in this book. The pronunciation key of the Second Edition is used, however. The G. & C. Merriam Company, publisher of Merriam-Webster dictionaries, refers to the simplified pronunciation key of the Third Edition as a "transitional compromise."

In a rapidly changing world, our spelling has remained relatively unchanged since the eighteenth century. The importance of spelling has changed, however. With the increasing volume of written communication in business and personal life, accuracy in spelling has become more important than it was in the 1700's, the 1800's, or in the early years of this century. Efforts at "spelling reform" have come to nothing and readers of this book may be confident that what they learn today is good for a lifetime.

Using *Word Studies*

For best results in spelling practice, you should get a pocket-size notebook, divide it into alphabetical sections, and record in the appropriate sections all the words that you misspell. To do this, you should have the notebook with you daily; it will become your personal speller.

Most important is your realization of the value of language to you. Development of word awareness and word mastery is likely to be a slow growth dependent upon sustained interest. Therefore, do not rush at these lessons in an impatient, do-or-die spirit; instead, be leisurely and observant in your approach, remembering that your usage of words tells a great deal about you, and therefore word study is worth your most careful attention.

The study of words is rewarding to those who recognize its importance. Failure to recognize its importance is almost certain to be expensive, since we communicate with others through words and we are consequently judged to some extent by the words we use and the way we use them.

The author believes that you will be more interested in words after you have read this book and completed the exercises in it. Words can be interesting, but they are like people—you have to know them to appreciate them.

Acknowledgments

Many authorities have contributed to the Sixth Edition of *Word Studies*. Three members of the California Writers' Club, in addition to the author, are represented. These eminently qualified writers have contributed lessons that are authoritative and up to date.

Miss Elizabeth Schwartz, Chairman of the English Department at the John F. Kennedy Senior High School in Sacramento, and co-author of a series of English textbooks;

Miss Victoria Schwartz, author of numerous articles and stories for young people and a writing aide for the Hospitalized Veterans Writing Project of the National Rehabilitation Service; and

Mr. Waldo T. Boyd, an electronics engineer and technical writer in engineering and business, author of *Your Career in the Aerospace Industry* (a 1966 selection of the Junior Literary Guild) and two subsequent books: *Your Career in Oceanology* and *The World of Cryogenics*.

The author is also indebted to the many teachers who have submitted comments and suggestions for this edition.

Marion M. Lamb
Sacramento, California

ABCDEFGHIJKLMNOPQRS CONTENTS
TUVWXYZABCDEF

PART 1   INTRODUCTION TO WORDS

Lesson   **Page**

   History of the English Language   3
1 Using the Dictionary   5
2 Vowel and Consonant Sounds   7
3 Classification of Words   8
4 Spelling Hints   9
5 **Review**   10

6 Phonetics   11
7 Phonetics   12

PART 2   WORD STRUCTURE

8 Prefixes   15
9 Suffixes   16
10 **Review**   17

11 Words Beginning With "Com," "Con," or "Co"   18
12 Words Beginning With "De" or "Ex"   19
13 Words Beginning With "Im" or "In"   20
14 Words Beginning With "Inter" or "Re"   21
15 **Review**   22

16 Words Beginning With "Mis" or "Dis"   23
17 Words Beginning With "Sub" or "Un"   24
18 Prefixes Signifying Numbers   25
19 Words Beginning With "Ante," "Fore," or "Pre"   26
20 **Review**   27

21 Words Ending in "Ance" or "Ence"   28
22 Words Ending in "Or"   29
23 Words Ending in "Ment"   30
24 Words Ending in "Tion," "Sion," or "Cian"   31
25 **Review**   32

26 Words Ending With "Able" or "Ible"   33
27 Words Ending With "Ar"   34
28 Words Ending With "Ant" or "Ent"   35
29 Words With "Ary," "Ory," or "Ery"   36
30 **Review**   37

Lesson		Page
31	Verbs Ending in "Ize," "Ise," or "Yze"	38
32	Verbs Ending in "Ate," "En"	39
33	Words Ending in "Ly," "Ward," or "Wise"	40
34	Words Ending in "Er"	41
35	**General Review**	42
36	Rules Governing Suffixing	44
37	Rules Governing Suffixing	45
38	Rules Governing Suffixing	46
39	Rules Governing Suffixing	47
40	**Review**	48
41	Use of the Hyphen	49
42	Use of the Hyphen	50
43	Word Division	51
44	Word Division	52
45	**Review**	53
46	Plural Forms of Nouns	54
47	Plural Forms of Nouns	55
48	Plural Forms of Nouns	56
49	Plural Forms of Nouns	57
50	**Review**	58
51	Plural Form of Nouns	59
52	Plural Form of Nouns	60
53	The Apostrophe	61
54	The Apostrophe	62
55	**General Review**	63

PART 3 BASIC WORDS

Lessons 56-75: Pronunciation

56	Pronunciation Symbols	67
57	Pronunciation of Vowels	68
58	Pronunciation of Consonants	69
59	Silent Consonants	70
60	**Review**	71
61	Syllable Trouble	72
62	The Nonexistent Syllable	73
63	Pronouncing Syllables Which Do Exist	74
64	Pronunciation Demons	75
65	**Review**	76

Lesson		Page
66	Words With Two Pronunciations	77
67	Noun or Verb?	78
68	Noun or Adjective?	79
69	Versatile Words	80
70	**Review**	81
71	Names of Well-known Persons	82
72	Places at Home and Abroad	83
73	Foreign Words and Expressions	84
74	Foreign Words and Expressions	85
75	**General Review**	86

Lessons 76-85: Homonyms, Antonyms and Synonyms

76	Homonyms, Antonyms, and Synonyms	88
77	Spelling of Homonyms	89
78	Function of Homonyms	90
79	Spelling of Homonyms	91
80	**Review**	92
81	Antonyms	93
82	Choosing the Right Synonyms	94
83	Meaning of Synonyms	95
84	Vocabulary Enrichment	96
85	**General Review**	97

Lessons 86-105: Troublesome Words

86	Words Often Misused	99
87	Words Which Sound Alike	100
88	Words Which Sound and Look Alike	101
89	Words Often Misused	102
90	**Review**	103
91	Words Often Misused	104
92	Choosing Appropriate Words	105
93	Correct Word Usage	106
94	Correct Word Usage	107
95	**Review**	108
96	Specific Words vs. General Words	109
97	Specific Words vs. General Words	110
98	Using Appropriate Words	111
99	Using Technical Words	112
100	**Review**	113

Lesson		Page
101	"Ie" and "Ei" Combinations	114
102	"Ie" and "Ei" Combinations	115
103	Words With Double Letters	116
104	Words Frequently Misspelled	117
105	**Review**	118

Lessons 106-110: States, State Capitals, and Abbreviations

106	States and Their Capitals	119
107	States and Their Capitals	120
108	Major Cities in the United States	121
109	Common Abbreviations	122
110	**General Review**	123

PART 4   ENRICHING YOUR VOCABULARY

111	Law	127
112	Government	128
113	Government	129
114	Politics	130
115	**Review**	131
116	Space Exploration	132
117	Nuclear Energy	133
118	Automation and Data Processing	134
119	Modern Technology	135
120	**Review**	136
121	Literature	137
122	Literature	138
123	Art and the Dance	139
124	Music	140
125	**Review**	141
126	Education	142
127	Education	143
128	Education	144
129	Religion	145
130	**General Review**	146
131	Theater	148
132	Food and Dining	149
133	Health	150
134	Clothing and Fashion	151
135	**Review**	152

Lesson		Page
136	Hobbies	153
137	Athletics	154
138	Recreation	155
139	Travel	156
140	**Review**	157
141	Communications	158
142	Radio and Television	159
143	Newspapers and Magazines	160
144	Printing and Publishing	161
145	**General Review**	162
146	Business	164
147	Bookkeeping and Accounting	165
148	Agriculture	166
149	Textiles	167
150	**Review**	168
151	Money and Banking	169
152	Investments	170
153	Risk and Insurance	171
154	Real Estate	172
155	**Review**	173
156	Labor and Industrial Relations	174
157	Marketing	175
158	Transportation	176
159	Transportation	177
160	**General Review**	178

Part 1

ABCDE
FGHIJKLMNO

Introduction to Words

Part One includes a brief history of the English language, followed by seven lessons on dictionary practice. Emphasis is given to word elements such as vowels, consonants, diphthongs, digraphs, blends, syllables, and phonetic markings of words. Also presented are suggestions for spelling improvement that require awareness of some of these word elements. Mastery of this first section will enable you to profit from later lessons in *Word Studies.*

A BRIEF HISTORY OF THE ENGLISH LANGUAGE

Modern English is to a great extent a Romance language, although historians classify it as a Germanic language. English is considered a Germanic language for two reasons: first, because the words of Old English were chiefly Germanic (sometimes called Teutonic); and second and probably more important, the short words of Old English that have survived the test of time are the ones that we use most in our daily lives. Words such as *mann* (man), *wīf* (wife), *cild* (child), *hūs* (house), mete (meat, food), *etan* (eat), *drican* (drink) and *libban* (live) are part of our everyday vocabulary.[1]

Modern English contains words from many countries and tribes involved in England's history, and more recently from those involved in American history. Development of the modern English language may be divided into three approximate periods, which were actually overlapping.

Old English	450 A.D. to 1150 A.D.
Middle English	1150 A.D. to 1500 A.D.
Modern English	1500 A.D. to the present time

In 43 A.D. Britain was invaded by the Romans. The Roman influence modified the Celtic language of upper-class Britons, but it did not greatly affect the speech of the peasants.

In the fifth century, after the Romans left Britain, the country was invaded by Teutonic tribes (about 410 A.D.)—the Jutes, the Angles, and the Saxons. They settled in Britain, naming the country Angle-land (later England). Anglo-Saxon became the language of the land.

We date the beginning of Old English from this Anglo-Saxon period. Before 500 A.D., written language was virtually unknown in Britain, and to have an accurate history, language must be recorded.

Middle English developed following the conquest of the English by the Norman French in 1066. English reflects the influence of three centuries during which French was the official language in Britain. Words such as *noble, dame, servant, feast, government, alliance, theology, prayer, apparel* and *jewel* indicate the Norman culture from which they came.[2]

Modern English dates from the Renaissance in England (around 1500) to the present time. During the Renaissance, with its emphasis on classical learning, many Latin and Greek words were added to the

[1] Albert C. Baugh, *A History of the English Language* (2nd ed., New York: Appleton-Century-Crofts, Inc., 1957), p. 63.
[2] *Ibid.*, pp. 201-203, 205.

English language. In our twentieth-century scientific world, we are still adding words derived directly from the Latin and the Greek: *astronaut, aquaplane, automobile, telephone, electronics, nuclear, atomic*—to mention just a few derivatives.

It has been said that an Englishman of 1300 would not have understood either the English of 500 A.D. or that of today. The language of a people changes with its history, and this fact can be seen in the history of our language. The English language has been enriched by words from every part of the world. Words such as *skunk, hickory, squash, caribou,* and *pecan,* for example, were adopted from the American Indians.

Diversity makes English a wonderful language to use, but a difficult one to learn. Not until the eighteenth century was a dictionary of English words available to standardize spelling. Samuel Johnson's *Dictionary of the English Language,* issued in 1775 was a milestone, although we consider it inadequate today. In 1828 Noah Webster's *American Dictionary of the English Language* was issued.

There are still many inconsistencies in our spelling. *Night, thought,* and *height*—to mention just three words—are not spelled according to pronunciation. At the time the spelling of these words was established, however, the *gh* sound was pronounced. Despite the fact that modern pronunciation is sometimes at variance with spelling, it is still useful to look for relationships between the two. Similarly, we look at word structure in an effort to determine meaning.

English is the native language of more people in the world than any other language except Chinese. It is a popular second language, and in many countries is considered necessary for those who aspire to positions of leadership. It is worthy of our best efforts.

The following illustration charts the development of English:

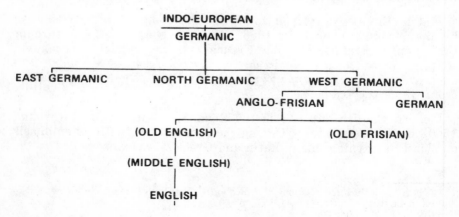

1

USING THE DICTIONARY

Do you know the types of information available to you in a good collegiate dictionary? In an unabridged dictionary? Examine the large dictionaries in your school library. Ask your librarian about the differences between the Second Edition and the Third Edition of *Webster's New International Dictionary of the English Language.* (Some authorities prefer the Second Edition.) Look at the portable dictionaries, starting with *Webster's Seventh New Collegiate Dictionary.* Which one would you like to own?

Specialized Dictionaries. There are many kinds of dictionaries. Some dictionaries trace word origins and histories. Others emphasize vocabulary for specialized areas such as business or medicine. *A Dictionary of Modern English Usage,* by H. W. Fowler, revised and edited by Sir Ernest Gowers, compares British and American usage and pronunciation. *The Reader's Digest Great Encyclopedic Dictionary* contains French, German, Spanish and English words, as well as sections on word origins, the history of writing, and American slang. There are dictionaries of geographical names and dictionaries of biographical names.

Many dictionaries include pictures, charts and maps to help explain the meaning and function of certain words. A list of abbreviations used in writing and printing, the names of the presidents of the United States, and the names of accredited colleges and universities may be included.

In *Word Studies,* we are concerned primarily about the spelling, pronunciation, and meanings of words so that they will be used more effectively. To be precise in using words that reflect our exact meaning, we need to know something about word origins and the structure of words. To be correct in writing words, we need to know not only spelling but also the rules for capitalization, syllabication, the use of hyphens in compound words, and other technical matters. All of this information is to be found in the *Merriam-Webster* dictionaries, for example, and in other dictionaries of comparable size and quality.

Syllabication. As you can see in the example on the following page, the correct syllabication of a word is shown when it has more than one syllable. The proper accents are also indicated for each word. A syllable is accented when it is stressed or pronounced with more force than the other syllables, as in *act' ed.* Some words have two syllables accented, as in *su' per in tend'.* The syllable receiving the greater stress is indicated by a heavy accent mark, called *the primary accent.* The syllable receiving only slight stress has *the secondary accent.* Syllabication of words helps in writing them correctly. Accenting the syllables aids in pronouncing the words correctly.

Locating a word in the dictionary. Study the example below taken from a page of *Webster's Seventh New Collegiate Dictionary:*

abdomen   2   abolitionist

syn RENOUNCE, RESIGN: ABDICATE implies a giving up of sovereign power or sometimes an evading of responsibility such as that of a parent; RENOUNCE may replace it but often implies additionally a sacrifice for a greater end; RESIGN applies to the giving up of an unexpired office or trust
ab·do·men \'ab-də-mən, ab-'dō-mən\ *n* [MF & L; MF, fr. L]
1 : the part of the body between the thorax and the pelvis; *also* : the cavity of this part of the trunk containing the chief viscera **2** : the posterior section of the body behind the thorax in an arthropod — **ab·dom·i·nal** \ab-'däm-ən-ᵊl\ *adj* — **ab·dom·i·nal·ly** \-ē\ *adv*
ab·dom·i·nous \ab-'däm-ə-nəs\ *adj* [L *abdomin-, abdomen*] : big‑bellied
ab·duce \ab-'d(y)üs\ *vt* [L *abducere*] : ABDUCT
ab·du·cent \ab-'d(y)üs-ᵊnt\ *adj* [L *abducent-, abducens,* prp. of *abducere*] *of a muscle* : ABDUCTING
ab·duct \ab-'dəkt\ *vt* [L *abductus,* pp. of *abducere,* lit., to lead away, fr. *ab-* + *ducere* to lead — more at TOW] **1** : to carry off

By permission. From *Webster's Seventh New Collegiate Dictionary* © 1970 by G. & C. Merriam Co., Publishers of the Merriam-Webster Dictionaries.

All words in the dictionary are arranged alphabetically. Using the example above, how would you locate the word *abduct?* First you would turn to the section devoted to words beginning with the same letter as the word you wish to find, in this case *a.* At the top of each page are two guide words; these are the first and the last words on the page. You will find *abduct* listed alphabetically between the guide words *abdomen* and *abolitionist.* This is the quickest method for locating a word in the dictionary. Notice that the word is printed first in heavy type. When two spellings are given in heavy type, both are correct.

Assignments

A. Write the exact name of your dictionary and its date of publication. Locate the following words, recording the guide words on the pages containing the words. Syllabicate and accent each word.

character	significant
effective	understanding
management	until
necessity	valid
ordinary	wholly

B. Look up the following words in your dictionary and record their meaning. Use each one in a sentence.

deficient	miscellaneous
discourse	negligible
fabricate	peripheral
integrity	reservoir
linguistic	transcend

ABCDEFGHIJK**LESSON** **2**

VOWEL AND CONSONANT SOUNDS

Pronunciation. In your dictionary, find the word *calculate*. Notice that the pronunciation of the word is shown in parentheses: (*căl′ cŭ lāte*). The pronunciation may be shown with diacritical marks, as in the above example, or the word may be spelled in phonetic symbols that correspond to the sound of each letter. Explanation of the pronunciation marks may usually be found in the introductory pages of the dictionary. To avoid confusion, phonetic spelling is used as little as possible in this book. Our emphasis is on the one correct spelling of each word or, in some cases, the two spellings allowed.

Vowel sounds. Vowels are the trouble-makers in spelling because they have so many sounds. Following is a list of the long and short vowel sounds. Other vowel sounds are presented in Lesson 7.

Long vowel sounds	Short vowel sounds
ā as in dāy, māke, lābor	ă as in ăm, măn, răndom
ē as in ēve, mēal, serēne	ĕ as in ĕnd, mĕnd, ĕxcuse
ī as in īce, mīle, sīgh	ĭ as in ĭll, mĭll, admĭt
ō as in ōar, ōld, bōld	ŏ as in ŏdd, nŏt, lŏt
ū as in dūe, mūte, tūbe	ŭ as in ŭp, tŭb, stŭdy
ȳ as in stȳle, mȳ, flȳ	y̆ as in pity̆, my̆th, busy̆

Consonant sounds. Following are the ways of marking consonant sounds used in this book:

s pronounced as *z* may be marked ṣ, as in wiṣdom
c ordinarily has the sound of *k*
c pronounced as *s* may be marked ç, as in niçe
g has a hard sound, as in game
g with a soft sound may be marked ġ, as in enġine
th has a soft sound, as in health
th with a heavy sound may be marked as t̶h̶, as in t̶h̶at

In this book silent consonants and vowels are italicized, with the exception of silent *e* at the end of a word. When two vowels come together with only one sounded, the vowel sounded is marked, and the silent vowel is not italicized.

Assignments

A. Indicate the correct pronunciation of each of the following words by marking vowel and consonant sounds.

facilitate	ghost	hypocrite	invalidate	khaki
fulfill	guarantee	initial	juice	manage

B. Syllabicate the following words, indicate accents, and mark vowel and consonant sounds:

animal	brought	encyclopedia	martyr
annual	certain	harmonious	material

CLASSIFICATION OF WORDS

Following is an example of a typical dictionary entry:

bar' rel   (băr' ĕl)   *n.* [*ME.* barel, *fr. OF.* baril]

Following the pronunciation of the word, the part of speech is indicated. The word *barrel* is shown to be a noun by the *n.* following its pronunciation. Three classes of words—(1) pronouns such as *he* and *it;* (2) conjunctions such as *but* and *or;* and (3) interjections such as *oh*—include words that are so common that they do not appear in this book. Some words may be classified as more than one part of speech depending upon their use. The following abbreviations of the parts of speech used by most dictionaries will be used:

adjective *adj.*	noun *n.*	verb *v.*
adverb *adv.*	preposition *prep.*	

The material in brackets traces the etymology of the word; i.e., its origin. In the example above, *ME.* is the abbreviation for *Middle English; fr.* stands for *from;* and *OF.* refers to *Old French.* The Middle English and the Old French spellings of the word are given in the brackets. These abbreviations and others are explained in the table of abbreviations in the first pages of the dictionary.

Verbs. In the following example, you will note that the principal parts of *rise* are given because *rise* is an irregular verb; it does not form its past and past perfect tenses in the usual way. The principal parts of *raise* are not given. It is a regular verb because its past forms follow the usual pattern: *raise, raised, raised.*

rise (rīz) *vi;* rose (rōz) ; ris en (rĭz' en) ; ris ing (rīz' ing)
      [*ME.* risen, fr. *O.E.* risan]

raise (rāz) *vt;* [*ME.* raīsen, fr. *ON.* reisa]

Verbs are further classified as either transitive (*t*) or intransitive (*i*). *Rise* is intransitive because it does not act upon an object, but *raise* is transitive because it can act upon an object.

The mists *rise.* The moon *rises* later each evening.
(There is no object acted upon in either sentence.)

She *raised* funds for the festival. I *raise* the window.
(Both sentences contain objects. Can you name them?)

Assignments

A. Indicate the parts of speech for the following words. Mark each verb as either *vt* or *vi.* (Some words may be used in various constructions; in these cases, indicate all parts of speech for the words.)

Example: mean, n ... adj ... vt ... vi ...

correct	expect	mean	perform	prove	retire	would
crowd	honor	occupy	please	rest	waste	yield

B. Indicate the etymology of *crimson, follow, finance, jute.*

8

SPELLING HINTS

The most important factor in developing spelling competence is the desire to improve. Notice words carefully. Read. Pronounce words carefully. If you mispronounce a word, you will probably misspell it. Have a clear mental picture of the word as it looks when spelled correctly. If you should see a word with which you are thoroughly familiar, such as *first* written *frist,* you would know immediately that it was misspelled because the word would look wrong. Knowing the spelling rules that are presented on the following pages—and applying them—will also help.

Steps in Spelling Improvement

1. Look carefully at the word so that you will have a mental picture of it.
2. Pronounce the word aloud. Think of its meaning.
3. Spell the word aloud, syllable by syllable, several times.
4. Give special attention to the vowels. If, for example, you have the word *specimen,* notice that it is spelled with *e* (men) not *a.* Also notice any silent letters in the word.
5. With eyes closed, pronounce the word. Try to recall how it looks. Spell it slowly.
6. Write the word from memory. Decide whether it looks right. Refer to the textbook to see whether it is correct. If you make an error, restudy the word.
7. Record each word you misspell syllable by syllable. Underscore the syllables that have been misspelled.
8. Look for a pattern in your errors and diagnose the reason for them. Do you skip syllables? Do you miss easy or difficult words? Learn from your mistakes.

Develop word awareness by listening to the words you hear each day. Improve your vocabulary by selecting precise words that best express your meaning. In most dictionaries, more space is devoted to the meaning of words than to any other type of information. It is essential to learn the various meanings of a word at the time that you learn to spell and pronounce the word.

Assignment

Following are twelve words that cause problems even for expert spellers. Copy the words. Beside each word write its pronunciation and meaning. Underscore the syllables likely to cause trouble in spelling.

ecstasy	irrelevant	privilege
exhilarate	liquefy	rarefy
hypocrisy	naive	sacrilegious
indispensable	pneumonia	supersede

REVIEW

A. Write the following words in syllables; insert accents and mark vowel and consonant sounds.

absolutely	coordination	received
accommodation	determine	reelect
accumulate	experiment	satisfaction
business	gasoline	scientific
cooperate	preempt	yesterday

B. The underlined words in the following sentences may be used as more than one part of speech. How are these words used in these sentences? Write the abbreviation for the part of speech of each underlined word.

1. Is this guarantee good for one year?
2. The average score was 88.
3. Please put these umbrellas in the corner.
4. Bill could not disguise his voice.
5. These votes should reflect individual preferences.
6. Why did you mention the error?

C. The word *allow* may mean (1) provide (2) permit (3) tolerate. Choose the definition that applies to each of the following sentences:

1. Allow an inch for the bottom margin of each page.
2. You are allowed to visit patients in the afternoon.
3. How much money have you allowed for the printing?
4. We will not allow safety hazards in this laboratory.

D. The word *exercise* may mean (1) activity (2) drill (3) use. Choose the definition that applies to each of the following sentences:

1. Have you completed the last exercise on page 14?
2. Walking to work provides enough exercise for me.
3. Will you exercise your option in this matter?
4. This finger exercise is excellent for typists.

E. The following words may be spelled in two ways. Give the alternate spelling for each word.

acknowledgment	gray	benefited
counselor	instill	peddler
good-by	medieval	judgment

LESSON **6**

PHONETICS

In phonetic spelling, we spell by sound. *Rough* becomes *rŭf*, *raise* is *rāz*; and *sale* is *sāl*. The diacritical marks over the vowels indicate the vowel sounds, and distinguishing marks or letters indicate the sound of consonants. In this book, we rely upon diacritical marks rather than phonetic spelling to indicate correct pronunciation.

The schwa. In many dictionaries, all unstressed vowels are represented by an inverted "e," called the *schwa*. This mark, "ə," is used for the "a" in *alone*, for example; the "e" in *listen*; the "i" in *clarity*; the "o" in *felon*; and the "u" in *bogus*.

Diphthongs. A vowel diphthong is formed by pronouncing one vowel after another in the same syllable, as in *oil*, *toy*, *out*, *now*. Imperfect or partial vowel diphthongs include "ew," "ue," "au," and "ŏŏ."

There are two consonantal diphthongs: "ch" as in *change,* and the letter "j," a combination of "d" and "zh."

Digraphs. A vowel digraph is a combination of two vowels with only one of the vowels pronounced, usually with the long vowel sound, as in *read, boat, mail.*

A consonant digraph also represents a single speech sound, but this sound is different from the sound of either of the consonants. Consonantal digraphs include final "gh" as in *tough*; "ng" as in *sing*; "sh" as in *wish*; voiced "th" as in *those*; voiceless "th" as in *thin*; "ph" as in *phrase*; "wh" as in *what*; and "wh" as in *who*.

In other words, consonants in a digraph combine to form a distinctive sound different from the individual consonants, whereas vowel digraphs have the long sound of one of the vowels.

Consonant digraphs are not to be confused with consonant blends. Consonant blends are common consonant combinations in which the letters retain their individual identity: "bl" as in *black*; "pl" as in *please*; and "spl" as in *splash*.

Assignment

Underline diphthongs once and digraphs twice.

believe	deceive	main
boys	diphthong	south
chain	fail	this
chair	laugh	mouth
contain	load	pamphlet

11

PHONETICS

Consonants. There are 25 consonant sounds in English. They are classified as voiced (heavy) and voiceless (light). For each voiceless consonant except "h," there is a corresponding voiced consonant.

Voiced	Voiceless	Voiced	Voiceless
b as in *bay*	*p* as in *pay*	*d* as in *do*	*t* as in *to*
g as in *gale*	*k* as in *kale*	*v* as in *van*	*f* as in *fan*
z as in *zinc*	*s* as in *sink*	*th* as in *either*	*th* as in *ether*
w as in *wear*	*wh* as in *while*	*zh* as in *treasure*	*sh* as in *wash*

Sometimes "h" is a voiced consonant, as in *hall*. Voiced consonants not listed above are "l," "m," "n," "r" and "y."

Vowels. Difficulties in reading and writing English words lie with the five vowels—"a," "e," "i," "o," "u"—plus "y," which is sometimes used as a vowel. In Lesson 2 we covered the long and short vowels, which are easy to recognize. Following is a list cf other vowel sounds, including vowel diphthongs that are preceded by an asterisk.

ã as in cowãrd
â as in âir, câre, pârent
ä as in ärm, fär, fäther
à as in àsk, gràss, plàster
a̤ as in a̤ll, ta̤lk, la̤wn
a̤ as in wa̤n, wha̤t, qua̤lity
á as in grádation, vácation
a as in allot, annual
*au as in author
ê as in thêir, whêre
ẽ as in hẽr, gẽrm, makẽr
e̥ as in pre̥y, obe̥y, de̥ign
é as in évent, dépend
ēe as in ēel, knēe, nēed
e as in apparel, silent
*ew as in few
ï as in pïque, polïce
ī as in fīrd, bīrd, shīrk

ī as in ice
õ as in minõr
ô as in ôrb, lôrd, côrk
ȯ as in dȯve, ȯther, sȯme
o as in woman
o̥ as in do̥, who̥, pro̥ve,
ó as in óbey, própose
ǒ as in sǒft, wrǒng
ōō as in ōōze, fōōd, mōōn
*o͝o as in fo͝ot, wo͝ol, bro͝ok
û as in ûrge bûrn, fûrl
u̥ as in ru̥de, ru̥ral, intru̥de
u as in put, full, push
ú as in únite, formúlate
ǔ as in previoǔs, circǔs
*ue as in blue
*oi, oy, as in oil, boy, toy
*ou, ow, as in out, owl

Assignment

Copy the following words, circling all voiced consonants and marking the sound of each vowel.

admire	early	growth	months
appeal	easier	losing	other
breath	dozen	kitchen	railroad
citizen	etch	machine	realize
cloth	edge	message	school

Part 2

Word Structure

Word families, like human families, branch from common ancestors. In the English language, these ancestors, known as word roots, come from many sources, with the most dominant influences from the Teutonic and the Romance languages. These roots combine with various prefixes and suffixes, most of which originated in Latin or Greek, to produce a variety of words. After you learn to recognize common word roots and affixes, you will be able to detect meaning in words unfamiliar to you.

ABCDEFGHIJKLESSON 8
PREFIXES

A prefix is a combination of letters placed before a word or word root to modify meaning. Among the common Latin prefixes are "ab," "ad," "bi," "com," "contra," "dis," "ex," "in," "inter," "intra," "intro," "per," "post," "pre," "sub," "super," and "trans." Some of the less common Greek prefixes are "anti," "apo," "dia," "hemi," "meta," and "para." Other prefixes that can be traced to Latin and Greek origins have been modified through usage in other languages: "a," "ac," "ag," "ant," "be," "col," "con," "de," "di," "mis," "pur," and "sup."

Consider the Latin word *vertere,* meaning "to turn." We have the word root in our language in two forms: "vert," and "vers." We can construct a variety of words, each with a different meaning, by adding prefixes to these roots.

con + vert = *convert,* a noun meaning *one who has turned with.*
dis + vert = *divert,* a verb meaning *to turn aside.*
re + vert = *revert,* a verb meaning *to turn back, return.*
ad + verse = *adverse,* an adjective meaning *turned against.*

Remember that a prefix modifies (that is, changes) the meaning of a word.

Assignments

A. Consult your dictionary for the meaning of the following prefixes:

col, com, con *with, near*   ex, e *without, out of* *free of*   intro *into, w/in* *inward*   re *back, again, anew*
de *away from, off*   im, in, un *no, not, non* *without*   pre *before* *in front of*   sub, sus, suf *under, below* *beneath*
dis *opposite, away, apart*   inter *between, among*   pro *before, forward* *for*   trans *across, over*

B. The following examples give the word root, its source, and one English derivative. Using the prefixes in Exercise A, build two more words for each word root.

Word Roots	Sources	English Derivatives	
duce, duct	ducere (L) (to lead)	produce	*product* *abduct*
fer	ferre (L) (to bear, place)	confer	*inferior* *infer*
ject	jacere (L) (to throw)	subject	*reject* *deject*
mitt	mittere (L) (to send)	transmit	*submit* *remit*
port	portare (L) (to carry)	import	*export* *report*

15

SUFFIXES

A suffix is a combination of letters added to the end of a word or word root. In Lesson 8, we changed the meaning of words by changing prefixes. In this lesson we shall see that suffixes indicate the function of words; i.e., their place in the sentence as nouns, adjectives, verbs, adverbs, or other parts of speech. These suffixes are known as *derivational suffixes.*

Prefix + Word	**Word + Suffix**
un + equal = unequal	equal + ity = equality (n.)
	equal + tion = equation (n.)
	equal + ate = equate (v.)
	equal + ly = equally (adv.)

There is another type of suffix, known as the *inflectional suffix.* This suffix gives more information about the word, such as person, number, tense or mood.

Did you see my son's papers? (person, number)
Have you seen my sons' papers? (tense, person, number)
Who saw my sons' paper? (tense, person)
Have you seen my son's paper? (tense, person)

In the sentences above we have examples of the inflectional suffixes "s," "'s," "s'," and "n." Explain the differences in meaning from sentence to sentence and you will understand the function of inflectional suffixes.

Common Derivational Suffixes

Noun-forming	Verb-forming	Adj.-forming	Versatile Suffixes
ance	ate	able	ant (n., adj.)
ancy	en	ible	ary (n., adj.)
ence	ise	al	ent (n., adj.)
ency	ize	ar	er (n., adj.)
ery		ful	ist (n., adj.)
hood	**Adverb-forming**	ish	ory (n., adj.)
ician	er	ive	
ment	ly	less	
ness	ward	ous	
or	wise	ual	
(s)ion			
(t)ion			

Assignment

From the prefixes and word roots in Lesson 8, build ten or more words by adding the suffixes listed in this lesson. *importance*

Example: port ... import ... importer *advertisement*
convertable
production
16 *introductory* *reduction*
subjective *introduction*
injection
rejection

ABCDEFGHIJK**LESSON 10**
REVIEW

A. Underline each prefix with one line and each suffix with two lines. Write the meaning of each word root and the meaning of the word.

> **Example:** conference—a meeting for an exchange or sharing of views
> fer (ferre)—to bear; act of bearing with or considering

conductor	production	preferred	projection
deduction	reduction	transferable	projected
education	deference	transfers	admitted
introduction	interference	injections	admissible

B. Place diacritical marks above the vowels in the following words, using the charts in Lessons 2 and 7.

coward	event	few	message
curious	following	industrial	national
every	forwarded	marriage	substantial

C. Place the letter "I" above the inflectional suffixes in the following words and the letter "D" above the derivational suffixes. When both are present, the inflectional suffix is the second one. Consult your dictionary for help.

>   I   D   D I
> **Examples:** reform*ed*   form*ative*   reform*ers*

conforming	information	informative
deformed	informant	performs
informers	informal	performers

D. Circle each voiced consonant in the following words:

balloon	loss	wear
daughter	model	while
decision	naturally	yellow
exact	quarter	yield
growth	reservoir	zero
juice	thank	zinc

E. Underline diphthongs once and digraphs twice:

deceive	block	south	fish
change	ring	fail	believe
maid	laugh	main	diphthong
cool	this	boys	load
pamphlet	mouth	contain	read

17

WORDS BEGINNING WITH "COM," "CON," OR "CO"

The prefixes "com," "con," and "co"—and their adapted forms "col" and "cor"—mean "with" or "together." In some words, a hyphen or a diaeresis is used after the prefix "co" to indicate the end of a syllable, as in *cooperate*, also written *co-operate, coöperate*.

combine	(cŏm bīne′)	v.	To unite; to join.
communicate	(cŏm mū′ nĭ cāte)	v.	To make known.
companion	(cŏm păn′ ion)	n.	An associate.
	yŭn		
compile	(cŏm pīle′)	v.	To collect.
complicate	(cŏm′ plĭ cāte)	v.	To make difficult.
compose	(cŏm pōşe′)	v.	To put together.
comrade	(cŏm′ răde)	n.	A companion.
conciliate	(cŏn çĭl′ ĭ āte)	v.	To reconcile.
condense	(cŏn dĕnse′)	v.	To make more compact.
confer	(cŏn fẽr′)	v.	To consult.
conform	(cŏn fôrm′)	v.	To adapt to.
connect	(cŏn nĕct′)	v.	To join.
consensus	(cŏn sĕn′ sŭs)	n.	Agreement.
consign	(cŏn sīgn′)	v.	To entrust with.
consolidate	(cŏn sŏl′ ĭ dāte)	v.	To unite; to combine.
construction	(cŏn strŭc′ tion)	n.	A putting together.
	shŭn		
coherent	(cō hẽr′ ĕnt)	adj.	Logically consistent.
coincidence	(cō ĭn′ cĭ dĕnçe)	n.	Unplanned concurrence of events.
coordinate	(cō ôr′ dĭ nāte)	adj.	Of the same rank.
co-workers	(cō-wõr′ kẽrs)	n.	Those working together.

Assignment

Copy the words in the first column, with definitions chosen from the second column.

1. compel   (a) hinder   (b) resist   (c) force
2. complex   (a) uniform   (b) intricate   (c) obvious
3. comprehensive   (a) extravagant   (b) inclusive   (c) understanding
4. compromise   (a) mutual concession   (b) continued debate   (c) wranglin
5. condolence   (a) expression of sympathy   (b) agreement   (c) warning
6. confirm   (a) strengthen   (b) destroy   (c) upset
7. conquer   (a) capitulate   (b) surrender;   (c) overpower
8. cooperate   (a) act with others   (b) enjoy   (c) obey
9. confiscate   (a) seize   (b) destroy   (c) return
10. conclude   (a) agree   (b) close   (c) argue
11. compassionate   (a) wild   (b) merciful   (c) agitated
12. concede   (a) start   (b) admit   (c) direct
13. conscious   (a) dutiful   (b) ignorant   (c) aware

WORDS BEGINNING WITH "DE" OR "EX"

The prefix "de" means "down" as in *decrease*, or "away" as in *detract*. What is the meaning of "de" in the following words?

decrepit	(dĕ crĕp′ ĭt)	*adj.* Broken down with age.
deduction	(dĕ dŭc′ tion)	*n.* That which is taken away.
degrade	(dĕ grāde′)	*v.* To reduce in rank.
departure	(dĕ pär′ tŭre)	*n.* A going away.
depreciation	(dĕ prē′ ci ā′ tion) shĭ	*n.* A lessening in value.
descend	(dĕ scĕnd′)	*v.* To go down.
despise	(dĕ spīṣe′)	*v.* To look down upon.
detach	(dĕ tăch′)	*v.* To part; to separate.
deteriorate	(dĕ tē′ rĭ ό rāte)	*v.* To grow worse.
deviate	(dē′ vĭ āte)	*v.* To turn aside from.

The prefix "ex" means "out of" as in *exhale* or *exile*. It also means "beyond" as in *excel* or *excess*.

exaggeration	(ex ag′ gēr ā′ tion) ĕg zăj′	*n.* An overstatement.
excel	(ĕx çĕl′)	*v.* To go beyond; to surpass.
exceptional	(ĕx çĕp′ tion ăl)	*adj.* Rare; out of the ordinary.
excessive	(ĕx çĕs′ sĭve)	*adj.* Beyond a just amount.
exhale	(ĕx hāle′)	*v.* To breathe out.
exile	(ĕx′ īle)	*v.* To banish.
exorbitant	(ĕx ôr′ bĭ tănt)	*adj.* Unreasonably high.
explode	(ĕx plōde′)	*v.* To burst noisily.
export	(ĕx pōrt′)	*v.* To send abroad.
expulsion	(ĕx pŭl′ sion)	*n.* A driving or forcing out.

Assignment

Copy the words on the right. Beside each word place the number of the definition that seems appropriate.

1. To reduce in rank.	*6* depreciation
2. To turn aside from.	*9* descend
3. Broken down with age.	*1* degrade
4. To grow worse.	*8* exhale
5. Unreasonably high.	*7* expulsion
6. Lessening in value.	*2* deviate
7. A driving or forcing out.	*4* deteriorate
8. To breathe out.	*10* exile
9. To go down.	*3* decrepit
10. One driven from his country.	*5* exorbitant
11. To surpass.	*12* despise
12. To look down upon.	*11* excel

ABCDEFGHIJK **LESSON 13**

**WORDS BEGINNING WITH "IM"
OR "IN"**

The prefix "in" and its various adaptations—"il," "im," "ir" have two meanings: "not," as in *immature* and *inadequate*: or "in," as in *within, into, income*. Usually "il" is used with words beginning with "l"; "im" with words beginning with "b," "m," or "p"; "ir" before words beginning with "r"; and "in" before other words.

illegible	(ĭl lĕġ′ ĭ ble)	*adj.* Impossible to read.
immaterial	(ĭm′ må tē′ rĭ ăl)	*adj.* Of no consequence.
immortal	(ĭm môr′ tăl)	*adj.* Undying.
impartial	(ĭm pär′ tial) shăl	*adj.* Not biased; just.
impassable	(ĭm pàss′ à ble)	*adj.* Cannot be passed.
imperfect	(ĭm pēr′ fĕct)	*adj.* Defective.
impersonal	(ĭm pēr′ sŏn ăl)	*adj.* Not involved.
impossible	(ĭm pŏs′ sĭ ble)	*adj.* Cannot be done.
improbable	(ĭm prŏb′ à ble)	*adj.* Unlikely to be true.
inadequate	(ĭn ăd′ é quate) kwĭt	*adj.* Insufficient.
incapable	(ĭn cā′ pà ble)	*adj.* Unable.
incapacitate	(ĭn′ cà păç′ ĭ tāte)	*v.* To disable.
inconvenient	(ĭn′ cŏn vēn′ ient) yĕnt	*adj.* Inopportune.
independent	(ĭn′ dé pĕnd′ ĕnt)	*adj.* Self-governing.
indirectly	(ĭn′ dĭ rĕct′ lў)	*adv.* Round-about.
inevitably	(ĭn ĕv′ ĭ tà blў)	*adv.* Unavoidably.
insensible	(ĭn sĕn′ sĭ ble)	*adj.* Without feeling.
insignificant	(ĭn′ sĭg nĭf′ ĭ cănt)	*adj.* Unimportant.
intolerant	(ĭn tŏl′ ēr ănt)	*adj.* Narrow-minded.
irresponsible	(ĭr′ ré spŏn′ sĭ ble)	*adj.* Not accountable.

Assignment

Complete each sentence by choosing a word from the above list to fill in the blank.

1. A person who could live forever would be *immortal*
2. Jack is financing his own education because he wants to be *independent* of his family.
3. Mr. Stokes was *insensible* to the complications his solution might create.
4. Betty is very *irresponsible*; she refuses to be accountable for her actions.
5. The mountain road is *impassable* since it is narrow with many deep holes.
6. All the bills cannot be paid with this *inadequate* sum of money.
7. The student's handwriting was so poor that his homework was *illegible*
8. People used to believe that it was *impossible* to go to the moon.
9. He *inevitably* gave away the answer by providing some clues.
10. Your argument is _____ to the debate. *immaterial*

20

14

WORDS BEGINNING WITH "INTER" OR "RE"

The prefix "inter" indicates relationship and means "between" or "among," as in *interact* and *international*. The prefix "re" means "back to" or "again," as in *return* and *restate*.

intercede	(ĭn' tẽr çēde')	*v.*	To act between parties.
intercept	(ĭn' tẽr çẽpt')	*v.*	To stop or interrupt.
intercollegiate	(ĭn' tẽr cŏl lē' ġĭ āte)	*adj.*	Between colleges.
interfere	(ĭn' tẽr fẽre')	*v.*	Meddle ; come between.
intermediate	(ĭn' tẽr mē' dĭ āte)	*adj.*	Between extremes.
intermingle	(ĭn' tẽr mĭn' gle)	*v.*	To mix together.
international	(ĭn' tẽr nă' tion ăl)	*adj.*	Between countries.
interrupt	(ĭn' tẽr rŭpt')	*v.*	To break into.
interval	(ĭn' tẽr văl)	*n.*	Space of time.
intervene	(ĭn' tẽr vēne')	*v.*	To come between.
reconcile	(rĕc' ŏn çīle)	*v.*	To bring back to harmony.
recover	(rḗ cȯv' ẽr)	*v.*	To take again ; to regain.
redeem	(rḗ dēēm')	*v.*	To buy back.
reelect	(rē' ḗ lĕct')	*v.*	To vote into office again.
reform	(rḗ fôrm')	*v.*	To bring from bad to good.
reinstate	(rē' ĭn stāte')	*v.*	To restore to former position.
remind	(rḗ mīnd')	*v.*	To cause one to remember.
replacement	(rḗ plāçe' mĕnt)	*n.*	Substitution.
reproduce	(rē' prṓ dūçe')	*v.*	To repeat.
reunion	(rḗ ūn' ion)	*n.*	A reuniting of persons.
	yŭn		

Assignments

A. Look up the following words in the dictionary. Write the complete history of each word.

interest   interlude   interrogate   remember   relieve

B. Copy the words listed below. Beside each word write its *antonym* (word having the opposite meaning) from the list above.

intracollegiate *intercollegiate*   discard *redeem*
national *international*   terminal *recover*
antagonize *reconcile*   forget *remind*
listen *interrupt*   lose *recover*
dismiss *reinstate*   corrupt *reform*

C. Copy the following definitions. Next to each one choose a word from the column on the right to which it refers.

1. To explain; translate.   *5* reappear
2. To vote into office again.   *4* interfere
3. To speak in behalf of others.   *1* interpret
4. To meddle.   *2* reelect
5. To come into sight again.   *3* intercede

21

A. Below are prefixes from Lessons 11-14 with some commonly used word roots. Build words to complete the following sentences. The word constructed for each sentence should agree in meaning with the word or words in parentheses.

Prefixes	Word Roots
con	cede (cedere—to go along) L.
com	cel (cellere—to rise) L.
de	cept (capere—to take) L.
ex	clude (claudere—to shut) L.
im	fere (ferre—to bear, place) L.
in	hale (halare—to breathe) L.
inter	part (partire—to divide) L.
re	pel (pellere—to drive) L.
	port (portare—to carry) L.

inhale, exhale 1. People (breathe in) oxygen and (breathe out) carbon dioxide.
intercede 2. Gregory will (plead) for Henry with Judge Henderson.
departure 3. Bill's (going away) made us sad.
will concede 4. I hope that Jim (will admit) victory to his opponent.
excel 5. Every adult should strive to (be above average) in one field.
6. The soldiers will (stop) the arms before they reach the enemy.
impel 7. Her parents will not (force) her to do all her homework.
export 8. The company will (send abroad) most of its goods this year.
interfere 9. It is not nice to (meddle) in other people's business.
conclude 10. How will you (close) the discussion?

B. Replace the underlined words in the following sentences with *synonyms* (words that have the same or nearly the same meaning) from Lessons 11-14.

concise 1. This detailed, inclusive report is excellent.
redeem 2. The man was able to buy back his watch.
condense 3. Can you shorten your term paper to five pages?
insufficient 4. The funds are not sufficient to cover our expenses.
exaggeration 5. That is an overstatement.
exhorbitant 6. Prices at this store are unreasonably high.
descend 7. Be careful as you go down those stairs.
co-operate 8. In order to work well with others on committee work, one
communicate should be able to express his ideas effectively.
deteriorate 9. The situation will get worse if you leave now.
illegible 10. Your writing is impossible to read.

C. Write one or more paragraphs on a topic of your choice. Include at least two words from each of the preceding four lessons. These words should be used correctly and sensibly. Underline the words from the lessons.

ABCDEFGHIJK LESSON 16

WORDS BEGINNING WITH "MIS" OR "DIS"

The prefix "mis" means "wrong," "bad," or "ill," as in *mischief*, *miserable*, and *misery*.

misapplication	(mĭs′ ăp plĭ cā′ tion)	*n.*	A wrong use.
misapply	(mĭs′ ăp plȳ′)	*v.*	To use wrongly.
misbehave	(mĭs′ bĕ hāve′)	*v.*	To act improperly.
misdeed	(mĭs dēed′)	*n.*	A wrong action.
misfortune	(mĭs fôr′ tŭne)	*n.*	Bad luck.
misgiving	(mĭs gĭv′ ĭng)	*n.*	Feeling of doubt.
mishandle	(mĭs hăn′ dle)	*v.*	To maltreat.
misleading	(mĭs lēad′ ing)	*adj.*	Deceiving.
mispronounce	(mĭs′ prŏ nounçe′)	*v.*	To say words incorrectly.
misspell	(mĭs spĕll′)	*v.*	To write words incorrectly.

The prefix "dis" implies separation, as in *dismiss* and *distribute*. In some nouns and adjectives, the prefix "dis" means the absence of a quality: *disunion, dissatisfaction, dishonest.*

disability	(dĭs′ à bĭl′ ĭ tȳ)	*n.*	Weakness.
disconnect	(dĭs′ cŏn nĕct′)	*v.*	To disunite.
discourage	(dĭs coûr′ age) ĭj	*v.*	To deter; dishearten.
discover	(dĭs cŏv′ ēr)	*v.*	To find for the first time.
discrepancy	(dĭs crĕp′ ăn çȳ)	*n.*	Difference.
discriminate	(dĭs crĭm′ ĭ nāte′)	*v.*	To mark as different.
discuss	(dĭs cŭss′)	*v.*	To talk about.
dispose	(dĭs pōṣe′)	*v.*	To distribute; to incline.
dispute	(dĭs pūte′)	*v.*	To quarrel.
distract	(dĭs trăct′)	*v.*	To divert, harrass.

Assignments

A. Choose ten words from the above list. Write the words, underlining all prefixes and suffixes. Use each word in a sentence.

B. Copy the following words. Beside each word write the affixes (prefix and/or suffix) needed to form a word related to this lesson.

dis able	*mis* deed	*mis* pronounce	*mis* take
dis agree	*mis* direct	*dis* regard	*mis* tend
dis appear	*mis* fortune	*dis* repute	*mis* trust
dis arm	*mis* giving	*dis* satisfy	*dis* taste
dis card	*mis* handle	*dis* service	*dis* tribute
dis content	*dis* honest	*dis* similar	*mis* understand
mis conception	*mis* leading	*dis* solve	*dis* unite
dis cover	*dis* miss	*dis* spell	*mis* use

23

WORDS BEGINNING WITH "SUB" OR "UN"

The prefix "sub" means "under," "below," or "inferior" as in *substandard*. This prefix appears as "sus," before the letters "c" (soft), "p," and "t," as in *susceptible, suspend*, and *sustain*.

subcommittee	(sŭb′ cŏm mĭt′ tée)	*n.*	Subdivision of a group.
subdued	(sŭb dūed′)	*adj.*	Reduced in force.
subjugate	(sŭb′ ju gāte)	*v.*	To bring under control of.
submarine	(sŭb′ mà rĭne′)	*n.*	Underwater ship.
submerge	(sŭb mērġe′)	*v.*	To put under water.
submit	(sŭb mĭt′)	*v.*	To yield; to surrender.
subordinate	(sŭb ôr′ dĭ nắte)	*adj.*	Holding an inferior rank.
subscribe	(sŭb scrībe′)	*v.*	To sign one's name.
subsoil	(sŭb′ soil′)	*n.*	Soil under the surface soil.
subway	(sŭb′ wāy′)	*n.*	Underground transportation system.

The prefix "un," meaning "not," is commonly used with adjectives. The prefixes "in," "im," and "non" are used with nouns and verbs, even when the related adjective begins with "un," as in *unable—inability; unbalanced—imbalance; uncooperative—noncooperation*.

unaffected	(ŭn′ ăf fĕct′ ĕd)	*adj.*	Genuine; plain; simple.
unavoidable	(ŭn′ à void′ à ble)	*adj.*	Inevitable.
uncertain	(ŭn çẽr′ taĭn)	*adj.*	Unsure.
unclaimed	(ŭn clāimed′)	*adj.*	Unasked for.
unconscious	(ŭn cŏn′ scious) shŭs	*adj.*	Unaware.
undivided	(ŭn′ dĭ vīd′ ĕd)	*adj.*	Unbroken.
uneventful	(ŭn′ é vĕnt′ ful)	*adj.*	Monotonous.
unfavorable	(ŭn fā′ vŏr à ble)	*adj.*	Adverse.
unlike	(ŭn līke′)	*adj.*	Dissimilar.
unnecessary	(ŭn nĕç′ ĕs sar y̆) sĕr′	*adj.*	Useless; unwarranted.

Assignment

Rewrite the following sentences, replacing the italicized word or words in each sentence with a *synonym* from the above list.

1. Surely they will never *yield* to such injustice. submit
2. The weather is *inclement* for a picnic. unfavorable
3. Elmer holds a *lowly* position in that company. subordinate
4. The colonists attempted to *conquer* the natives. subjugate
5. Louise has a *plain* manner that inspires confidence. an unaffected
6. You seem *unsure* about the exact amount deposited. uncertain
7. Our vacation was *calm* but beneficial. uneventful
8. He developed a plan for *an underground transportation* system. a subway
9. Good *underwater ships* are of first importance in oceanography. submarines
10. He was *unaware of his surroundings* after the fall. unconscious of his surroundings

24

PREFIXES SIGNIFYING NUMBERS

The following prefixes indicate number when affixed to words or word roots.

Prefix	Meaning	Prefix	Meaning
bi	two	mon, mono	one, single, alone
tri	three	poly	many, much
semi	half	deca, dec	ten

bicuspid	(bī cŭs′ pĭd)	*n.* A double-pointed tooth.
bicycle	(bī′ çў cle)	*n.* Vehicle with two wheels.
biennial	(bī ĕn′ *n*ĭ ăl)	*adj.* Every two years.
biped	(bī′ pĕd)	*n.* A two-footed animal.
triangle	(trī′ an′ *g*le) ăng′	*n.* Figure with three angles.
triennial	(trī ĕn′ *n*ĭ ăl)	*adj.* Every three years.
tripod	(trī′ pŏd)	*n.* A three-legged stand.
trisect	(trī′ sĕct′)	*v.* To divide into three parts.
semiannual	(sĕm′ ĭ ăn′ *n*ŭ ăl)	*adj.* Twice a year.
semicircle	(sĕm′ ĭ çīr′ cle)	*n.* A half circle.
semidetached	(sĕm′ ĭ de tăched′)	*adj.* Partially connected.
semiprecious	(sĕm′ ĭ prĕ′ cious) shŭs	*adj.* Lesser value.
monarch	(mŏn′ ārch)	*n.* Supreme ruler.
monogamy	(mó nŏg′ à mў)	*n.* Having one wife or husband.
monotony	(mó nŏt′ ó nў)	*n.* Lack of variety producing boredom.
polygamy	(pó lўg′ à mў)	*n.* Having many spouses.
polytheism	(pŏl′ ў thē ĭsm)	*n.* Belief in many gods.
decade	(dĕc′ āde)	*n.* Period of ten years.
decathlon	(dé căth′ lŏn)	*n.* Composite athletic contest of ten events.

Assignments

A. One or more words in each sentence contains a prefix from this lesson. Write the meaning of those words.

1. <u>December</u> has not always been the twelfth <u>month</u> of the year. *10ᵗʰ month*
2. <u>Polysyllabic</u> humor evokes laughter by the <u>misuse</u> of long words. *many syllables*
3. <u>Monotony</u> is harder to endure than hard work. *lack of variety*
4. A <u>polygon</u> with eight sides is called an octagon. *many sided*
5. Our <u>biennial</u> meetings were replaced with <u>semiannual</u> meetings. *~~twice~~ once in 2 yrs.* *2 times a year*

B. Use each of the following words in a sentence:

bicentennial	bicuspid	semidetached
semiweekly	trisect	semiprecious

19

WORDS BEGINNING WITH "ANTE," "FORE," OR "PRE"

These three prefixes—"ante," "fore," and "pre" mean "before." "Ante" means "before in space or time"; "fore" means "front, ahead of time"; and "pre" means "prior to" or "in advance of."

antecedent	(ăn' tḗ ced' ĕnt)	n.	That which precedes.
antedate	(ăn' tḗ dāte')	v.	Precede in time.
ante meridian	(ăn' tḗ mḗ rĭd' ĭ ăn)	adj.	Before noon; written a.m.
anteroom	(ăn' tḗ rōōm')	n.	A waiting room.
forearm	(fōrḕ' ärm')	n.	Part of the arm between the elbow and the wrist.
forebears	(fōrḕ' bẹârs)	n.	Ancestors.
foreboding	(fōrḕ bōd' ĭng)	n.	Sign or feeling for future, especially of evil.
forecast	(fōrḕ càst')	v.	To predict.
foreclose	(fōrḕ clōse')	v.	To take away the right to redeem a mortgage or pledge.
forefathers	(fōrḕ' fä' thẽrs)	n.	Men of the past of common heritage.
forefinger	(fōrḕ' fĭn' gẽr)	n.	First finger, next to thumb.
foremost	(fōrḕ' mōst')	adj.	First.
forerunner	(fōrḕ' rŭn' nẽr)	n.	Predecessor; ancestor.
precaution	(prḗ cau' tion)	n.	Measure taken beforehand to secure good results.
precede	(prē çède')	v.	To go before; be in front of.
precedence	(prḗ cēd' ĕnçe)	n.	Priority in rank.
precocious	(prḗ cō' cious)	adj.	Prematurely developed mentally.
preconception	(prē' cŏn cĕp' tion)	n.	Opinion formed beforehand.
predecessor	(prĕd' ḗ cĕs' sŏr)	n.	Previous holder of a certain position or title.
preeminent	(prḗ ĕm' ĭ nĕnt)	adj.	Above others.

Assignment

Replace the word(s) in parentheses with a word from the above list.

forecasts 1. Harold (predicts) the weather after the five o'clock news.
forefathers 2. Did your (ancestors) settle in this state?
precedence 3. Capt. Morrow should be given (priority in rank) over Lt. Jones.
precocious 4. Benjamin is (mentally beyond his age group).
precaution 5. You should take every possible (measure) to avoid accidents.
foreboding 6. Tom had repeated (presentiments of trouble) before we started for Alaska.
forearm 7. Louise broke her right (arm between the elbow and the wrist).
precede 8. You should (be in front of) Dr. Bell in the faculty procession.
anteroom 9. The doctor's (waiting room) was filled with patients.
9:00 am. 10. It was approximately (three hours before noon) when we left.

26

ABCDEFGHIJKLESSON 20
REVIEW

A. Copy the entry words given below. Choose the best *synonym* and write it beside the entry word.

1. **disability** (a) detect (b) unlike (c) weakness (d) belittle
2. **subscribe** (a) write (b) underneath (c) yield (d) support
3. **forebears** (a) patience (b) ancestors (c) carries (d) measures
4. **unaffected** (a) adverse (b) controlled (c) unable (d) genuine
5. **forecast** (a) foretell (b) decide (c) premature (d) precede

B. Each of the following statements suggests a word found in Lessons 16-19. Number your paper from one to ten. Beside each number write the word that corresponds in meaning to the word or words underscored in that sentence.

1. Have you heard the weather prediction for tomorrow? *forcast*
2. Joan had already formed her opinions before she came. *pre conceptions*
3. Dr. Allerton is above all others in the field of psychiatry. *foremost*
4. Can you come to my office at 9:30 in the morning? *a.m.*
5. Anna should break her habit of saying words incorrectly. *mispronunciation*
6. Did you notice the difference between your final figures and mine? *discrepancy*
7. I have feelings of doubt about the success of this venture. *misgivings*
8. The Social Committee was so large that it was broken up into several subdivisions. *subcommittees*
9. During the next ten years, we shall see some radical changes. *decade*
10. Many men and women in this group say that they believe in *monogamy* one life-time marriage, but their actions will indicate that they believe in having several wives or husbands. *polygamy*

C. Write contrasting words (antonyms) for each of the following words by changing or adding prefixes:

Word	Antonym
assent	dissent
attract	*detract*
conscious	*unconscious*
detached	*attached*
divided	*undivided*
emerge	*submerge*
encourage	*discourage*
fortune	*misfortune*
impose	*compose*
monosyllable	*polysyllabic*
monotheism	*polytheism*
postdate	*predate*
post meridian	*ante meridian*

27

WORDS ENDING IN "ANCE" OR "ENCE"

In the next five lessons, we shall consider some of the common noun-forming suffixes. The first of these are the suffixes "ance," and "ence"; they mean "act of" or "state of," as in *resistance* and *absence*. The suffixes "ancy" and "ency" have the same meanings.

acceptance	(ăc çĕpt' ănçe)	*n.*	Approval.
alliance	(ăl lī' ănçe)	*n.*	Union; partnership.
assurance	(ăs sur' ănçe)	*n.*	Promise; pledge; guarantee.
endurance	(ĕn dūr' ănçe)	*n.*	Ability to continue.
fragrance	(frā' grănçe)	*n.*	A pleasing odor.
insurance	(ĭn sŭr' ănçe)	*n.*	Protection against loss.
observance	(ŏb şĕrv' ănçe)	*n.*	Act of following a custom.
performance	(pẽr fôrm' ănçe)	*n.*	Deed; action.
temperance	(tĕm' pẽr ănçe)	*n.*	Moderation; restraint.
absence	(ăb' sĕnçe)	*n.*	State of not being present.
benevolence	(bĕ nĕv' ŏ lĕnçe)	*n.*	Act of kindness.
conference	(cŏn' fẽr ĕnçe)	*n.*	Discussion; consultation.
confidence	(cŏn' fĭ dĕnçe)	*n.*	Trust.
correspondence	(cŏr' rĕ spŏnd' ĕnçe)	*n.*	Written communication.
experience	(ĕx pē' rĭ ĕnçe)	*n.*	Living through events.
independence	(ĭn' dĕ pĕnd' ĕnçe)	*n.*	Not controlled by others.
innocence	(ĭn' nŏ çĕnçe)	*n.*	Lack of knowledge of evil.
residence	(rĕş' ĭ dĕnçe)	*n.*	Dwelling place.
reverence	(rĕv' ẽr ĕnçe)	*n.*	Profound respect; awe.
silence	(sī' lĕnçe)	*n.*	Lack of sound; quiet.

Assignment

Form words to replace the word or phrase underscored in the following sentences. Add one of the suffixes from this lesson to one of the roots below, using prefixes as needed.

Prefixes

ac
bene
con
ob
per
re

Word Roots

cept (capere—to take) L.
fer (ferre—to bear, place) L.
form (fournir—to furnish) F.
serv (servare—to save) L.
ver (vereri—to fear) L.
vol (volent—wishing) L.

1. Mary's favorable response to the invitation surprised us. *acceptance*
2. Did you attend the Governor's meeting on education. *conference*
3. The parishioners look upon the minister with deep respect. *reverence*
4. His actions while in the race proved him to be too slow. *performance*
5. The stranger's act of kindness was overwhelming. *benevolence*
6. In celebration of the Fourth of July, many cities hold parades. *observance*

22

WORDS ENDING IN "OR"

The suffix "or" designates an agent (person, thing or quality), and it may also indicate a condition or activity. Generally "or" rather than "er" is used after the letter "t."

actor	(ăc′ tŏr)	n.	One who plays a part.
administrator	(ăd mǐn′ ǐs trā′ tŏr)	n.	One who manages affairs.
bachelor	(băch′ ĕ lŏr)	n.	An unmarried man.
collector	(cŏl lĕc′ tŏr)	n.	One who gathers or obtains.
conductor	(cŏn dŭc′ tŏr)	n.	A director.
distributor	(dĭs trĭb′ ú tŏr)	n.	An agent or agency that distributes.
doctor	(dŏc′ tŏr)	n.	A physician.
editor	(ĕd′ ĭ tŏr)	n.	One who supervises the writing of publications.
elevator	(ĕl′ ĕ vā′ tŏr)	n.	A hoisting machine or lift.
error	(ĕr′ rŏr)	n.	Mistake.
governor	(gŏv′ ĕr nŏr)	n.	Highest elected official of a state.
inspector	(ĭn spĕc′ tŏr)	n.	One who views critically.
inventor	(ĭn vĕn′ tŏr)	n.	One who creates something new.
originator	(ŏ rĭg′ ĭ nā′ tŏr)	n.	One who starts something new.
possessor	(pŏs sĕss′ ŏr)	n.	One who occupies or controls.
proprietor	(prŏ prī′ ĕ tŏr)	n.	One who owns.
protector	(prō tĕc′ tŏr)	n.	A person or device that guards.
radiator	(rā′ dĭ ā′ tŏr)	n.	That which radiates heat.
senator	(sĕn′ à tŏr)	n.	Member of the Senate.
visitor	(vĭs′ ĭ tŏr)	n.	One who pays a call; guest.

Assignments

A. Define the following words:

benefactor	contractor	prospector
retractor	detector	selector
separator	mediator	legislator
calculator	debtor	depositor
dictator	duplicator	solicitor
incinerator	refrigerator	incubator

B. Combine the prefixes and/or suffixes with the word roots listed below to derive at least five words listed on this page, preferably more.

Prefixes	Word Roots and Meanings	Suffix
bene	fact (facere—to do) L.	or
con	spect (specere—to look, see) L.	
de	tect (tegere—to cover) L.	
in	tract (trahere—to draw, pull) L.	
pro	ven, vent (venire—to come) L.	
re		

benefactor
contractor
detector
inspector
protector

29

23

WORDS ENDING IN "MENT"

The suffix "ment" is used mainly to form nouns from verbs: commit (v.) + ment = commitment (n.). The suffix "ment" denotes a "concrete result," an "action," or a "condition."

accomplishment	(ăc cŏm' plĭsh mĕnt)	n.	Achievement.
adjournment	(ăd joûrn' mĕnt)	n.	Ending a meeting.
adjustment	(ăd jŭst' mĕnt)	n.	Restoring of harmony.
agreement	(à grēe' mĕnt)	n.	Harmony of opinion.
amusement	(à mūşe' mĕnt)	n.	Pleasurable diversion.
assignment	(ăs sīgn' mĕnt)	n.	Designated task.
confinement	(cŏn fīne' mĕnt)	n.	Restraint within limits.
development	(dĕ vĕl' ŏp mĕnt)	n.	Unfolding; promotion of growth.
disappointment	(dĭs' ăp point' mĕnt)	n.	Defeat of expectation or hope.
discernment	(dĭs cern' mĕnt) zērn'	n.	Keenness of insight.
encouragement	(ĕn coûr' age mĕnt) ij	n.	Help; inspiration.
enlargement	(ĕn lärġe' mĕnt)	n.	Increase in size.
environment	(ĕn vī' rŏn mĕnt)	n.	Surroundings.
establishment	(ĕs tăb' lĭsh mĕnt)	n.	Settled arrangement or order.
fulfillment	(fu̧l fĭll' mĕnt)	n.	Complete realization of hopes.
government	(gȯv' ērn mĕnt)	n.	Ruling administration.
improvement	(ĭm pro̧ve' mĕnt)	n.	Enhanced value; better state.
measurement	(mĕaş' ure mĕnt) ēr	n.	Determination of extent, degree, or quantity.
punishment	(pŭn' ĭsh mĕnt)	n.	Penalty imposed on offender.
refinement	(rĕ́ fīne' mĕnt)	n.	Purification; improvement.

Assignment

Copy the words on the right. Beside each word place the number of the best definition from the left column.

1. Defeat of expectations or hopes.
2. Ending a meeting.
3. Designated task.
4. Keenness of insight.
5. Promotion of growth.
6. Complete realization of hopes.
7. Ruling administration.
8. Surroundings.
9. Feeling; an opinion.
10. Help; inspiration.

10 encouragement
9 sentiment
4 discernment
7 government
1 disappointment
8 environment
6 fulfillment
2 adjournment
3 assignment
5 development

24

**WORDS ENDING IN "TION,"
"SION," OR "CIAN"**

The suffix "ion" and its variations "tion," "sion" and "cian" form nouns from verbs. The endings "tion" and "sion" indicate an "act" or "process"; a "state" or "condition." The phonetic pronunciation of "tion" is "shun."

agitation	(ăg' ĭ tā' tion)	n.	Anxiety.
alteration	(al' tĕr ā' tion)	n.	Modification.
exhibition	(ĕx' hĭ bĭ' tion)	n.	Public showing.
indication	(ĭn' dĭ cā' tion)	n.	Sign; hint; suggestion.
recollection	(rĕc' ŏl lĕc' tion)	n.	Act of calling to mind.
reduction	(rĕ dŭc' tion)	n.	Change to lower level.
repetition	(rĕp' ĕ tĭ' tion)	n.	Reiteration.
restriction	(rĕ strĭc' tion)	n.	Limitation.

The ending "sion" is pronounced "shun," after a consonant, as in *mission*, but after a vowel it is pronounced "zhun," as in *confusion*.

allusion	(ăl lū' sion)	n.	Indirect reference.
confusion	(cŏn fū' sion)	n.	State of disorder.
discussion	(dĭs cŭs' sion)	n.	Exchange of ideas.
extension	(ĕx tĕn' sion)	n.	Spreading out; stretching.
mission	(mĭs' sion)	n.	Assignment; a service.
occasion	(ŏc cā' sion)	n.	An occurrence.
omission	(ŏ mĭs' sion)	n.	Something left undone.
permission	(pĕr mĭs' sion)	n.	Consent.
possession	(pŏs sĕs' sion)	n.	Ownership; control.

The suffix "cian" indicates "one skilled in," and is pronounced "shun."

magician	(mà ġĭ' cian)	n.	One skilled in magic.
politician	(pŏl' ĭ tĭ' cian)	n.	One skilled in politics.
technician	(tĕch nĭ' cian)	n.	One skilled in technical details.

Assignment

Rewrite the following sentences, replacing the italicized word in each sentence with a *synonym* from the words above.

1. Our commanding officer was sent on a Government *task*. mission
2. Unless we adhere to the rules, we will have *turmoil*. confusion
3. We were mystified by the performance of the *conjurer*. magician
4. Mary's *anxiety* was due to her illness. agitation
5. The dancers will perform at the *public display* next week. exhibition
6. Are there any *limitations* on the use of firearms? restrictions
7. A *person skilled in politics* usually has more power than *one skilled in technical details*. politician technician
8. Mr. Payne made no *reference* to the unfortunate incident. allusion
9. I listened to their *exchange of ideas* about the election. discussion
10. Congenial guests made this *event* a memorable affair. occasion

31

ABCDEFGHIJKLESSON 25
REVIEW

A. Combine the prefixes and/or suffixes with the word roots listed below to construct five words from Lessons 21 and 22.

Prefix	Word Roots and Meanings	Suffixes
ac	cap, cept (capere—to take, catch) L.	ance
bene	dur (durare—to last) L.	ence
con	fact (facere—to do) L.	or
en	fer (ferre—to bear) L.	
in	serv (servare—to save) L.	
per	spec, spic (specere—to look, see) L.	
pro	tect (tegere—to cover) L.	
re	tract (trahere—to draw) L.	
	ven, veni (venire—to come) L.	

acceptance
benefactor
conference
endurance
inspector

B. Number your paper from one to ten. Beside each number write the word from Lesson 21 or 22 that corresponds to the meaning of the sentence bearing that number.

1. An unmarried man is called a *bachelor* .
2. A person who starts something new may be called an *inventor*
3. When the room is completely quiet, there is *silence*
4. A physician is more commonly known as a *doctor*.
5. If you own something, you are the *owner* of it. *proprietor*
6. To continue a task despite fatigue is known as *endurance*
7. Protection against loss is the purpose of *insurance*
8. A person's dwelling place is known as his *residence*
9. Truly profound respect may approach *reverence*
10. Freedom from evil is virtue; lack of its knowledge is *ignorance*

C. Copy the definitions on the right and choose the number of the word, in the left column, that it best defines.

1. allusion   *3* Spreading out.
2. occasion   *5* One skilled in politics.
3. extension   *1* Indirect reference.
4. technician   *4* One skilled in technical details.
5. politician   *2* An occurrence.

D. Build at least five words ending with "ment" from the following prefixes and word roots. A word may have only a suffix, or both a prefix and a suffix. In some words, letters must be inserted.

Prefixes	Word Roots and Meanings	Suffix
ac, ad	amuse (amuser—to cause to muse) OF.	ment
dis	appoint (apointier—to prepare) OF.	
	cern (cernere—to separate) L.	
	complish (complere—to fill up) L.	
	just (justus—right) L.	

amusement
adjustment   *discernment*
accomplishment
appointment

32

ABCDEFGHIJK**LESSON** # 26

WORDS ENDING WITH "ABLE" OR "IBLE"

This lesson and the one following introduce several common adjective-forming suffixes. The suffixes "able" and "ible" form adjectives meaning "able to"; "fit to be"; or "worthy to be." No definite rule governs the use of "able" in preference to "ible"; however, "able" is more frequently used.

acceptable	(ăc çĕpt' à ble)	*adj.*	Allowable.
available	(à vāil' à ble)	*adj.*	Able to be used; attainable.
dependable	(dĕ pĕnd' à ble)	*adj.*	Reliable.
innumerable	(ĭn nū' mĕr à ble)	*adj.*	Beyond counting.
laudable	(laud' à ble)	*adj.*	Worthy of being commended.
notable	(nō' tà ble)	*adj.*	Remarkable.
passable	(păss' à ble)	*adj.*	Able to be passed; mediocre.
respectable	(rĕ spĕct' à ble)	*adj.*	Correct in behavior.
valuable	(văl' ú à ble)	*adj.*	Worth a relatively high price.
venerable	(vĕn' ēr à ble)	*adj.*	Worthy of honor.

The suffix "ible" is usually used after words or word roots ending in "s" or the "s" sound, as in *permissible*; the soft sound of "g" as in *legible*; and after "t," as in *convertible*.

accessible	(ăc çĕs'sĭ ble)	*adj.*	Within reach; obtainable.
convertible	(cŏn vērt' ĭ ble)	*adj.*	Transformable.
credible	(crĕd' ĭ ble)	*adj.*	Worthy of belief.
edible	(ĕd' ĭ ble)	*adj.*	Fit to be eaten.
feasible	(fēa' sĭ ble)	*adj.*	Able to be done.
indefensible	(ĭn' dĕ fĕn' sĭ ble)	*adj.*	Beyond justification.
indestructible	(ĭn' dĕ strŭct' ĭ ble)	*adj.*	Cannot be demolished.
invisible	(ĭn vĭs' ĭ ble)	*adj.*	Incapable of being seen.
irresistible	(ĭr' rĕ sĭst' ĭ ble)	*adj.*	Overpowering.
susceptible	(sŭs çĕp' tĭ ble)	*adj.*	Impressionable.

Assignment

Copy the words on the right. Beside each word place the number of the word(s) from the left column that best defines the word.

1. Transformable.
2. Worthy of honor.
3. Fit to be eaten.
4. Believable.
5. Possible; able to be done.
6. Beyond justification.
7. Impressionable.
8. Enduring; cannot be destroyed.

4 credible
7 susceptible
5 feasible
3 edible
6 indefensible
1 convertible
8 indestructible
2 venerable

33

WORDS ENDING WITH "AR"

Another adjective-forming suffix we shall consider is "ar." In adjectives, this suffix means "of the nature of," "of," or "belonging to." There are many nouns also ending in "ar," but few verbs.

angular	(ăn′ gú lär)	*adj.*	Sharp-cornered.
beggar	(bĕg′ gär)	*n.*	One who lives by asking alms.
circular	(cir′ cú lär) sûr′	*adj.*	Round.
columnar	(có lŭm′ när)	*adj.*	Referring to a line of figures or symbols; resembling a pillar.
familiar	(fà mĭl′ iär)	*adj.*	Well-known.
globular	(glŏb′ ú lär)	*adj.*	Shaped like a sphere.
insular	(ĭn′ sú lär)	*adj.*	Pertaining to an island; isolated.
irregular	(ĭr rĕg′ ú lär)	*adj.*	Not in line with rules.
linear	(lĭn′ ē är)	*adj.*	Consisting of lines.
lunar	(lū′ när)	*adj.*	Pertaining to the moon.
molecular	(mó lĕc′ ú lär)	*adj.*	Consisting of molecules.
particular	(pär tĭc′ ú lär)	*adj.*	Attentive to details.
peculiar	(pé cūl′ iar)	*adj.*	Queer; strange.
polar	(pō′ lär)	*adj.*	Spherical; pertaining to region.
popular	(pŏp′ ú lär)	*adj.*	Widely accepted by the public.
secular	(sĕc′ ú lär)	*adj.*	Pertaining to worldly matters.
similar	(sĭm′ ĭ lär)	*adj.*	Having a general likeness.
singular	(sin′ gú lär) sĭng′	*adj.*	Unusual.
vehicular	(vé hĭc′ ú lär)	*adj.*	Pertaining to means of transportation.
vulgar	(vŭl′ gär)	*adj.*	Low; common; boorish.

Assignments

A. Copy the words listed below. Beside each word write its *antonym* from the above list.

crowded *insular*   religious *secular*   refined *vulgar*
square *circular*   unlike *similar*   disliked *popular*
regular *irregular*   usual *singular*   round *angular*

B. Copy the following words, placing after each word the abbreviation indicating the part of speech: noun or adjective.

calendar *n - adj*   dollar *n*   lunar *adj.*
caterpillar *n*   familiar *adj.*   molar *n - adj.*
cedar *n - adj.*   grammar *n*   muscular *adj.*
globular *adj.*   regular *adj.*   pillar *n*
burglar *n*   particular *adj.*   vernacular *adj.*
popular *adj.*   scholar *n*   vehicular *adj.*

34

ABCDEFGHIJK LESSON

28

**WORDS ENDING WITH "ANT"
OR "ENT"**

The suffixes "ant" and "ent" are used to form both adjectives and nouns. The nouns denote a "person" or "thing" acting as an "agent," as in *occupant* and *detergent*; whereas the adjectives describe the "condition" or "act" of the verb or word root, as in *ignorant* and *corpulent*.

abundant	(à bŭn' dănt)	*adj.* Abounding; plentiful.
applicant	(ăp' plĭ cănt)	*n.* One seeking an opportunity.
assistant	(ăs sĭst' ănt)	*n.* One who helps; helper.
attendant	(ăt tĕnd'ănt)	*n.* One who accompanies.
brilliant	(brĭl' liănt)	*adj.* Sparkling; very bright.
ignorant	(ĭg' nŏ̇ rănt)	*adj.* Lacking knowledge.
inhabitant	(ĭn hăb' ĭt ănt)	*n.* One living in a designated place.
occupant	(ŏc' cŭ pănt)	*n.* One who has the use or possession of something.
pleasant	(plĕaş' ănt)	*adj.* Agreeable.
apparent	(ăp păr'ĕnt)	*adj.* Visible.
component	(cŏm pō' nĕnt)	*adj.* Comprising. *n.* A part.
convenient	(cŏn vēn' iĕnt)	*adj.* Comfortable; handy.
correspondent	(cŏr' rĕ̇ spŏnd' ĕnt)	*n.* One who communicates by letter.
diligent	(dĭl' ĭ ġĕnt)	*adj.* Perseveringly attentive; industrious.
equivalent	(ĕ́ quĭv' à lĕnt)	*adj.* Having the same value.
obedient	(ŏ́ bē' dĭ ĕnt)	*adj.* Willing to accept control.
opponent	(ŏp pō' nĕnt)	*n.* Adversary.
permanent	(pēr' mà nĕnt)	*adj.* Lasting; abiding.
persistent	(pēr sĭst' ĕnt)	*adj.* Enduring.
resident	(rĕ̇ş' ĭ dĕnt)	*n.* One who dwells in a particular place.

Assignment

Combine the prefixes and/or suffixes with the word roots listed below to build ten words from the above list. Use each word in a sentence.

Prefixes	Word Roots and Meanings	Suffixes
as, ap, at	gnor (gnoscere—to know) L.	ant
con, com	hab (habitare—to dwell) L.	ent
in	man (manere—to remain) L.	
per	par (parere—to come forth) L.	
re	plic (plicare—to twist together) L.	
	pon (ponere—to put, set) L.	
	sed, sid, sis (sedere—to sit) L.	
	sist (sistere—to stand) L.	

permanent
applicant
consistant
resistant
persistant
assistant
insistant
resident
component

35

29

WORDS WITH "ARY," "ORY," OR "ERY"

In adjectives, "ary" means "of," "belonging to," or "connected with," as in *sedentary* (connected with sitting). In nouns, "ary" means the same thing, but the meaning applies to a person or object, whereas the adjective usually refers to a quality or condition.

beneficiary	(bĕn′ ĕ fi′ ci ar′ ў) fĭsh ĭ ĕr	*n.*	One who receives a benefit or advantage.
granary	(grăn′ à rў)	*n.*	Storehouse for grain.
mortuary	(môr′ tŭ ăr′ ў)	*n.*	A funeral home.
notary	(nō′ tà rў)	*n.*	Public officer who certifies papers as to authenticity.
reactionary	(rĕ ăc′ tion ăr′ ў)	*n.*	One who favors return to an older order.
revolutionary	(rĕv′ ό lū′ tion ăr′ ў)	*n.*	One who fights for drastic change.
sanitary	(săn′ ĭ tăr′ ў)	*adj.*	Hygienic; healthful.
sedentary	(sĕd′ ĕn tăr′ ў)	*adj.*	Characterized by sitting.
temporary	(tĕm′ pό răr′ ў)	*adj.*	Not permanent.

"Ory" means "of," "relating to," or "characterized by" when it appears in adjectives; in nouns, it indicates "place of" or "for."

auditory	(au′ dĭ tō′ rў)	*adj.*	Pertaining to hearing.
factory	(făc′ tό rў)	*n.*	Production plant.
lavatory	(lăv′ à tō′ rў)	*n.*	Bathroom.
preparatory	(prĕ păr′ à tō′ rў)	*adj.*	Introductory.
promissory	(prŏm′ ĭs sō rў)	*adj.*	Conveying an assurance.
regulatory	(rĕg′ ŭ là tō′ rў)	*adj.*	Concerned with making rules.

"Ery" is a noun-forming suffix meaning "art" or "practice," "state" or "condition."

archery	(ärch′ ĕr ў)	*n.*	Sport using bow and arrows.
finery	(fīn′ ĕr ў)	*n.*	Showy clothes; ornaments.
monastery	(mŏn′ ăs tĕr′ ў)	*n.*	A cloister.
scenery	(scĕn′ ĕr ў)	*n.*	Landscape.
snobbery	(snŏb′ bĕr ў)	*n.*	Rank-conscious conduct.

Assignment

Choose words from the above list to answer the following questions.

1. What did she call the bathroom? *lavatory*
2. What is another name for a plant that produces goods? *factory*
3. Where are the dead bodies placed before burial? *mortuary*
4. How would you describe rank-conscious conduct? *snobbery*
5. How would you describe the political ideas of someone who favors a return to the past? *reactionary*

ABCDEFGHIJKLESSON 30
REVIEW

A. Form words to complete the following sentences by using the prefixes, suffixes, and word roots listed below. The words chosen should substitute for the words in parentheses.

Prefixes	Word Roots and Meanings	Suffixes
ac, as	audi (audire—to hear) L.	able, ible
in	cept (capere—to take) L.	ant, ent
ir	gis (gerere—to carry) L.	ar
per	hab (habitare—to dwell) L.	ary, ory, ery
re	man (manere—to remain) L.	
sus	reg (regere—to guide) L.	
	san (sanus—healthy) L.	
	sed, sid, sis (sedere—to sit) L.	
	sist (sistere—stand) L.	
	vis (videre—to see) L.	

1. Good will is an (unseen) asset.
2. The judge ruled that Arthur's testimony was not (allowable) *acceptable*
3. The university (officer) enrolled the students. *official*
4. His actions were (not in line with the rules).
5. The doctor said it would be a (lasting) disability.
6. The (person living here) is not at home.
7. Jim lost his (hearing) capability.
8. The environment of a hospital should be (hygienic).
9. The teacher appointed (a helper) to record grades.
10. Ann has (an impressionable) mind to outside influences.

B. Replace the underlined words in the following sentences with synonyms. These synonyms should be taken from Lessons 26-29.

1. Senator Adams was a formidable enemy in debate.
2. The defendant's guilt was obvious to all.
3. John has gained weight because of his inactive life.
4. This food is not fit to be eaten.
5. Allen's story was not only believable; it was convincing.
6. We stopped at the place where the priests live in the hope of seeing Father Andrew.
7. My older brother works in a storehouse for grain during the summer.
8. This philosopher has some strange ideas about life.
9. Harry is a very reliable person.
10. These house plans are comparable to yours.

C. Write one or more paragraphs on a topic of your choice. Include at least two words from each of the preceding four lessons. These words should be used correctly and sensibly, showing that you understand their meaning. Underline the words as you use them.

ABCDEFGHIJK LESSON 31

VERBS ENDING IN "IZE," "ISE," OR "YZE"

Usually when the first part of the word is a word in itself, use "ize," as in *itemize*. When the first part of the word is not a word in itself, use "ise," as in *surmise*. A few words of Greek derivation use "yze" or "yse." These suffixes mean "to subject to," "to become," or "to practice."

advertise	(ăd′ vẽr tīse)	v.	To make known publicly.
chastise	(chăs tīse′)	v.	To punish.
despise	(dĕ spīse′)	v.	To loathe; scorn.
exercise	(ĕx′ ẽr çīse)	v.	To practice.
analyze	(ăn′ à lȳze)	v.	To separate into elements.
paralyze	(păr′ à lȳze)	v.	To make motionless.
authorize	(au′ thōr īze)	v.	To empower.
characterize	(chăr′ ăc tẽr īze′)	v.	To distinguish.
civilize	(cĭv′ ĭ līze)	v.	To educate; refine.
localize	(lō′ căl īze)	v.	To confine to one place.
mobilize	(mō′ bĭ līze)	v.	To prepare for active use.
modernize	(mŏd′ ẽrn īze)	v.	To bring up to date.
philosophize	(phĭ lŏs′ ŏ phīze)	v.	To search for the meaning of fundamental beliefs.
recognize	(rĕc′ ŏg nīze)	v.	To acknowledge a person or thing previously known.
standardize	(stănd′ ärd īze)	v.	To bring into conformity.
summarize	(sŭm′ mà rīze)	v.	To present briefly.
synchronize	(sȳn′ chrŏ nīze)	v.	To cause to take place at the same time.
temporize	(tĕm′ pŏ rīze)	v.	To comply with the time.
visualize	(vĭs′ ú ăl īze)	v.	To form a mental image of.
vitalize	(vī′ tăl īze)	v.	To endow with energy.

Assignments

A. Combine the prefixes and/or suffixes with the word roots listed below to derive words from the list above.

Prefixes	Word Roots and Meanings	Suffixes
syn	chron (chronos—time) L.	ise
ad	cogn (cognoscere—to know) L.	ize
re	soph (sophos—wisdom) Grk.	yze
phil	vert (vertere—to turn) L.	

B. Copy the words listed below. Beside each word or phrase write its *antonym* from the word list.

1. Reward.
2. Synthesize.
3. Mobilize.
4. Adore.
5. Take away power.

38

VERBS ENDING IN "ATE," "EN"

The suffixes "ate" and "en" have identical meanings; the first is a Latin suffix and the second Anglo-Saxon. Both are found in verbs and adjectives, but in this lesson we shall concentrate on the verbs. In verbs, the suffixes mean "to make" or "to act," as in *captivate* and *weaken*. In adjectives, the suffixes mean "having the quality of," as in *affectionate* and *woolen*.

accelerate	(ăc çĕl′ ĕr āte)	v.	To cause to move faster.
accommodate	(ac cŏm′ mố dāte)	v.	To adapt; to oblige.
accumulate	(ac cū′ mu lāte)	v.	To collect; to pile up.
annihilate	(an nī′ hĭ lāte)	v.	To reduce to nothing.
appreciate	(ap prē′ çĭ āte)	v.	To set a just value on.
calculate	(căl′ cŭ lāte)	v.	To determine; to estimate by mathematical processes.
conciliate	(cŏn çĭl′ ĭ āte)	v.	To cause to agree.
exaggerate	(ĕx ăǵ′ gĕr āte)	v.	To overstate the truth.
inculcate	(ĭn cŭl′ cāte)	v.	To implant; to teach.
irritate	(ĭr′ rĭ tāte)	v.	To excite impatience and anger.
retaliate	(rế tăl′ ĭ āte)	v.	To return like for like.
separate	(sĕp′ ȧ rāte)	v.	To disconnect; to sever; take away.
vacillate	(văç′ ĭl lāte)	v.	To waver; to hesitate.
brighten	(brīght′ en)	v.	To cause to shine.
fasten	(fȧs′ ten)	v.	To attach or join.
moisten	(mois′ ten)	v.	To make slightly wet.
quicken	(quĭck′ ĕn)	v.	To make alive; to revive.
strengthen	(strĕngth′ ĕn)	v.	To make more durable.
tighten	(tīght′ en)	v.	To fix securely and firmly.
weaken	(wēak′ ĕn)	v.	To lessen in strength.

Assignment

Rewrite the following sentences, replacing the italicized word or words with synonyms from the above list:

1. How did Charles *amass* so much money in three years?
2. I would like to *oblige* you, but we have no rooms available.
3. How did you *determine* your loss on investments for 1969?
4. Claire's tendency to *overstate the truth* has resulted in a credibility gap she cannot bridge.
5. To *insist upon "an eye for an eye"* in time of trouble is usually not wise.
6. We shall have to *take* the children *away* from their parents during the ceremony.
7. To *waver* now is to lose the opportunity.
8. Teachers should try to *implant* values of honest and industry.
9. Their aim was not to defeat their enemies but to *kill* them.
10. Your disregard of nutrition *affected* your health.

**WORDS ENDING IN "LY,"
"WARD," OR "WISE"**

Of these three suffixes used to form adverbs, "ly" is the most common. Adverbs answer the questions "how" (in what manner), "when," and "where." Which of these three questions does each of the following adverbs answer?

awkwardly	(awk′ wãrd lў)	*adv.*	In a clumsy manner.
cautiously	(cau′ tious lў) shŭs	*adv.*	Carefully avoiding danger.
easily	(ēaṣ′ ĭ lў)	*adv.*	Without difficulty.
entirely	(ĕn tīre′ lў)	*adv.*	Completely; wholly.
frequently	(frĕ′ quĕnt lў)	*adv.*	Often.
indistinctly	(ĭn′ dĭs tĭnct′ lў)	*adv.*	Obscurely; not clearly.
promptly	(prŏmpt′ lў)	*adv.*	Without delay.
quietly	(quī′ ĕt lў)	*adv.*	Free from noise; calmly.
skillfully	(skĭll′ fụl lў)	*adv.*	Proficiently.
unusually	(ŭn ū′ ṣụ ăl lў)	*adv.*	Uncommonly; rarely.

clockwise	(clŏck′ wīṣe′)	*adv.*	Moving as the hands of the clock move.
lengthwise	(lĕngth′ wīṣe)	*adv.*	Longitudinally.
likewise	(līke′ wīṣe′)	*adv.*	In like manner; also.
otherwise	(oth′ ĕr wīṣe′) uth	*adv.*	In a different manner.
sidewise	(sīde′ wīṣe′)	*adv.*	Viewed from the side.

afterward	(aft′ ẽr wãrd)	*adv.*	At a later time.
downward	(down′ wãrd) dou	*adv.*	In a descending course.
forward	(fôr′ wãrd)	*adv.*	Toward the front.
homeward	(hōme′ wãrd)	*adv.*	In the direction of home.
upward	(ŭp′ wãrd)	*adv.*	From lower to higher.

Assignments

A. Choose ten words from the above list. Write the words, underlining the adverb-forming suffixes. Write the part of speech of the word that remains when the suffix is removed. Use your dictionary.

B. Are adverb-forming suffixes classified as derivational or inflectional? Explain.

C. Write a paragraph using four of the words from the above list. Each word should be used correctly and sensibly. Underline the four words as you write them.

34

WORDS ENDING IN "ER"

The suffix "er," in nouns, signifies "one who" or "that which." It also shows the comparative degree of adjectives, as in *sweeter,* and the comparative degree of adverbs, as in *nearer.* Some of the following words are used both as adjectives and adverbs.

Nouns

adviser	(ăd vīṣ′ ẽr)	*n.*	One who recommends.
customer	(cŭs′ tóm ẽr)	*n.*	One who buys.
designer	(dĕ ṣīgn′ ẽr)	*n.*	One who determines form.
laborer	(lā′ bõr ẽr)	*n.*	One who does physical work.
photographer	(phō tŏg′ rȧ phẽr)	*n.*	One who takes pictures.
purchaser	(pûr′ chȧs ẽr)	*n.*	One who buys.
reminder	(rĕ mīn′ dẽr)	*n.*	Something that causes one to remember.

Adjectives

earlier	(ẽar′ lǐ ẽr)	*adj.*	Preceding in time.
friendlier	(friĕnd′ lǐ ẽr)	*adj.*	More favorably disposed.
happier	(hăp′ pǐ ẽr)	*adj.*	More pleased with one's well-being.
prettier	(pret′ tǐ ẽr)	*adj.*	More attractive.
simpler	(sǐm′ plẽr)	*adj.*	Less complex.
smoother	(smōōth′ ẽr)	*adj.*	Less irregular.

Adverbs

faster	(fȧst′ ẽr)	*adv.*	More quickly.
harder	(härd′ ẽr)	*adv.*	More difficult; harsher.
later	(lāt′ ẽr)	*adv.*	In the future; after delay.
nearer	(nẽar′ ẽr)	*adv.*	Closer.
quicker	(quĭck′ ẽr)	*adv.*	With greater speed.
slower	(slōw′ ẽr)	*adv.*	More sluggish.
sooner	(sōōn′ ẽr)	*adv.*	At an earlier date.

Assignment

Choose a word from the above list to substitute for each group of italicized words in the following sentences.

1. You have to drive *more rapidly* than 40 m.p.h. on the freeway.
2. I suggest that you come *at an earlier date.*
3. Lola is *more favorably disposed towards others* now.
4. *Those who buy* should check sales claims.
5. Mr. Allen is *one man who takes good pictures.*
6. Do you think that Vivian is *more attractive* than Vera?
7. This machine is *less complex* than yours.
8. This photograph is a *remembrance* of our picnic on July 4.
9. We will continue this conversation *in the future.*
10. This stone is *freer from irregularities* than that one.

35

GENERAL REVIEW

Section I: Review of Lessons 31-34

A. Combine affixes and word roots to form at least ten words from the previous four lessons. In some cases, it is necessary to insert extra letters to complete the word:

Prefixes	Word Roots and Meanings	Suffixes
a, ad	cul (calcare—to tread) L.	ate
de, dis	civ (civis—civil) L.	ize, ise
e, ex, ec	duco (ducere—to lead) L.	ly
in, on	graph (graphein—to write) Grk.	er
photo	mot, mov, mob (movere—to move) L.	
	sign (signum—to mark, sign) L.	
	stinct (instigare—to incite) L.	
	temp (tempus—time) L.	
	vers, vert (vertere—to turn) L.	
	vid, vis (videre—to see) L.	
	vita (vita—life) L.	

B. Copy the words in the right-hand column. Beside each word place the number of the definition that applies:

1. To punish.
2. To separate into elements.
3. To form a mental image of.
4. To reduce to nothing.
5. To set a just value on.
6. Longitudinally.
7. One who takes pictures.
8. In a clumsy manner.
9. To adapt; to oblige.
10. One who informs and recommends.

annihilate
analyze
appreciate
awkwardly
chastise
photographer
lengthwise
visualize
adviser
accommodate

C. Copy the words listed below. Beside each one write its *antonym* from Lessons 31-34.

1. To reward.
2. To synthesize.
3. To brutalize.
4. To decelerate.
5. Gracefully.
6. To empower.
7. To understate.
8. To please.
9. Seldom.
10. Dangerously.
11. To keep secret.
12. To take away energy.
13. To soothe.
14. Generalize.
15. Ignore.
16. Combine.
17. Commonly.
18. Backward.
19. One who sells.
20. Less difficult.

Section II: General Review of Lessons 1-34

A. Copy the affixes on the right. Beside each, place the number of the word from the left column that best defines the affix.

1. To subject to, become, practice.
2. Between.
3. Before.
4. State, act.
5. With, together.
6. Down, away.
7. One who, that which.
8. Able to be.
9. Art, state, condition.
10. Not, in, on.

de-
-er
-ery
inter-
im-, in-
-able, -ible
-ance, -ancy
-ize, -ise, -yze
pre-
com-, con-, co-

B. Listed below are suffixes having the meaning of "state," "quality," and "act," with one example for each suffix. Give two other examples for each suffix.

Suffix	Example
ance	resistance
ence	competence
ent	diligent
ery	snobbery ·

C. Listed below are suffixes having the meaning of "one who," "that which," with one example for each suffix. Give two other examples for each suffix.

Suffix	Example
ant	consultant
er	adviser
ent	resident
or	possessor

D. Copy the words listed below. Change the prefix in each word to form a word different in meaning. Write the meaning of each revised word.

consign   submit   reform   intercede
  deduction   monotheism   dispose   export

E. Copy the words listed below. Change the suffix in each word to form a word different in meaning. Write the meaning of each revised word.

actor   registrar   mortuary   credible
  circular   auditory   indication   sanitary

RULES GOVERNING SUFFIXING

In the next five lessons, we shall study the rules that govern the joining of suffixes to words. As you study the rules, remember that all rules have exceptions.

Rule 1: When a one-syllable word ends in a consonant preceded by a vowel, double the consonant if the suffix begins with a vowel. Do not double the consonant if the suffix begins with a consonant. Example: *ship + ed =* shipped; *ship + ment =* shipment. Since there are very few suffixes that begin with consonants, it is the first part of the rule that is of special interest.

Assignments

A. Add the indicated suffixes to the words listed below:

ing	en, on	er
clip	bid	bit
drag	bit	cut
get	glad	drum
knit	glut	fat
let	hid	hot
run	mad	job
sit	rid	quit
stir	rot	slip

ed	y *	ly
ban	bag	dim
chop	bat	glad
fan	chat	grim
hop	fun	hot
mob	fur	low
scrub	fog	neat
sin	nut	sad
step	spot	trim

* The letter *y* is considered a vowel when it is sounded as a vowel.

B. Add suffixes to the words below to form words which will illustrate Rule 1. Note that almost all suffixes begin with vowels. (This is not true of prefixes, many of which begin with consonants.)

blot	flip	pet	ship
clap	gun	pin	shop
clip	jog	put	shut
clot	lag	putt	slum
dim	man	quiz	snub
dip	split	rub	spit
strut	stop	war	trip

RULES GOVERNING SUFFIXING

In this lesson we are concerned about two-syllable words ending in a consonant preceded by a single vowel, such as the word *permit*. Some of these words are accented on the second syllable, as in *refer*. Most of them end in "l," "r," or "t," with occasional exceptions ending in other consonants, as "d" in *forbid*.

Rule 2: When a suffix beginning with a vowel is added to a two-syllable word ending in a consonant preceded by a single vowel, the final consonant is doubled. Example *refer* + *ed* = referred. The final consonant is not doubled, however, if the new word does not retain the same accent as the basic word. Example: *refer* + *ence* = reference. (An exception to this rule is found in *excel, excelled, excellence*.)

Assignments

A. Following the above rule, add the suffixes indicated to the words:

ing	ed	ance, ence
befit	demur	concur
commit	deter	confer
compel	omit	infer
equip	submit	prefer
forbid	transmit	recur
incur	repel	remit
abut	allot	occur
ballot	annul	temper
alter	barrel	allow

B. Circle the words below which follow Rule 2. Explain why the rule applies to them, and why it does not apply to others.

reverent	deferral
bestowed	admission
misfitted	expelled
transferee	averred
borrowing	ironed
propellor	localize
admittance	unveiled
refitting	following

C. The words *equip* and *prevail* are similar in that the final consonant is preceded by two vowels and the accent is on the second syllable of each word. The past tense of these words is *equipped* and *prevailed*. Similarly, the present participle is *equipping* and *prevailing*. Why is the final consonant doubled in one word and not in the other? (Clue: Look to your rules for pronunciation.)

RULES GOVERNING SUFFIXING

Rule 3: If a word ends in "e," the "e" is retained before a suffix beginning with a consonant. The "e" is dropped before a suffix beginning with a vowel.

Many words ending in "ce" or "ge" retain the "e" before all suffixes except those beginning with "e," "i," or "y," to keep the soft sound of "c" or "g": *notice . . . noticeable*; but the "i" in *noticing* keeps the "c" soft, and therefore the final "e" is dropped. Some words ending in "g" preceded by "d" may drop the final "e" before a suffix, since the "d" softens the "g": *acknowledge . . . *acknowledgment*.

Can you explain the spelling of the following words?

> change . . . changing . . . changeable
> charge . . . charger . . . chargeable
> amuse . . . amusing . . . amusement
> *judge . . . judging . . . judgment

* In recent dictionaries, the spellings *judgement* and *acknowledgement* are acceptable.

In words ending in "ue," the final "e" is dropped before a suffix.

> argue . . . argument . . . arguing
> continue . . . continuing . . . continual
> pursue . . . pursuer . . . pursuance

Assignments

A. Copy the following verbs in the left hand column. Form a noun, adjective or adverb from each verb by adding a suffix from the right hand column. Explain the relationship of these derivatives to Rule 3.

Words	Suffixes
abridge	able
accommodate	er
budge	ing
displace	ion
engage	less
move	ment
sacrifice	
trace	

B. Copy the following sentences, correcting any italicized word that is misspelled.

1. That salesman's rudeness was *unexcuseable.*
2. Most rumors are *basless* in fact.
3. No *retaliateory* action was taken by the soldiers.
4. Much repair work is needed before the house will be *liveable.*
5. We *trudgd* five miles through the mud to reach our campsite.

RULES GOVERNING SUFFIXING

Rule 4: In a word ending in "y" preceded by a consonant, the "y" is changed to "i" when adding all suffixes except those beginning with "i." The "y" is retained before suffixes beginning with "i."

Examples: supply . . . supplied *but* supplying . . . supplier

Rule 5: In a word ending in "y" preceded by a vowel, the "y" is retained when adding a suffix.

Examples: annoy . . . annoyance; attorney . . . attorneys

(Irregular verbs do not follow this rule, as in pay . . . paid; say . . . said.)

Rule 6: Comparison of adjectives ending in the letter "y" requires the changing of "y" to "i" when a consonant precedes the "y."

Examples: pretty . . . prettier . . . prettiest

Assignments

A. Write the present participle and past tense of each of the verbs in the following list.

Example: apply . . . applying . . . applied.

comply	fry	marry	signify
vary	hurry	query	supply
verify	justify	worry	try
convey	deploy	stay	satisfy

B. Use the suffixes: "able," "ible," "ous," "al" and "ing" to form adjectives from the following nouns.

Example: beauty . . . beautiful; fury . . . furious

charity	glory	hurry
courtesy	horror	hypocrisy
terror	sanctify	victory

C. Write the plural forms of the following nouns:

Example: university . . . universities

bureaucracy	lavatory	factory
candy	monastery	galaxy
dictionary	alley	journey

D. Write nouns formed from the following adjectives:

Example: holy . . . holiness

busy	happy	kindly
catty	icy	lovely
friendly	nasty	lowly

A. Form the present participle of each of the following verbs:

awake	fade	praise	shine
choose	freeze	put	stay
drag	give	repel	submit
drink	lose	ride	take
drive	play	rise	throw
excel	please	see	try

B. Combine the suffixes and words listed below to form at least fifteen words from Lessons 36-39. Use each suffix at least once. Identify the rule governing the formation of each new word.

Words	Suffixes
abridge	able, ible
accommodate	al
ban	ance, ence
bureaucracy	es, s
engage	ion
horror	less
hypocrisy	ly
lovely	ment
mad	ness
neat	ous
omit	
prefer	
sanctify	
slice	
trace	

C. Number your paper from one to ten. Beside each number write the word from the right column that corresponds to the definition in the left column.

1. Beyond number.	amenable
2. Cannot be destroyed.	innumerable
3. Beyond control; delinquent.	impressionable
4. Unfailing; unerring.	laudable
5. Worthy of honor.	venerable
6. Credible.	accessible
7. Within reach; obtainable.	indestructible
8. Easily influenced.	infallible
9. Willing to yield.	believable
10. Worthy of praise.	incorrigible

ABCDEFGHIJKLESSON **41**

USE OF THE HYPHEN

A hyphen is sometimes used in words formed by the addition of an affix and in compound words formed by combining two or more separate words.

Rule 1: A compound may be written as one word, two or more words, or as a hyphenated word: *bookkeeping, attorney general,* and *court-martial.* A hyphenated compound that comes into everyday use is likely to be written eventually as one word.

Rule 2: Compound numbers from *twenty-one* to *ninety-nine* are hyphenated.

Rule 3: When a prefix is inserted before a proper noun or adjective, a hyphen is used: *pro-American, pre-Johnson.*

Rule 4: The prefixes "vice" and "ex" and the suffixes "elect" and "designate" are hyphenated in titles: *ex-president, vice-chairman, congressman-elect, ambassador-designate.*

Assignments

A. In the words listed below, the elements of compound words have been separated. Write the correct spelling of each word. Refer to your dictionary when in doubt.

anti Communist	inter national	pro U.N.
book keeper	labor saving	ready made
broad minded	lake side	secretary elect
brother in law	master piece	six teen
cold blooded	master plan	there after
ex port	never the less	thirty nine
ex president	news caster	thorough bred
fire engine	news stand	top notch
fire proof	non Government	trans Atlantic
first class	over due	un American
forty six	post marked	up and coming
gate way	post master	vice president
grand daughter	pre Armistice	way laid
grand stand	pre scription	with hold
head quarters	pre serve	work shop
hit and run	pre Shakespearian	world war
ice cream	pre Victorian	yard stick
inter American	pro Nixon	year round

B. For each of the rules listed above, choose two additional words that illustrate the rule and use them in a sentence.

USE OF THE HYPHEN

Rule 5: When a prefix is added to a word, the combination is generally written as one word: *misspell, prepay.* Some exceptions are *semi-indirect, anti-intellectual.* These words are hyphenated to indicate correct pronunciation of repeated vowels.

Rule 6: The hyphen is sometimes used after the prefix "re" to avoid confusion between two words with the same spelling but different meanings: *re-cover* and *recover,* for example.

Rule 7: The prefix "self" is always followed by a hyphen; the suffix "self" is joined to the word: *self-esteem, himself.*

Rule 8: When adding a suffix causes a letter to occur three consecutive times, the suffix is hyphenated: *wall-less, bell-like.*

Assignment

Write the correct form of each compound that appears in parentheses.

1. Is (self government) successful at your college?
2. You can partially overcome (self consciousness) by good grooming.
3. Nancy always thought of (her self) as her best friend.
4. In the dim light, it appeared to be a (ball like) figure.
5. The snake bite proved to be (harm less).
6. Our efforts must be (co ordinated) if they are to succeed.
7. The coach decided to (re treat) the team to another round of sodas.
8. Dr. Simmons prescribed an (anti biotic) to stop the infection.
9. His father became a (semi invalid) shortly after the accident.
10. In spite of all their tugging, the rope remained (semi attached) to the pier.
11. When Harry gets out of the United States Army, he hopes to (re establish) his law practice in town.
12. In a utopia, we would all live in a (jail less) society.
13. The man was (semi intoxicated) when his car ran off the road.
14. It is important never to lose your (self esteem).
15. The candidate demanded a (re count) of the ballots.
16. (Self reliance) was important on the American frontier.
17. The politician, being a practical and realistic man, was (anti idealist).
18. The company's mail was (mis sorted) and sent to the wrong departments.
19. Their studio apartment is (hall less), consisting of only one large room.
20. Mary and Jane could blame only (them selves) for arriving so late.
21. A (dis proportionate) amount of money was allotted for the decorations.
22. The encounter was (pre arranged) by intermediaries.
23. Why do you (dis trust) Anne?
24. Try to do the homework by (your self).
25. Does this painting (pre date) the Renaissance?

WORD DIVISION

When it is necessary to divide words at the end of the writing line, a hyphen is inserted between syllables at the point of division. The following rules are helpful.

Rule 1: Words of one syllable, such as *length* and *book*, should not be divided.

Rule 2: A prefix of three or more letters may be separated from the rest of the word at the end of a line: *pre-diction, over-work*. Similarly, a suffix of three or more letters may be separated from the rest of the word: *grace-ful, home-less*.

Rule 3: When double consonants are contained within a word, the word may be hyphenated between the consonants unless the basic word ends with a double consonant: *get-ting, permis-sion,* but *cross-ing, pass-able*.

Rule 4: The suffixes "cion," "cian," "gion," "sion," "tion," "tive," and "sive" are kept as syllables regardless of word structure: *coer-cion, musi-cian, conta-gion, impres-sion, correc-tion, protec-tive, permis-sive*.

This rule does not apply to other suffixes: *stop-ping, wrap-per, dili-gent*.

Rule 5: Compounds written as one word should be divided only between words: *over-coat, pains-taking, beach-comber*.

Rule 6: Hyphenated words should be divided only at the hyphen: *court-martial, father-in-law*.

Assignment

Assume that you have come to the end of a writing line with three or four letters written for each of the following words. Indicate with a hyphen the division point for each word.

attitude	forever
authority	furniture
basketball	instruction
believable	machinery
category	memory
condition	operation
connection	passenger
considerable	population
direction	questionnaire
dollar	sergeant at arms

ABCDEFGHIJK LESSON **44**

WORD DIVISION

Rule 7: Words should be divided so that there are at least three letters before the hyphen and after the hyphen, preferably more: *gen-eral,* not *gener-al; deci-sion,* not *de-cision.*

Rule 8: Long vowels are usually found in "open" syllables; that is, the vowel ends the syllable. If the vowel is short, the syllable is usually "closed" by a consonant; this is especially likely to be true if the syllable is accented: *mi-ser, mis-ery; na-ture, nat-ural; mu-sic, mus-lin.*

Rule 9: When two consonants or two vowels are pronounced as one sound, they are not divided. When consecutive vowels are pronounced separately, they may be divided: *nei-ther, teach-able;* but *cre-ative, tri-ennial.*

Rule 10: Some words and abbreviations are so closely related that they should be divided carefully for readability.

Examples:

Mr. Richard-Brown, *not* Mr.-Richard Brown, *or* Mr. Rich-ard Brown

T. H. Jones, D.D.S., *not* T. H. Jones,-D.D.S., *or* T. H.-Jones, D.D.S.

Cincinnati,-Ohio 45227, *not* Cin-cinnati, Ohio   45227, *or* Cincinnati, Ohio-45227

Rule 11: Avoid dividing figures, abbreviations, and words or figures containing apostrophes.

Examples:

$25,000 *not* $25,-000 *or* $-25,000

A.T. & T. *not* A.T.- & T.; 1970's *not* 1970-'s

Assignment

Copy the following list of words or phrases, dividing them in accordance with the above rules.

New Jersey	324 Pine Street
achieved	Mary Smith
appreciate	Maryanne
appreciation	Mr. Howard
only	technical
scientific	capitalization
records	July 4, 1776
dominate	Mike's
school	essentials
8:00 o'clock	coupon
Provo, Utah 84601	into

ABCDEFGHIJK LESSON **45**
REVIEW

A. The following paragraphs contain mistakes in word division and in the use of the hyphen. Recopy the paragraphs, correcting all errors.

The Chinese New-Year celebration begins two-weeks before their New Year's Day and closes with the Lantern Festival two-weeks after New Year's Day. The Chinese New-Year falls between January 21 and February 19 most years.

During this period, accounts are settled and households thoroughly cleaned. On New Year's Eve, members of the family gather to-gether for feasting and reminiscing. Incense is burned to honor ancestors, and at midnight fire-crackers are exploded to welcome the spirits. The spirits are believed to return between 11 P.M. on New Year's Eve and 1 A.M. on New Year's morning.

New Year's Day is spent in calling on friends and in family reunions. Gifts are exchanged, including money for luck in the New-Year.

The Dragon Dance is a feature of the Lantern Festival. Men in a dragon costume dance to drums and gongs and exploding firecrackers to dramatize man's struggle with the universe, and to bring New Year's festivities to a memorable con-clusion.

B. Copy the words listed below as they appear here. Circle those words that are incorrectly hyphenated, or divided as if at the end of a line. Write the number of the rule that applies in each case.

Hyphenation	Word Division
brother-in-law	crea-tion
her-self	self-dis-cipline
self-esteem	should-n't
semiattached 6	stand-ard
thirty-nine	sta-ture
un-American	Mon-tana
ex-port	Mr. R.V.-Taylor
bell-like	Teuton-ic
ice cream	topsy-tur-vy
pre-scription	to-wards
pre-Shakespearian	Vati-can
newsstand	vertical-ly
over-due	Wedg-wood
secretary-elect	Wednes-day
grand daughter	West-Virginia
nine-teen	direct-ion
nevertheless	cross-ed

53

PLURAL FORMS OF NOUNS

The next ten lessons deal with rules involved in forming the plurals and the possessives of nouns. (Consult Lesson 9 for a quick review of inflectional suffixes.) As you consider these rules, keep in mind that no rule is without exceptions.

Rule 1: The singular form of most nouns is changed to the plural by the addition of "s."

Example: book . . . books; invitation . . . invitations; rail . . . rails

Rule 2: Plurals of nouns ending in "s," "x," "z," "ch," "sh," or "ss" are formed by adding "es."

Examples: bus . . . buses or busses; tax . . . taxes; buzz . . . buzzes

bench . . . benches; lash . . . lashes; mass . . . masses

Rule 3: Proper nouns form their plurals in the same way as common nouns: an "s" is added to the end of the word. If the proper noun ends in "s," "x," "z," "ch," "sh," or "ss," the plural is formed by adding "es."

Examples: Smith . . . Smiths: Fox . . . Foxes

Thanksgiving . . . Thanksgivings

Assignments

A. Form the plurals of the following words and write the number of the rule that applies in each case.

hunch	Christmas	Charles
lunch	Tuesday	church
Brown	sex	class
brush	mix	blotter
tax	pass	box
cross	desk	flash
quiz	dance	guess
lobby	canoe	sneeze

B. Use each of the words below in a sentence, correcting any words that are misspelled.

dishes	Joneses
glasses	ranches
schooles	fixis
servicess	wishes
Mondays	passes

54

47

PLURAL FORMS OF NOUNS

Rule 4: In nouns ending in "y" preceded by a vowel, the plural is formed by adding "s." In nouns ending in "y" preceded by a consonant, plurals are formed by changing the "y" to "i" and adding "es." When a proper name ends in "y," the plural is formed by adding "s."

Examples: attorney . . . attorneys; journey . . . journeys

army . . . armies; lady . . . ladies

Mary . . . Marys: The four Marys worked together.

Rule 5: Most nouns ending in "f" or "fe" form the plural by adding "s."

Examples: chief . . . chiefs; hoof . . . hoofs; safe . . . safes

Rule 6: Some nouns are exceptions to Rule 5, forming the plural by changing "f" or "fe" to "ves."

Examples: calf . . . calves; knife . . . knives; half . . . halves

Assignments

A. Copy the following words. Beside each word write its plural form and the number of the rule involved.

journey	handkerchief	alloy	safe
life	industry	Betty	chimney
shelf	company	inquiry	wife
story	country	inventory	yourself

B. Correct incorrect plurals as you copy the following sentences:

1. "Honor among thiefs" has been questioned many times.
2. Two halfs make a whole.
3. The sound of pounding hoofs was common in the Old West.
4. The new convoys of men will reach the front line soon.
5. The consumer surveies proved helpful in our research.
6. These tile rooves are attractive but expensive.
7. Do you have the knifes and forks?
8. We should take care of these bills ourselfs.
9. The children attended four parteys last week.
10. The Darveys are happily married.
11. We have a committee to clean up the alleys.
12. We spent part of our vacation picking berries.
13. Friends and enemys alike fled before the advancing armys.
14. The chiefs ruled their territories with a firm hand.
15. How many inquiries have you received?

48

PLURAL FORMS OF NOUNS

Rule 7: Nouns ending in "o" *preceded by a vowel* form the plural by adding "s."

Examples: curio . . . curios; cameo . . . cameos; rodeo . . . rodeos

Rule 8: *Most* other nouns ending in "o," especially nouns related to music, form the plural by adding "s."

Examples: alto . . . altos; piano . . . pianos; Eskimo . . . Eskimos

Rule 9: *Some* nouns ending in "o" *preceded by a consonant* form the plural by adding "es."

Examples: echo . . . echoes; Negro . . . Negroes; potato . . . potatoes

Assignments

A. Write the correct plural for each word in parentheses in the following sentences. Check the dictionary if you are unsure.

1. (Radio) are popular among teen-agers.
2. You can exchange this diamond for three choice (cameo).
3. We brought six (kimono) from Japan.
4. Do you like mashed (potato) as well as rice?
5. Tonight we honor our football (hero).
6. Several (volcano) are still active.
7. Many (tobacco) have contributed to this blend.
8. (Tornado) seldom occur in California.
9. Hammond High School bought two new (piano).
10. Three children played piano (solo) at the concert.
11. Five (trio) have entered the contest.
12. The teacher writes daily (motto) on the chalkboard.
13. Few (studio) offer such opportunities.
14. (Mosquito) don't like me, I'm glad to say.
15. Do you like to play (domino)?
16. Our apartment is filled with (curio) from many countries.
17. Do you approve of our (embargo)?
18. We are studying (ratio) in mathematics.
19. (Patio) are pleasant settings for parties.
20. The (alto) should stand here, and the (soprano) over there.

B. The words in the following list have been written in their plural form. Copy these words, correcting any spelling errors.

shampoos	zeros	portfolios
memoes	taboos	haloes
vetoes	cellos	avocados
zoos	flamingos	mementoes
proes	igloos	toes

49

PLURAL FORMS OF NOUNS

Rule 10: There are some nouns that form the plural irregularly by making a change within the word.

Examples: child . . . children; foot . . . feet; woman . . . women

Rule 11: Hyphenated compound nouns and compound nouns of more than one word form the plural by adding "s" to the main word, usually the noun.

Examples: court-martial . . . courts-martial

mother-in-law . . . mothers-in-law

Rule 12: One-word compound nouns, as a rule, form the plural by adding "s" to the end of the word. In some compounds, the second element has an irregular plural.

Examples: cupful . . . cupfuls; football . . . footballs

housewife . . . housewives; workman . . . workmen

Rule 13: When an adverb or preposition is hyphenated to a noun, the plural is formed by making the noun plural.

Examples: goings-on; hangers-on; runners-up

Rule 14: When neither word of a compound is a noun, the second element of the word takes the plural form.

Examples: come-ons; go-betweens; higher-ups; run-ins

put-ons; write-ups; drop-outs; tie-ins

Assignments

A. Copy the plurals in parentheses, making any necessary corrections.

1. He lost three (teeths) in the accident.
2. The wagons were drawn by strong (ox).
3. The recipe calls for two (cupsful) of flour.
4. There aren't any (notary publics) in this building.
5. All (post offices) sell money orders.

B. Copy the following words. Beside each word write its plural and the number of the rule that applies.

attorney-at-law	set-to
cross-examination	sister-in-law
governor general	well-wisher

C. The following nouns form their plurals by changing the vowels. Give the plural forms and use them in sentences: *man, mouse, goose, louse.*

ABCDEFGHIJKLESSON 50

REVIEW

A. Copy the following words. Write the plural form and the number of the rule that applies.

adjutant general   child   ghetto
army   Chinese   inspector general
attorney   commander in chief grant-in-aid
bill of fare   fish   journey
cameo   frequency   Negro

B. Copy the following sentences, correcting any misspelled plurals in parentheses.

1. We have had only two (adjutant generals) in thirty-two years.
2. Many (Negroes) have made important contributions to American life.
3. I like two (teaspoonfuls) of sugar in tea.
4. Our nation has placed (embargoes) on many shipments to foreign countries.
5. From the top of the Empire State Building, one can see across the (rooves) of New York City.
6. I need two (loafs) of bread.
7. Boys standing on the corner watch (passerbys).
8. Bill's remarks are always spoiled by unpleasant (innuendos).
9. Several (wives) left the convention hall to shop.
10. Someone must have put the silver (knifes) on one of the top (shelves).
11. You should get rid of the (flies) that are buzzing around the (tomatoes).
12. In all of our (journies), we have never spent more than five days in each of the foreign (countries).

C. Supply the correct plural form of the words in parentheses.

1. The two (survey) resulted in different conclusions.
2. Bill has visited many (lady) from this office.
3. I know two (Molly) and three (Harry).
4. We appreciate the (courtesy).
5. The six (Smith) went to the shore together.
6. Mary is willing to sing with the (soprano).
7. Do not take shortcuts through the (alley).
8. These (banjo) should be returned to Mr. Shriver.
9. Add two (cupful) of sugar to the batter.
10. The (Eskimo) originally came from Asia.
11. The (daughter-in-law) were more helpful than the daughters.
12. All the (bench) are occupied.
13. (Albino) must be careful not to get sunburned.
14. Which of the two (dairy) did you prefer?
15. At the picnic we played (domino) and told (story).

58

PLURAL FORMS OF NOUNS

Rule 15: Some nouns have the same form for both the singular and the plural: *sheep . . . sheep; series . . . series.*

Rule 16: Some foreign nouns retain their original plurals. Others have English equivalents and in some cases both are acceptable. The English plural is usually preferred.

Word	Original Plural	English Plural
alumna (female graduate)	alumnae (L.)	(none)
alumnus (male graduate)	* alumni (L.)	(none)
formula	formulae (L.)	formulas
index	indices (L.)	indexes

* When referring to male and female graduates together, use *alumni.*

Rule 17: Form the plural of a letter, sign, or symbol by adding an apostrophe and "s":

Examples: The *6's* in this column should be *5's.*

There were four *A's* today.

Assignments

A. Write the correct plural for each word in parentheses. Check your answers with the dictionary.

1. There are many (formula) for success.
2. My brother caught three (salmon) in an hour.
3. The military_and naval (corps) coordinate their defense efforts.
4. When you have gathered the (datum), you can write the report.
5. We invested in stocks in the (1950).
6. Five (20) are equal to two (50).
7. Two (C.P.A.) were assigned to audit our accounts.
8. Our mathematics teachers are (Ph.D.).
9. Why don't you cross those (t) and dot those (i)?
10. The State College (Alumnus) Association sent us two additional (memorandum).

B. Copy the following words. Beside each word write its plural and the number of the rule that applies.

criterion	Chinese	parenthesis
ABC	curriculum	species
fish	crisis	tableau
appendix	gross	sheep
deer	analysis	thesis
1970	series	index

59

PLURAL FORMS OF NOUNS

Rule 18: Some nouns and expressions always require a plural verb regardless of the final letter: *grounds, goods, clothes, cattle, assets, glasses.*

Rule 19: Some nouns such as *molasses, whereabouts,* and *news* are singular even though they end in "s."

Rule 20: A collective noun names a collection of individual items or persons that may be considered together as a group or individually.

When the collective noun refers to the group as a unit it takes a singular verb, but if the individuals or the items in the group are considered separately, the plural verb is used. Some common collective nouns are: *class, committee, crowd, group, herd,* and *jury.*

Examples: The jury were debating the man's innocence among themselves.

The jury was silent while the prosecutor spoke.

Assignments

A. Cross out the incorrect verb in each of the following sentences.

1. When the game was over, the team (was, were) photographed.
2. The council (has, have) come to blows over the budget.
3. The Board of Directors (is, are) filing a protest.
4. The Committee on Foreign Affairs (is, are) not in agreement about the distribution of money for foreign aid.
5. The American delegation (has, have) been divided into three committees by the International Council.
6. News of the tornado (was, were) suppressed for five hours.
7. Scissors (was, were) found on the floor beside the body.
8. A gross of pencils (was, were) taken from the stockroom.
9. The whereabouts of the speaker (are, is) unknown.
10. More statistics (are, is) needed to document your report.

B. Copy the following words. Beside each word write either "S" for *Singular* or "P" for *Plural.* Give the number of the rule involved. (Consider collective nouns as singular, since they are singular in form even though they sometimes require a plural verb.)

clothes	alms	billiards
company	army	breeches
contents	flock	tongs
crowd	gallows	whereabouts
faculty	herd	band (music)
pliers	nuptials	apparatus
suds	pants	community
team	belongings	luggage

53
THE APOSTROPHE

The apostrophe is used to indicate contractions and possessives.

Contractions

We may combine some common words, leaving out one or more letters and using an apostrophe to show the omission. The resulting word is called a contraction. Contractions are used in informal writing and in daily speech.

Examples: can't (cannot); won't (will not); wasn't (was not)

they're (they are); they'd (they would)

Possessives

Rule 1: To form the possessive case of nouns, both singular and plural, that do not end in "s," add an apostrophe and "s."

Examples: I have the children's books. This is Mr. Smith's office.

Rule 2: Singular nouns of one syllable ending in an "s" sound, such as "s," "x," and "z," form the possessive by adding " 's." Singular nouns of more than one syllable, ending in an "s" sound, add only an apostrophe to form the possessive, unless the possessive will sound unnatural without the final "s."

Examples: Nouns of one syllable—Mr. Cox's thesis.

Nouns of more than one syllable—Miss Adams' keys.

"S" added to retain expected sound—Cortez's armies.

Rule 3: The possessive of a plural noun that ends in "s" is formed by adding an apostrophe only.

Examples: The boys' books are here. This is a millionaires' club.

Assignments

A. Copy the following words. Beside each word write the singular and plural possessives, and the number of the rule involved.

subscriber	acquaintance	minute
tourist	agency	pioneer
woman	hour	Polynesian

B. Combine the following pairs of words into contractions:

I am	we are	is not	they will
you are	I will	could not	we would
he is	he would	it is	that is

ABCDEFGHIJKLESSON 54

THE APOSTROPHE

Rule 4: Pronouns form their possessive case through irregular spelling changes. The apostrophe is not used in possessive pronouns.

Examples: they . . . theirs; who . . . whose; he . . . his; she . . . hers
we . . . ours; you . . . yours; * it . . . its; my . . . mine

* Do not confuse *its* with *it's*, the contraction of *it is*.

Rule 5: Compound words form the possessive by adding " 's" to the last word. For plural possessives of compound words, an "of" phrase indicates possession.

Examples: The commander in chief's estate was seized.
The estates of the commanders in chief were seized.

Our sister-in-law's husband was absent.
The husbands of the sisters-in-law were absent.

Rule 6: Joint ownership or authorship is indicated by making the last noun possessive: *Lewis and Clark's expeditions.*

Separate possession is indicated by making each noun possessive: *Byron's and Shelley's poetry.*

Rule 7: Do not use the possessive case for nouns denoting inanimate objects: The pages of the book, *not* the book's pages.

However, in common idiomatic expressions, the possessive may be used, as in *earth's surface; razor's edge; wit's end.*

Assignments

A. Write the correct possessive form for each phrase in parentheses.

1. No one disagreed with the (school board) recommendation.
2. Everyone wanted to hear the (park ranger) lecture.
3. (Tom and Bill) car has been stolen.
4. (Florida and California) oranges are preferred above others.
5. The abstract picture is (my work).

B. Copy the following sentences, correcting any mistakes in the italicized words.

1. *This county's park system* is one of the best in the state.
2. Our dog always buries *it's* bones.
3. The *vice-chairman's* role was to conduct the meetings when the chairman was absent.
4. *Twain and Poe's* books are examples of American literature.
5. The chairs are *theirs* but the table is *ours.*

ABCDEFGHIJKLESSON 55

GENERAL REVIEW

Section I: Review of Lessons 51-54

A. Write the correct possessive for each italicized word or phrase.

1. This paper is *you*.
2. The *commander in chief* decision saved us.
3. *Mr. Smith* shoes need cleaning.
4. Has the Community Council announced *it* plan?
5. Is this *Mr. Jones* house?
6. In less than a *minute* time, he was there.
7. I have three *month* time to devote to the project.
8. Meet me in the *D. A.* office.
9. We have *Rex* will in the office safe.
10. *Dr. Franz* car is beyond repair.

B. Beside each word write its singular possessive, its plural, and its plural possessive.

ambassador	employee	sergeant at arms
animal	employer	brother-in-law
association	genius	C.P.A.
bear	heroine	M.D.
cashier	humorist	Government
citizen	league	Charles
civilization	lieutenant	sheep
commentator	nephew	corps
company	organization	jury
cousin	physicist	president-elect

C. Copy the following sentences, crossing out the incorrect possessives.

1. I told the Randalls that the luggage was (theirs, their's).
2. Did she say that the wallet was (hers, her's)?
3. The decision should be (theirs, theirs'), not (ours', ours).
4. There is a sale at (Mark & Lee's, Mark's & Lee's) Department Store.
5. The (passersby's, passersby) testimony was helpful.
6. The sale was held in (White's, Inc.; White, Inc.'s) warehouse.
7. We had a (gentlemans', gentlemen's) agreement.
8. Mark (Twain's, Twains') novels are still popular.
9. The (Writer's, Writers') Conference was held in Vermont.
10. (Frances's, Franceses') report was typed on our machine.

D. Write the contractions for the following words:

you are	was not	cannot
they would	that is	have not
he is	they will	you would

Section II: General Review of Lessons 36-54

A. Correct the following words as you write them. They all contain errors in suffixing.

consistant	incured
controled	occassion
conveniance	planing
courtious	prominant
depositer	regreted
familar	responsable
friendlyness	steping-stone
incidently	successfull
improvment	untill
jewelery	visiter

B. You are at the end of a writing line with only three or four letters of each of the following words typed on the page. Indicate with a hyphen where you would divide each word.

beautiful	protective
bookkeeping	questionnaire
court-martial	re-enact
diligent	self-esteem
granddaughter	semi-direct
himself	stopping
international	suspicion
musician	undertake
newsstand	vice-president
permission	workmen

C. Write the correct plural for each word in parentheses.

1. The (ranch) are in dire need of rain.
2. How many (Christmas) have you spent overseas?
3. The (church) will help us in this venture.
4. The (bus) are not running tonight.
5. Many of our (fish) died while we were on vacation.
6. Our (tax) are higher this year.
7. We have eight (glass) of orange juice in the refrigerator.
8. The two (brother-in-law) are congenial.
9. (Tornado) and erupting (volcano) attest to Nature's violence.
10. May I have two (cupful) of sugar and three (box) of matches?
11. A committee was appointed to review all (curriculum) for the coming year.
12. Frontier schools concentrated on the three (R).
13. My brother raises white (mouse) as a hobby.
14. There were two (runner-up) in the contest.
15. Dick manages several art (studio).

ABCDEFGHIJKLMNOPQRSTUVWXYZ

Part ABCDE 3
FGHIJKLMNO

Basic Words

In Part 3 you will review many words basic to a good vocabulary.

Lessons 56-75 deal with pronunciation: They present important words, famous names and places, and foreign expressions now part of our ever-growing language. All of these words are commonly mispronounced.

Lessons 76-85 deal with homonyms, antonyms, and synonyms.

Lessons 86-105 clarify many of the troublesome words often misused and misspelled.

Lessons 106-110 present a glossary of the states and their capitals.

PRONUNCIATION SYMBOLS

You will remember that the pronunciation of a word may be shown by either phonetic symbols or diacritical marks. This text uses the diacritical marking system of *Webster's New International Dictionary, Second Edition.* (See Lessons 1-7, Part 1.) Five of the most commonly use diacritical marks are discussed below. You should know them by name.

The macron (mā′ crŏn) is the horizontal line used over a vowel (‾) to indicate a long sound: (rē′ ăl ĭsm), (stāte), (cūte), (līne), (knōw).

The breve (brēve) is commonly used to mark short vowels (˘): (păck), (lĕt), (mĭll), (lŏt), (tŭb).

The tilde (tĭl′ dĕ) is used to indicate a vowel sounded as "er" in an unaccented syllable (˜): (māk′ ẽr), (mīn′ ẽr).

The dieresis (dī ĕr′ ĕ sĭs) is the double dot (¨) used over an "a" to indicate the "ah" sound: (ärm), (fär), (fä′ thẽr).

The circumflex (cîr′ cŭm flĕx), (ˆ) is used to indicate the following sounds: "a" as in (câre) and (pârent); "e" as in (thêir); "o" as in (ôrb) and (côrk); and "u" as in (ûrġe) and (bûrn).

Assignment

Copy the following words and place a diacritical mark over each vowel. Check your answers with the dictionary. Your dictionary may use the schwa (inverted "e," ə) for unaccented vowels. Do you understand the vowel markings?

accordingly	people	maybe	general
admire	policy	merely	going
alone	possess	numerous	happiness
attempt	prize	o'clock	headache
began	railroad	appear	tomorrow
brought	realize	opposite	tried
chosen	speech	original	usually
consider	straight	owing	various
device	suppose	enjoy	very
during	therefore	escape	view
easily	influence	field	waste
effort	dying	forest	window
yield	fork	stare	rather
zero	purge	churn	letter
idea	create	performer	farm

PRONUNCIATION OF VOWELS

We accept the fact that words such as *ought, brought, night, either* and *neither* used to be pronounced differently than they are today—a fact that accounts for their spelling. The pronunciation of words continues to change; pronunciations once considered wrong are now acceptable because they are in general use. This is why we say that language is a living and growing part of our culture.

It is wise to learn the traditional spelling and pronunciation of words for formal use. However, remember that other spellings and pronunciations are sometimes allowed in the most recent dictionaries. Vowels present the greatest difficulty in pronunciation. Syllabication of words usually indicates correct pronunciation of vowels. In "open syllables"—syllables ending with a vowel—the vowel usually has a "long" sound.

Assignments

A. Syllabicate the following words and indicate the vowel sounds. Then refer to a dictionary, indicating the pronunciation it gives for each word. In doing this, you will see the importance of usage in determining that which is acceptable. Be sure to record the name and edition of the dictionary you use, since variations in pronunciation do occur.

apparatus	catch	rabid
patronage	data	aviator
err	forehead	implacable
apricot	creek	gratis
blatant	just	gala
finance	penalize	economics

You have found that two pronunciations are given for some of the above words. Usually one pronunciation has been established by rule, the other by popular usage.

B. Write a sentence for each of the above words, circling the vowels that cause you problems in spelling.

C. Copy the following list of words, correcting any mistakes that have been made in syllabication and adding diacritical marks.

uni form	per u sal
tot al	sta tus
trac tor	sup ple
te le graph	ge nu ine
dit to	doc u ment
di verse	co lumn
ben e fit	Bi ble
bi cy cle	as sure
pro vide	us able

ABCDEFGHIJKLESSON **58**

PRONUNCIATION OF CONSONANTS

Watch those consonants! Some consonants and consonantal diph-thongs have more than one possible pronunciation. The words below contain consonants that may cause trouble.

The letter "g" followed by "i," "e," or "y" usually has the "j" sound; "g" followed by "a" or "u" has the "gay" sound. "Ch" may have the "k" sound, the "sh" sound, or the regular "ch" sound. (For further details concerning consonants, review Lessons 6 and 7.)

agenda	(å ģĕn′ då)	n.	List of things to be done.
archipelago	(är′ chĭ pĕl′ å gō)	n.	Group of islands.
architect	(är′ chĭ tĕct)	n.	One who plans buildings.
archives	(är′chĭves)	n.	Public records.
brochure	(brŏ çhụre′)	n.	A pamphlet.
chandelier	(chăn′ dĕ liĕr′)	n.	A lighting fixture.
character	(chăr′ ăc tēr)	n.	Distinctive quality.
congratulate	(cŏn grăt′ ụ lāte)	v.	To wish joy.
diphtheria	(dĭph thēr′ ĭ å)	n.	A disease of the throat.
gigantic	(ģī găn′ tĭc)	adj.	Huge.
gist	(ģĭst)	n.	The main point.
kindergarten	(kĭn′ dēr gär′ tĕn)	n.	School for small children.
length	(lĕngth)	n.	Measured distance.
naphtha	(năph′ thå)	n.	A flammable liquid.
niche	(nĭche)	n.	Recess in a wall.
picture	(pĭc′ tụre)	n.	Representation in art or words.
quantity	(quạn′ tĭ tў)	n.	An amount; a portion.
rough	(rough) rŭf	adj.	Coarse; not smooth.
sword	(swōrd)	n.	Weapon; rapier.
towards	(tŏ′ wărds)	prep.	In the direction of.

Assignments

A. Copy the above words. In each word, circle the consonants that might cause you to misspell the word.

B. Insert missing consonants to form complete words. Then read the sentences aloud.

1. I couldn't get the ____ist of his argument.
2. Are you planning to send Billie to kindergar____en?
3. This bro____ure on consumer education is helpful.
4. Have you measured the le____th of this rug?
5. The surface of the track was too rou____ for racing.
6. What is the a____nda for our meeting today?
7. This scenery would make a beautiful pic____ure.
8. Irene congra____ulated Merrell on his promotion.
9. His attitude to____ards us is unfriendly.
10. The ar____itect's estimate is the first item on the a____enda.

ABCDEFGHIJKLESSON **59**

SILENT CONSONANTS

Do not sound silent consonants. A silent consonant is usually found with another consonant preceding it or following it. The following words are typical: dou*b*t, *k*now, clim*b*, *p*neumonia, g*h*ost. The same is true of French-derived words in which the silent consonant, usually, final "s" or "t," follows a vowel: debu*t*, debri*s*, apropo*s*.

asthma	(ăs̱*th*′ mà)	*n.*	A respiratory disease.
chasten	(chās′ *t*en)	*v.*	To discipline; to punish.
chestnut	(c*h*ĕst′ nŭt)	*n.*	A tree; a nut.
christen	(chrĭs′ *t*en)	*v.*	To baptize; to name.
cupboard	(cŭ*p*′ boārd)	*n.*	Closet for dishes.
depot	(dē′ pō*t*)	*n.*	A delivery station.
epistle	(é pĭs′ *t*le)	*n.*	A letter.
glisten	(glĭs′ *t*en)	*v.*	To sparkle or shine.
gnash	(*g*năsh)	*v.*	To grind the teeth together.
handkerchief	(hănd′ kĕr chĭef)	*n.*	A cloth used to wipe the face.
hasten	(hās′ *t*en)	*v.*	To urge forward; to hurry.
indict	(ĭn dīct′)	*v.*	To charge with an offense.
irrigate	(ĭr′ rĭ gāte)	*v.*	To supply with water.
moisten	(mois′ *t*en)	*v.*	To make slightly wet.
pneumonia	(*p*neú mō′ nĭ à)	*n.*	A disease of the lungs.
scintillate	(scĭn′ tĭl lāte)	*v.*	To gleam, spark.
solder	(sŏl′ dĕr)	*n.*	Metal used to join other metals. *v.* To unite.
subtle	(sŭb′ tle)	*adj.*	Delicate; acute; keen.
wrench	(*w*rĕnch)	*n.*	A tool that tightens and loosens. *v.* To twist; jerk.
wring	(*w*rĭng)	*v.*	To squeeze, twist.

Assignments

A. Copy the words listed below, circle silent letters, and choose one word from the above list to add to each group.

Examples	Additional Words
doubt, climb	
kick, science	
ghastly, ghoul	
gnaw, knife	
calm, salmon	
watch, hasten	
write, wrap	
psychology, pneumatic	

B. Indicate the pronunciation of each of the following words. Use each word in a sentence: *asthma, corps, knight, plumber, raspberry, wrench.*

70

ABCDEFGHIJK LESSON **60**
REVIEW

A. Using the diacritical marks discussed in Lesson 56, indicate the correct pronunciation of the following words:

reptile	alias	irrevocable
subsidiary	brooch	menu
column	textile	morale
deaf	transient	demise
de luxe	statistics	deteriorate
naive	genuine	donor
poinsettia	irreparable	yield

B. Insert missing vowels in the following sentences and indicate the pronunciation of each vowel.

1. To ____r is human.
2. How are you planning to f____nance your new business?
3. This water is j____st tepid, not hot.
4. C____n you obtain the d____ta for us?
5. ABC Company is a subsidi____ry of XYZ, Inc.
6. Elaine comes from a long-l____ved family.
7. I have quoted his comments verb____tim.
8. Send us the c____pons in today's mail.
9. The boys are wading in the cr____k.
10. This leather is more s____pple than plastic.

C. Be prepared to write these sentences from dictation. Pay special attention to the underlined words.

1. There are eight major islands in the Hawaiian archipelago.
2. Naphtha is a dangerous liquid to keep in the home.
3. The quantity of food Lloyd can consume is amazing.
4. Diphtheria is no longer a common disease among children.
5. Rita is an independent person with a great deal of character.
6. The hotel manager bought a new chandelier for the lobby.
7. The archives of the United States are in Washington, D.C.
8. These gigantic rocks must be removed before the road can be completed.
9. Alice contracted pneumonia while on vacation.
10. Her jewelry seemed to scintillate in the moonlight.
11. Robert is going to solder the pipe now.
12. Space science has made rapid advancements in the last decade.
13. David's asthma keeps him from qualifying for the track team.
14. Are you sure you can fit all those dishes into the cupboard.
15. Mrs. Miller will have to chasten her children if they continue to misbehave.

ABCDEFGHIJKLESSON 61

SYLLABLE TROUBLE

Current usage permits more latitude in accenting syllables than was formerly permitted. In personal speech, it is perhaps wise to choose the traditionally preferred accents. Accenting the wrong syllable and incorrect syllabication cause difficulties in learning the correct spelling of words.

Assignments

A. Copy the words below. Say each word, stressing the accented syllables. If the word is incorrectly accented or syllabicated, rewrite it properly. Consult the dictionary.

ad dress'	fa mous'	mis chie' vous
ad mira' ble	fin' ance	op' er a' ting
af' flu ence'	for' mi da ble	pref' er a ble
al ly'	for fei' ture	quant i' ties
ap' plic able	fran ti' cal ly	rea di' ly
broad' cas ter	fur' i ous	re gis' tr a tion
burst	gen' u ine	reg' u lar
cin' e ma	hos' pit al' i ty	soph' o more
com' par a ble	in' te grate	sup' er flu ous
con' tin u ous' ly	in' ter est	syl la' ble
de' tail	jew el ry'	to' wards

B. Be prepared to write these sentences from dictation. Pay special attention to the underlined words.

1. Do you consider these investments comparable?
2. We were confronted by a formidable group of dissenters.
3. The Allens are known for their hospitality.
4. Elizabeth will inherit the family jewelry because the only other heir is a bachelor.
5. Do you believe that France will ally its interests with those of any other country?
6. Their attitude towards this country illustrates interesting changes in public opinion.
7. We have quantities of literature on this subject.
8. Do you have the address of the cinema?
9. Nancy's term paper is an admirable piece of research.
10. My two younger brothers are very mischievous.
11. Your ideas are perfectly clear, but they are contrary to most adult thinking.
12. The broadcaster burst with excitement as he announced the final score.
13. A genuine effort was made to eliminate some of the detail.
14. Tomorrow is registration day for the sophomores.
15. If an emergency arises, the equipment will be readily available.

72

ABCDEFGHIJK LESSON 62

THE NONEXISTENT SYLLABLE

The following three lessons contain words frequently mispronounced. Study these words carefully since mispronunciation leads to misspelling. This lesson is concerned with the tendency to add extra letters and syllables when pronouncing the words listed below.

analogous	(à năl' ố goŭs)	*adj.* Corresponding to something else.
athletic	(ăth lĕt' ĭc)	*adj.* Pertaining to sports.
disastrous	(dĭ sȧs' troŭs)	*adj.* Ill-fated.
drowned	(drowned)	*v.* Suffocated in water.
	dround	
elm	(ĕlm)	*n.* A tree.
endeavor	(ĕn dĕav' ŏr)	*v.* To strive.
film	(fĭlm)	*n.* A thin layer.
foundry	(foun' drȳ)	*n.* A building for casting metals.
grievous	(griĕv' oŭs)	*adj.* Distressing; severe.
handling	(hăn' dlĭng)	*n.* The method of using something.
heartrending	(heärt' rĕnd' ĭng)	*adj.* Causing grief.
height	(heīght)	*n.* Elevation.
hindrance	(hĭn' drănce)	*n.* Obstruction.
hungry	(hŭn' grȳ)	*adj.* Desire for food.
integral	(ĭn' tĕ grăl)	*adj.* Composite. *n.* A totality.
laundry	(laun' drȳ)	*n.* A place for washing.
lightning	(līght' nĭng)	*n.* Discharge of electricity from clouds.
remembrance	(rĕ mĕm' brănce)	*n.* Recollection; a reminder.
sacred	(sā' crĕd)	*adj.* Holy.
umbrella	(ŭm brĕl' *l*à)	*n.* A shade from rain or sun.

Assignments

A. Copy the list below, correcting any misspelled words. Next to each word, write its proper pronunciation.

laundery	hungary	analogous
drownded	sacred	heighth
umbrella	filum	handeling

B. Copy these sentences, correcting any underlined word that is misspelled. Write the correct pronunciation for each underlined word.

1. Julie saved the corsage as a <u>remembrance</u> of the dance.
2. Thunder and <u>lightning</u> accompanied the storm.
3. The newspaper reported a <u>heartrendering</u> account of the accident.
4. <u>Atheletic</u> competition between neighboring schools is common.
5. Our class visited a <u>foundry</u> last week.

63

PRONOUNCING SYLLABLES WHICH DO EXIST

A common error in pronunciation is the failure to pronounce all letters or syllables that should be sounded. The words listed below are often misspelled because of such faulty pronunciation.

arctic	(ärc′ tĭc)	*adj.*	Relating to the North Pole.
auxiliary	(aux il′ ia rў)	*adj.*	Helping; secondary.
	ŏg zĭl yȧ		
boisterous	(bois′ tēr oŭs)	*adj.*	Loud; turbulent.
boundary	(bound′ ȧ rў)	*n.*	That which fixes a limit.
February	(Fĕb′ rṳ ăr′ ў)	*n.*	Second month of the year.
heavily	(hĕav′ ĭ lў)	*adv.*	As if burdened with a great weight.
ivory	(ī′ vŏ rў)	*ŋ.*	Material of mammals' tusks.
liable	(lī′ ȧ ble)	*adj.*	Obliged by law; answerable.
library	(lī′ brar′ ў)	*n.*	A collection of books kept for study.
	brĕr		
licorice	(lĭc′ ŏ rice)	*n.*	A plant used as a flavoring.
literature	(lĭt′ ĕr ȧ tŭre)	*n.*	Group of writings.
maintenance	(māin′ tĕ nȧnçe)	*n.*	Upkeep; support.
massacre	(mȁs′ sȧ cre)	*n.*	Slaughter of many people.
	kĕr		
military	(mĭl′ ĭ tăr′ ў)	*adj.*	Pertaining to an army.
strength	(strĕngth)	*n.*	Capacity for exertion or endurance.
temperament	(tĕm′ pēr ȧ mĕnt)	*n.*	Disposition.
temperature	(tĕm′ pēr ȧ tŭre)	*n.*	Measured degree of heat.
theory	(thē′ ŏ rў)	*n.*	Hypothesis.
variegate	(vâr′ ĭ ĕ gāte)	*v.*	To diversify.
vegetable	(vĕġ′ ĕ tȧ ble)	*n.*	A plant grown for food.

Assignments

A. Be prepared to dictate the following sentences to your classmates.

1. The military auxiliary will meet again in February.
2. Libraries house all types of literature.
3. Elephants are the largest suppliers of ivory.
4. A landlord is liable for the maintenance of his buildings.
5. These variegated flowers are most unusual.

B. Copy the list below correcting any misspelled words. Next to each one write its proper pronunciation.

temperment	boisterous	massacre
vegetable	artic	boundry
licrice	strenth	heavily

ABCDEFGHIJK LESSON 64

PRONUNCIATION DEMONS

The words listed below present special problems in pronunciation and, therefore, spelling. In studying these words, avoid making the common mistakes of transposing letters so that perform would become preform; changing letters and spelling congratulate as congradulate; or omitting letters in spelling that are silent in pronunciation, for example the "t" in often.

asthma	(as̱th′ mȧ)	n.	A respiratory disease.
buffet	(bu̱f fet′) fā	n.	A sideboard; a cupboard.
corps	(cōrps)	n.	An organized body of people.
cupboard	(cŭp′ bōard)	n.	A cabinet for dishes.
debris	(dĕ bris′) brē	n.	Ruins; remains.
definitely	(dĕf′ ĭ nĭte lў)	adv.	Distinctly; certainly.
herb	(hĕrb)	n.	A plant used for seasoning.
indict	(ĭn dīct′)	v.	To charge with an offense.
jeopardy	(jĕop′ ārd ў)	n.	Peril; risk.
parliament	(pär′ lĭa mĕnt)	n.	A legislative body.
prejudice	(prĕj′ ŭ dĭçe)	n.	Bias; disadvantage.
prescription	(prē scrĭp′ tion)	n.	A written direction.
pseudonym	(pseū′ dŏ nўm)	n.	An assumed, second name.
raspberry	(rȁs̱p′ bĕr rў)	n.	A berry and its plant.
rescind	(rĕ́ scĭnd′)	v.	Annul; cancel.
sacrilegious	(săc′ rĭ lē′ gious) jŭs	adj.	Profane; desecrating.
salmon	(sȁlm′ o̱n)	n.	A large fish.
subtle	(sŭb′ tle)	adj.	Refined; artful.
vehicle	(vē′ hĭ cle)	n.	A conveyance.
Wednesday	(Wĕdne̱s′ daў)	n.	The fourth day of the week.

Assignments

A. Syllabicate the following words, give the meaning of each one, and circle the letters likely to cause trouble in pronunciation and spelling. Consult your dictionary where necessary.

jeopardy	Wednesday	preserve
alignment	vehicle	herb
kiln	raspberry	cupboard
parliament	asthma	sacrilegious
pseudonym	committee	benign
gourmet	indict	corps
congratulate	villain	debris

B. Write one or more paragraphs on a topic of your choice. Include at least ten of the words in this lesson, underlining each word as you use it. (These words should be used correctly and sensibly.)

75

ABCDEFGHIJKLESSON 65
REVIEW

A. Underscore the accented syllable of each word in parentheses.

1. It would be (extravagant) of me to go on such an expensive vacation.
2. Prosperity has made us an (affluent) society.
3. Her (forfeiture) of the prize was unexpected.
4. It is difficult to (integrate) all these ideas into one essay.
5. Is your past experience (applicable) to this new assignment?
6. Helen became (furious) at the (mischievous) behavior of her classmates.
7. Each (syllable) is pronounced separately.
8. Did you know her (fiancé) is a (famous) writer?
9. They are (frantically) searching for the lost (jewelry).
10. The rabbit ran away, (towards) the forest.

B. Pronounce each word below. Does the word look right? Does its spelling relate to the correct pronunciation? Copy the words, correcting any which are misspelled.

sacred	strength	jeopardy
hinderance	ivry	pregudice
disastrous	temperature	definately
elm	Febuary	recind
endeveor	arctic	perscription
lightening	auxiliary	sutle
laundery	boisterous	vehicle
drowned	liable	cupboard

C. Copy the following sentences, noting the underlined words. Practice pronouncing and spelling them so that you are prepared to write these sentences from dictation.

1. Registration for the next term will begin tomorrow.
2. John's handling of his formidable opposition was admirable.
3. Samuel Clemens' novels were published under the pseudonym "Mark Twain."
4. It is difficult for someone with asthma to participate in athletic events.
5. We usually have salmon for dinner on Wednesdays.
6. I don't think that the two situations are analogous.
7. The British legislative body is known as Parliament.
8. The military corps prevented a possible massacre.
9. His lack of height was a hindrance in winning the basketball scholarship.
10. Our dog was so hungry that she ate all the licorice.

ABCDEFGHIJK LESSON **66**

WORDS WITH TWO PRONUNCIATIONS

This series of four lessons introduces 40 words, each of which may be used as different parts of speech. In this lesson we are concerned with words that may be either nouns or verbs, depending upon the placement of accent marks.

accent	(ăc′ çĕnt)	*n.* A mark of emphasis.
	(ăc çĕnt′)	*v.* To emphasize.
conduct	(cŏn′ dŭct)	*n.* Behavior.
	(cŏn dŭct′)	*v.* To guide.
contest	(cŏn′ tĕst)	*n.* A struggle.
	(cŏn tĕst′)	*v.* To debate; argue.
digest	(dĭ′ ġĕst)	*n.* Summation; compilation.
	(dĭ ġĕst′)	*v.* To assimilate; comprehend.
escort	(ĕs′ côrt)	*n.* A guard.
	(ĕs côrt′)	*v.* To accompany.
insult	(ĭn′ sŭlt)	*n.* An affront; an indignity.
	(ĭn sŭlt′)	*v.* To assault verbally.
object	(ŏb′ jĕct)	*n.* Something tangible.
	(ŏb jĕct′)	*v.* To oppose.
produce	(prŏd′ ūçe)	*n.* Farm crops.
	(prŏ́ dūçe′)	*v.* To make.
reprint	(rē′ prĭnt′)	*n.* A second or later printing.
	(rē prĭnt′)	*v.* To print again.
transfer	(trăns′ fĕr)	*n.* A removal or conveyance.
	(trăns fĕr′)	*v.* To change; move.

Assignment

Copy the sentences below. Underline all words which appear on the above list. Above each underlined word indicate the part of speech. Use abbreviations.

1. Are you going to contest this case in court?
2. If you accent the correct syllable, you will pronounce the words properly.
3. The farmer brings his agricultural produce to market twice a month.
4. The platoon received a transfer to replace the soldier who was going home.
5. Training and ability are required to conduct an orchestra.
6. You may find this reprint helpful in your research.
7. This digest contains most of the information you will need.
8. Will you escort the ladies tonight?
9. Bob considered your remark an insult.
10. The object of the lesson was to teach self-reliance.

77

ABCDEFGHIJKLESSON **67**

NOUN OR VERB?

Listed below are ten additional words that may be either nouns or verbs, depending upon which syllable is stressed in pronunciation.

attribute   (ăt′ trĭ būte)   *n*. Inherent characteristic.
            (ăt trĭb′ úte)   *v*. To ascribe.

conflict   (cŏn′ flĭct)   *n*. A struggle.
        (cŏn flĭct′)   *v*. To oppose.

convict   (cŏn′ vĭct)   *n*. One under prison sentence.
       (cŏn vĭct′)   *v*. To find guilty.

extract   (ĕx′ trăct)   *n*. Excerpt.
       (ĕx trăct′)   *v*. To draw out.

ferment   (fĕr′ mĕnt)   *n*. Turbulence; disorder.
       (fĕr mĕnt′)   *v*. To agitate.

insert   (ĭn′ sĕrt)   *n*. A thing placed between.
      (ĭn sĕrt′)   *v*. To place between.

permit   (pĕr′ mĭt)   *n*. Warrant; license.
      (pĕr mĭt′)   *v*. To allow.

present   (prĕş′ ĕnt)   *n*. A gift.
       (prĕ̗ şĕnt′)   *v*. To introduce; give.

project   (prŏj′ ĕct)   *n*. A plan.
       (prŏ̗ jĕct′)   *v*. To extend.

recess   (re′ çes*s*)   *n*. A suspension of activity; indentation.
      (re çes*s*′)   *v*. To temporarily interrupt a procedure.

Assignment

Copy the sentences below. Replace each underlined word or phrase with its synonym from the list above. Insert accent marks to indicate the part of speech of each new word.

1. Did you obtain the hunting <u>license</u> for our trip?
2. After the performance, we will <u>give</u> a bouquet of roses to her.
3. We will <u>suspend</u> this meeting until tomorrow.
4. This <u>addition</u> should be placed between the first two pages.
5. The jury needs sufficient evidence to <u>judge</u> him <u>guilty</u>.
6. The <u>turbulence</u> was caused by a debate between political foes.
7. The <u>excerpt</u> from his speech summarized the most important points.
8. Is it possible to <u>extend</u> these plans into the future?
9. How did this local dispute escalate into a major <u>struggle</u>?
10. Many people <u>ascribe</u> his success to years of hard work.

78

ABCDEFGHIJKLESSON 68

NOUN OR ADJECTIVE?

Many words may be used as either nouns or adjectives. Unlike noun-verbs, most of these words do not vary their pronunciation according to function.

amateur (ăm′ à teûr′)   *n.* Novice; not a professional.
                                 adj. Unprofessional.

ancient (ān′ cient)   *n.* A venerable elder.
          shĕnt   *adj.* Old; primitive.

capital (căp′ ĭ tăl)   *n.* Upper case letter; seat of government; reinvested wealth.
                                 adj. Paramount; major.

invalid (in′ và lĭd)   *n.* One who is sickly.
        (ĭn văl′ ĭd)   *adj.* Not true; no basis in fact.

juvenile (ju̩′ vé nĭle)   *n.* Child; adolescent.
    or (ju̩ vé nĭle)   *adj.* Youthful; immature.

leisure (lēi′ sure)   *n.* Convenience.
        zhĕr   *adj.* Free; unoccupied time.
    or (lĕzh′ ĕr)

material (mà tēr′ ĭ al)   *n.* Any substance.
                           adj. Tangible; essential.

minute (mĭn′ ŭte)   *n.* One-sixtieth of an hour.
      (mī nūte′)   *adj.* Small; minor; petty.

official (ŏf fi′ cĭal)   *n.* Holder of a government position.
        fĭsh′   *adj.* Formal; recognized.

original (ố rĭġ′ ĭ năl)   *n.* The primary source or cause.
                          adj. First; primary.

Assignments

A. Use each of the following words in two sentences, once as a noun and once as an adjective: *material, official, juvenile, amateur, leisure.*

B. Copy the sentences below. Underline all words which appear on the preceding list. Above each underlined word write the abbreviation for its part of speech.

1. Ed is too concerned with minute details.
2. Archeologists study ancient ruins of past civilizations.
3. Murder is a capital offense.
4. Your conclusions are invalid since they are based on conjecture.
5. Even experts in art sometimes have difficulty distinguishing between an original and a reproduction.

ABCDEFGHIJK LESSON 69

VERSATILE WORDS

Each of the following words may be used as more than one part of speech. In some cases the meaning and/or pronunciation vary but the spelling remains the same. Where variations in pronunciation exist, note them since they may determine meaning.

absent	(ăb′ sĕnt)	*adj.* Not present.
	(ăb sĕnt′)	*v.* To withdraw (oneself).
address	(ăd drĕss′)	*n.* A speech; designation for delivery.
		v. To direct speech or attentions; to mark for delivery.
aerial	(á ēr′ ĭ ăl)	*adj.* Pertaining to the air.
or	(âer′ ĭ ăl)	*n.* Antenna.
catalog or **catalogue**	(căt′ là lŏg)	*n.* Index; register. *v.* To classify.
compound	(cŏm′ pound)	*adj.* Composite; complex. *n.* A mixture.
	(cŏm pound′)	*v.* To combine; to add to.
content	(cŏn tĕnt′)	*adj.* Satisfied. *n.* Happy. *v.* To please; gratify.
	(cŏn′ tĕnt)	*n.* The text of written material.
rebel	(rĕb′ ĕl)	*adj.* Insurgent. *n.* A revolutionary.
	(ré bĕl′)	*v.* To revolt.
record	(rĕc′ ŏrd)	*n.* Written account.
	(ré côrd′)	*v.* To write.
separate	(sĕp′ à răte)	*adj.* Distinct.
	(sĕp′ à rāte)	*v.* To divide.
subject	(sŭb′ jĕct)	*adj.* Liable; prone. *n.* One under authority.
	(sŭb jĕct′)	*v.* To expose to.

Assignment

Copy the sentences below. Replace the underlined word or phrase with a synonym from the list above. Indicate the part of speech of each word you substitute.

1. Ellen will make a written account of the proceedings.
2. Are you going to speak to the businessmen's luncheon today?
3. The insurgent forces were able to capture the village.
4. I am satisfied with the present situation.
5. These plans pose two distinct problems.

A. Use the following words as nouns in sentences and be prepared to read them aloud.

accent	conduct	extract	project	reprint
address	content	object	record	subject

B. Use the following words as verbs in sentences and be prepared to read them aloud.

attribute	convict	escort	present	recess
catalog	digest	insult	rebel	transfer

C. Use the following words as adjectives in sentences and be prepared to read them aloud.

aerial	capital	invalid	material	original
ancient	compound	juvenile	official	separate

D. Underscore the accented syllable of each of the words in parentheses and indicate the function of each word (part of speech). Be prepared to read the sentences aloud.

1. The grocer bought his (produce) from a farmer.
2. Can you (produce) enough vegetables for your family?
3. Be sure to (insert) a circular in each envelope.
4. Between what pages should this (insert) be placed?
5. Did you obtain the necessary (permit)?
6. (Permit) me to help you with this problem.
7. Crushed grapes are allowed to (ferment) in order to make wine.
8. There was a (ferment) of activity at the airport.
9. John cannot accept a fee if he wants to keep his (amateur) status.
10. Although I enjoy golf, I am still an (amateur).

E. The italicized words in the following sentences may be used as more than one part of speech. Write the abbreviation for the part of speech of each italicized word.

1. The wind blew down our *aerial* last night.
2. Will you *absent* yourself from next week's meeting?
3. Mark's greatest *attribute* is his humility.
4. Her mother has been an *invalid* since her illness last year.
5. Did you buy enough *material* for both dresses?
6. Our plans for a picnic are *subject* to weather conditions.
7. Do you have the correct *address* for my new home?
8. It will be necessary to *extract* the tooth.
9. Bill acted as her *escort* to the dance.
10. You should *accent* the second syllable.

ABCDEFGHIJK LESSON **71**

NAMES OF WELL-KNOWN PERSONS

This lesson lists some of the famous persons of the past and present. As you learn the significance of each person, concentrate on the correct spelling and pronunciation of his name.

Aristotle	(Ăr′ ĭs tŏt′ le)	Greek philosopher (384-322 B.C.)
Bunche, Ralph	(Bŭnche)	U.N. Under Secretary General.
Curie, Marie	(Cŭ riē′)	French chemist; discovered radium.
Freud, Sigmund	(Freud) Froid	Austrian neurologist; father of psychoanalysis.
Gandhi, Mohandas	(Găn′ dhi)	Indian political and religious leader.
King, Martin Luther	(Kĭng)	American civil rights leader.
Kosygin, Aleksei	(Ko sў′ gɪn)	Soviet Premier.
Mao Tse-tung	(Mä′ ổ Tṣĕ-tung′)	Chinese Communist leader.
Marshall, John	(Mär′ shăll)	Chief Justice of the United States (1801-1835).
Michelangelo	(Mĭ′ chĕl ăn′ ġĕ lō)	Italian sculptor; artist (1475-1564).
Nobel, Alfred	(Nổ bĕl′)	Swedish inventor; donor of the Nobel Prizes.
Omar Khayyam	(Ō′ mär Kha yyäm′) Kī	Persian poet (?-1123).
Pulitzer, Joseph	(Puļ′ ĭt zēr)	American journalist.
Roosevelt, Franklin D.	(Rōo ṣĕ vĕlt)	President of the United States (1933-1945).
Salk, Jonas	(Sälk)	Physician who developed polio vaccine.
Schweitzer, Albert	(Schweī′ tzēr)	Musician; clergyman; medical missionary.
Shakespeare, William	(Shāke′ spēare)	English dramatist and poet (1564-1616).
Socrates	(Sŏc′ rà tēṣ)	Greek philosopher (469-399 B.C.)
Stalin, Josef	(Stä′ lĭn)	Russian Communist leader (1929-1953).
Thant, U	(Thȧnt)	Secretary General of the United Nations.

Assignment

Complete the following sentences. Practice reading them aloud to make sure that you can pronounce the names correctly.

1. President R_____'s economic program was known as the New Deal.
2. U T_____ succeeded Dag Hammersjkold as U.N. Secretary General.
3. F_____ is sometimes called the father of modern psychiatry.
4. O_____ K_____'s poetry urges us to enjoy the present.
5. Have you ever seen M_____'s painting in the Sistine Chapel?

ABCDEFGHIJKLESSON 72

PLACES AT HOME AND ABROAD

This lesson contains names of well-known places at home and abroad. The following names of historic and scenic sites in the United States are likely to be misspelled or mispronounced.

Alamo	(Ăl' à mō)	Site of battle during the Texan War of Independence.
Appomattox	(Ăp' pŏ măt' tox) ŭks	Civil War brought to a close here; in Virginia.
Chesapeake Bay	(Chĕs' à pēake)	Body of water between Virginia and Maryland.
Gettysburg	(Gĕt' ty̆s bûrg)	Pennsylvania battlefield of the Civil War.
New Orleans	(Ôr' lĕ ăn̩s)	City of French heritage in Louisiana.
Niagara Falls	(Nī ăg' à rà)	North American waterfalls.
Philadelphia	(Phĭl' à dĕl' phĭ à)	First capital of the United States; in Pennsylvania.
Roanoke Island	(Rō' à nōke)	First English settlement; in North Carolina.
Sequoia National Park	(Sĕ quoi' à) kwoi	Park of world's largest and oldest trees; in California.
Yosemite	(Yŏ sĕm' ĭ tĕ)	Scenic park in California.

Check your spelling and pronunciation of the names listed below. Because they are foreign, they present spelling hazards.

Cairo	(Caī' rō)	Capital of Egypt.
Caribbean	(Căr ĭb bē' ăn)	Body of water southeast of Florida.
Iran	(Ī rän')	In southeastern Asia; formerly known as Persia.
Iraq	(Ĭ raq') räk	In southwestern Asia; Moslem culture.
Kenya	(Kĕn' yà)	Nation in East Africa.
Philippines	(Phĭl' ĭp pīne̩s)	Republic in the Pacific.
Prague	(Prägue)	Capital of Czechoslovakia.
Rio de Janeiro	(Rĭ' ō dĕ Jà nĕi'rō)	Cultural center of Brazil.
Saigon	(Saī gŏn')	Capital of South Vietnam.
Tel Aviv	(Tĕl' Â vĭv)	Major city in Israel.

Assignment

Choose the word from the list above which best corresponds to each of the following statements.

1. A fort which became a battle cry for the Texans.
2. A group of waterfalls separating Canada from New York.
3. Atlantic Ocean between The West Indies, North and South America.
4. Former capital city of Brazil.
5. Persian and Moslem states, often confused.

73
FOREIGN WORDS AND EXPRESSIONS

In this lesson we shall consider some French and Latin expressions used in our daily life but often mispronounced and misspelled.

avant-garde	(à' vänt' gàrde')	Out in front; offbeat.
bon voyage	(bôn' vo' yage')	Have a good journey.
	vwa yazh	
carte blanche	(cärte' blänche')	Unconditional power.
coup d'état	(coup d'e tat')	A sudden overthrow of government.
	kōo dá tà	
cuisine	(cui ṣine')	Style of cooking.
	kwĕ	
debonair	(dĕb' ó nâir')	Lighthearted; gracious.
encore	(en cōre')	Once more; again.
	än	
esprit de corps	(ĕs' prï*t*' dĕ côr*ps*)	Group spirit.
et cetera	(ĕt çĕt' ēr à)	And so on; and so forth.
fait accompli	(fait' ac' com' pli')	An accomplished fact.
	fĕ' tà' côn' plē'	
faux pas	(fau*x*' pa*s*')	A mistake.
	fō	
hors d'oeuvres	(*hôrs* d'oeu' vres)	Appetizers.
	dû' vres	
laissez faire	(lais' sez' fâire')	Noninterference.
	lĕ sā	
per annum	(pēr än' *n*ŭm)	By the year.
per capita	(pēr căp ĭ tà)	By the head.
raison d'être	(rắi' ṣôn' d'ê' tre)	Reason for existing.
résumé	(ré' ṣŭ mé')	A summary.
	rā mā	
status quo	(stā' tŭs quō)	Existing state of affairs.
tête-à-tête	(tête' à tête')	Private conversation.
	tāt à tāt	
vice versa	(vī' çḗ vēr' sà)	The reverse.

Assignments

A. Replace the italicized words with synonyms from the above list.

1. The cook has *complete freedom* in planning meals.
2. We like French *cooking*.
3. Before dinner we had some *appetizers* with our cocktails.
4. Have you written a *summary* of the plot?
5. Our Government no longer follows a policy of *noninterference*.

B. Complete the following sentences:

1. The carefully planned c_____ d'e_____, was a fiasco.
2. Mary is a great believer in the s_____ q_____.
3. We pay $1,800 p_____ a_____ for these accommodations.
4. We went to the airport to wish them b_____ v_____.
5. It was a f_____ a_____ by the time we found out.

74

FOREIGN WORDS AND EXPRESSIONS

Here are some additional **French** and **Latin** words that have been incorporated into our vocabulary. Be sure you know their proper pronunciation and spelling.

ad hoc	(ăd hŏc)	For this purpose only.
à la carte	(ä' lä cärte')	A meal chosen dish by dish.
aplomb	(à plŏmb')	Self assurance.
café	(cà' fé')	A coffeehouse; restaurant.
cause célèbre	(cauȿe çé' lĕ bre)	A notorious event.
exposé	(ĕx' pŏ ȿé)	A revelation of something
	ā	discreditable.
finesse	(fĭ nĕsȿe')	Subtlety; cunning.
genre	(ġën' re)	A style; type.
in toto	(ĭn tō' tō)	Entirely; all together.
ipso facto	(ĭp' sō făc' tō)	By the fact itself.
joie de vivre	(joie' dē vĭ' vre)	Joy of living.
	zhwȧ	
motif	(mŏ' tĭf')	Theme; pattern.
noblesse oblige	(nŏ' blĕsȿe' ŏ' blĭġe')	Privilege has its obligations.
per diem	(pēr dī' ĕm)	By the day.
per se	(pēr se)	By, of, or in itself.
	ā	
protégé	(prō tĕ ġé)	One under the protection of another.
pro tempore	(prō tĕm' pŏ rĕ́)	For the time being.
rendezvous	(ren' dĕȥ vouȿ)	A meeting place; a meeting
	rän	by appointment.
sans	(săņȿ)	Without.
savoir faire	(sà'voir' fâire')	Experience; sophistication.

Assignments

A. Copy the sentences below, replacing each italicized word with its synonym from the list above.

1. Do you prefer ordering *items from the menu* instead of ordering a full dinner?
2. Victoria handled the matters with *sophistication*.
3. Healthy children should be full of *the joy of living*.
4. In addition to salary, John receives $25 *per day* for traveling expenses.
5. They faced the crises *without* fear.

B. Complete the following sentences:

1. Too many people have abandoned the principle of n_____ o_____.
2. The candidate answered all the questions with the a_____ of a veteran.
3. Helen will serve as secretary p_____ t_____.
4. In what m_____ would you like the room decorated?
5. The president appointed an a_____ h_____ committee to plan the reception.

ABCDEFGHIJKLESSON 75

GENERAL REVIEW

Section I: Review of Lessons 71-74

A. Copy the names on the left. Beside each one place the number of the statement from the right column that best identifies the name.

Freud	1. Famous journalist; donor of prizes.
Gandhi	2. Physician who developed polio vaccine.
Mao Tse-tung	3. Greek philosopher who taught by questioning.
King	4. Civil Rights leader who preached nonviolence.
Schweitzer	5. Famous Italian painter and sculptor.
Pulitzer	6. Chinese Communist leader.
Nobel	7. Swedish inventor; donor of prizes.
Socrates	8. Medical missionary to Africa.
Michelangelo	9. Austrian neurologist; father of psychoanalysis.
Salk	10. Indian political and religious leader.

B. Listed below are the names of American states and foreign countries. Name a major city, historic or scenic site for each one.

Texas	California	Brazil
Virginia	South Vietnam	Czechoslovakia
Pennsylvania	Israel	Egypt

C. Define each of the following words and use it in a sentence.

tête-à-tête	status quo	motif
faux pas	encore	genre
et cetera	vice versa	protégé
café	savoir faire	cuisine

D. Complete the following sentences with foreign words or expressions that have been incorporated into our vocabulary.

1. Mary's trial became a c_____ c_____ when all the major newspapers reported it.
2. The testimony of the witness resulted in an e_____ of the criminal organization.
3. This can be proved i_____ f_____.
4. David attempted to convince them with great f_____.
5. A well written r_____ of your past experience will help you find a better job.
6. To bring order to society is the r_____ d'ê_____ of laws.
7. The p_____ c_____ income rose over the last six months.
8. Student e_____ d_____ c_____ is high because of favorable publicity.
9. He was a courteous and entertaining host; quite d_____.
10. The second officer of the Senate is known as the President P_____ T_____.

Section II: General Review of Lessons 56-74

A. Define each of the following diacritical marks. For each one, list two words that would make use of the mark in pronunciation: *macron, breve, tilde, dieresis* and *circumflex.*

B. Each of the following words contains troublesome consonants that may have more than one pronunciation or may be silent. Copy the following words, underlining any such consonants.

archives	asthma	picture	wrench
brochures	subtle	congratulate	depot
length	solder	agenda	hasten

C. Copy the sentences below, correcting any words in parentheses that are misspelled.

1. Will your little brother be a (hinderance) if he comes along?
2. The (film) will be developed in a few days.
3. The patient's (temperture) was normal for the second day.
4. We would like to get the northern (boundry) extended.
5. They expect the captain to (rescind) his order.
6. Their actions were considered (sacrilegious).
7. Nancy said that she would (definately) leave by Monday.
8. The weatherman explained the cold front as an (artic) air mass moving southward.
9. Don't forget your (umbreller).
10. Jim was cited for a motor (vehicle) violation.

D. Indicate the various parts of speech for each of the following words and write a sentence for each one.

reprint	insert	material	subject
object	attribute	minute	record
produce	capital	invalid	address

E. Copy the words on the left. Beside each place the number of the statement from the right column that best identifies it.

U Thant	1. Soviet Premier.
Mao Tse-tung	2. Noninterference.
Iraq	3. The reverse.
New Orleans	4. Chinese Communist leader.
vice versa	5. Theme; pattern.
laissez faire	6. A secretary general of the United Nations.
motif	
in toto	7. Entirely; all together.
Kosygin	8. City in Louisiana of French background.
Yosemite	9. National Park in California.
	10. Middle Eastern country.

HOMONYMS, ANTONYMS, AND SYNONYMS

Lessons 76-85 cover three classes of words: *homonyms, antonyms,* and *synonyms.* Many people are confused by these terms because they do not understand the differences among them. You should be familiar with *antonyms* and *synonyms,* since these terms have appeared in previous lessons. For review, their definitions are given with the meaning of a new term, *homonym.*

Homonym—a word that sounds like another word, but differs in meaning and spelling.

Examples: weigh and way; right and write; already and all ready.

Antonym—a word that has the opposite meaning of another word.

Examples: black and white; cold and hot; early and late.

Synonym—a word that is similar in meaning to another word.

Examples: novice and amateur; large and big; wealthy and rich.

Assignment

Write one homonym, one synonym, and one antonym for each of the following words:

Words	Homonyms	Synonyms	Antonyms
bored	board	indifferent	interested
capital			
coarse			
fair			
here			
male			
peace			
principal			
idle			
break			
buy			
foul			
pain			
vain			
mind			
raise			
steal			
right			
lone			

SPELLING OF HOMONYMS

Homonyms don't look alike but they sound alike. Since they sound alike, they are often misspelled. Therefore, to avoid the confusion caused by these troublemakers, identify meaning with exact spelling.

bail	(bāil)	*v.* To set free on security. *n.* Security.
bale	(bāle)	*n.* Large bundle.
cereal	(çēr' ē ăl)	*n.* Foodstuff of grain.
serial	(sēr' ĭ ăl)	*n.* Writing published in successive parts.
cession	(çĕs' sion)	*n.* A yielding or surrender.
session	(sĕs' sion)	*n.* A meeting or series of meetings.
forth	(fōrth)	*adv.* Forward.
fourth	(fōurth)	*adj.* Next after third.
gilt	(gĭlt)	*n.* Goldlike material.
guilt	(guĭlt)	*n.* Fact of having violated a law.
morning	(môr' nĭng)	*n.* First half of the day.
mourning	(mōurn' ĭng)	*n.* Grieving.
rite	(rīte)	*n.* Ceremony.
wright	(wrīght)	*n.* Workman.
serge	(sērġe)	*n.* Twilled fabric.
surge	(sûrġe)	*v.* To rise; to swell. *n.* A sweeping forward.
steak	(steāk)	*n.* A certain cut of meat.
stake	(stāke)	*n.* Pointed piece of wood or iron.
stair	(stâir)	*n.* A step or series of steps.
stare	(stâre)	*v.* To gaze fixedly.

Assignment

Copy the following sentences, selecting the correct homonym in parentheses.

1. Is the Legislature in (session, cession)?
2. He claimed to be a ship (rite, wright) by trade.
3. What (cereal, serial) do you eat most often for breakfast?
4. The blue (serge, surge) suit needs relining.
5. They are (morning, mourning) the death of her brother.
6. The picture frame was painted with (guilt, gilt).
7. Kathy was the (forth, fourth) person in line.
8. We drove a (steak, stake) into the ground.
9. The prisoner was released on $1,000 (bale, bail).
10. I saw him (stare, stair) incredulously at the speaker.

78
FUNCTION OF HOMONYMS

As you learn the spelling and meaning of the following homonyms, notice also the function of these words in sentences. Learning the part of speech of a homonym will help you to use it correctly.

allowed	(ăl lowed')	v. Permitted.
aloud	(ă loud')	adv. With the speaking voice.
bolder	(bōld' ẽr)	adj. More courageous.
boulder	(bōuld' ẽr)	n. Large rock.
cite	(çīte)	v. To quote.
sight	(sīght)	n. Spectacle. v. To see.
site	(sīte)	n. Location; place.
forward	(fōr' wărd)	adv. Onward. adj. Front.
foreword	(fôre' wôrd')	n. Preface.
hear	(hēar)	v. Listen to.
here	(hēre)	adv. At this place.
lessen	(lĕss' en)	v. To reduce; to decrease.
lesson	(lĕs' son)	n. Exercise assigned to students.
loan	(lōan)	v. To lend. n. That lent or borrowed.
lone	(lōne)	adj. Solitary.
marshal	(mär' shăl)	n. Officer. v. To direct.
martial	(mär' tial) shăl	adj. Warlike; military.
medal	(mĕd' al)	n. Commemorative award.
meddle	(mĕd' dle)	v. To interfere.
stationary	(stā tion ãr' ў)	adj. Motionless.
stationery	(stā ' tion ẽr' ў)	n. Writing paper.

Assignment

Substitute words from the above list for the words in parentheses.

1. The (location) of the plant has been chosen. *site*
2. We expect to stay (in this place) if we are (permitted) to do so. *here, allowed*
3. Is your name on your personal (letter paper)? *stationery*
4. We will go (ahead) with the project. *forward*
5. Let us look at the (assignment) for tomorrow. *lesson*
6. (A large rock) crashed down the mountain. *boulder*
7. You shouldn't (interfere) in their affairs. *meddle*
8. Those people are known for their (military) spirit.
9. That (solitary) figure out there is my cousin. *lone*
10. He will soon be out of (view). *sight*

SPELLING OF HOMONYMS

The best way to remember the spelling of homonyms is to associate meaning with the spelling itself.

Examples: *Alta* in *altar* means high—a place for sacrifices.
Bert slept in the *berth*.
The only *carrot* that *rots* is *carrots*.
Usually a *minor* is neither man *nor* child.

aisle	(aīsle)	*n.* Passageway between rows.
isle	(īsle)	*n.* A small island.
altar	(ạl′ tãr)	*n.* Pillar; stand.
alter	(ạl′ tẽr)	*v.* To change.
berth	(bẽrth)	*n.* A narrow bed on a ship or train.
birth	(bĭrth)	*n.* Act of being born.
cannon	(căn′ *n*ŏn)	*n.* Piece of artillery.
canon	(căn′ ŏn)	*n.* Rule; law.
carat	(căr′ ăt)	*n.* Unit of weight for jewels.
caret	(căr′ ĕt)	*n.* Proofreader's mark.
carrot	(căr′ *r*ŏt)	*n.* Plant with an edible root.
cede	(çēde)	*v.* To yield; to give up.
seed	(sēēd)	*n.* That from which anything springs.
council	(coun′ çĭl)	*n.* Assembly for consultation.
counsel	(coun′ sĕl)	*n.* Advice. *v.* To advise.
miner	(mĭn′ ẽr)	*n.* One who extracts minerals.
minor	(mī′ nŏr)	*n.* One not yet granted adult status. *adj.* Inferior; less.
rain	(rāin)	*n.* Precipitation.
reign	(reign) rān	*n.* Period of monarch's rule. *v.* To govern; to prevail.
waive	(wāive)	*v.* To relinquish a claim or right.
wave	(wāve)	*n.* Swelling motion. *v.* To flutter.

Assignment

Copy the words on the right. Beside each word place the number of the answer from the left column that best defines the word.

1. Act of coming into life.
2. That from which life springs.
3. To give up; to yield.
4. Unit of weight for precious stones.
5. Rule or law.

cede 3
carat 4
birth 1
seed 2
canon 5

ABCDEFGHIJKLESSON 80
REVIEW

A. Some of the homonyms in the following sentences are misspelled. As you copy these sentences, correct misspelled words. Consult your dictionary when you are in doubt.

1. Our City Counsel will meet tonight.
2. Have you seen our Capitol Building in our nation's capital?
3. It is against my principals to let Alice work hear.
4. Since she is a miner, she is too young for such responsibilities.
5. The cite of their house is the best along the shore.
6. Mr. Adams, Principle of Norwood High School, told the entire cast of the senior play that their requests were in vein.
7. You should wave those requirements, for they are too high.
8. Do you watch any of the western cereals on television?
9. The umpire ruled that the ball was a fowl.
10. The senator's compromises lessoned opposition to the bill.

B. Copy the words on the right. Beside each word place the number of the answer from the left column that best defines the word.

1. To interfere.
2. Writing paper.
3. Large rock
4. Chief; main.
5. Motionless.
6. To quote; bring forward.
7. More courageous.
8. Spectacle; to see.
9. Water from clouds.
10. Award of merit.

6 cite
10 medal
7 bolder
5 stationary
9 rain
2 stationery
8 sight
3 boulder
4 principal
1 meddle

C. Underline the homonyms from the preceding four lessons. Above each homonym, indicate its part of speech with the appropriate abbreviation.

1. Martial music filled the air.
2. Spectators surged towards the circus tent.
3. Friends and acquaintances waved to each other, and even the lone men and women smiled at the children.
4. Children laughed aloud as they moved forward through the gates.
5. Clowns would stare ferociously at the little children, and then their faces would break into smiles.
6. No one could be bored on such a fair day.
7. Marshals kept the crowd moving.
8. Animals were the principal attraction, but the clowns and the children reigned supreme.
9. Everyone stared as an acrobat was shot from a cannon.
10. Men walked down the aisles selling popcorn and balloons.

92

81
ANTONYMS

Antonyms are words of opposite meanings. You may better understand the meaning of a new word if you are already familiar with one of its antonyms. For example, you may not know the meaning of the word *affluence* but you may be familiar with the word *poverty*. If you learn that they are antonyms, your knowledge of one will help you to understand its opposite.

Study the following antonyms. What additional words could be added to each set?

antipathy	(ăn tĭp′ à thў)	*n.*	Aversion; incompatibility.
sympathy	(sўm′ pà thў)	*n.*	Agreement in feeling.
approbation	(ăp′ prô bā′ tion)	*n.*	Commendation.
disapproval	(dĭs′ àp prōv′ ăl) proŏv	*n.*	Censure.
castigate	(căs′ tĭ gāte)	*v.*	Punish; criticize severely.
reward	(rḗ wạrd′)	*v., n.*	Recompense.
complaisant	(cŏm plāi′ şănt)	*adj.*	Inclination to please or oblige.
defiant	(dḗ fī′ ănt)	*adj.*	Disposition to resist or challenge.
feigned	(feiɡned)	*adj.*	Not real; insincere.
genuine	ā (ġĕn′ ủ ĭne)	*adj.*	Authentic; sincere.
heterogeneous	(hĕt′ ẽr ŏġ′ ḗ noŭs)	*adj.*	Differing in kind.
homogeneous	(hŏ′ mŏ ġē′ nḗ oŭs)	*adj.*	Alike; similar.
instigate	(ĭn′ stĭ gāte)	*v.*	To stimulate; provoke.
restrain	(rḗ strāin′)	*v.*	To calm; deter.
mundane	(mŭn′ dāne)	*adj.*	Ordinary; earthly.
heavenly	(hĕav′ ĕn lў)	*adj.*	Ideal; exceptional.
recondite	(rĕc′ ȯn dīte)	*adj.*	Hidden; obscure.
obvious	(ŏb′ vĭ oŭs)	*adj.*	Easily discovered.
temperate	(tĕm′ pẽr ăte)	*adj.*	Moderate; restrained.
excessive	ĭt (ĕx çĕs′ sĭve)	*adj.*	Extreme; unreasonable.

Assignment

Add another antonym to the one already listed for each word.

Words	Antonym 1	Antonym 2
complaisant	defiant	*feigned*
eager	indifferent	
recondite	obvious	
regret	rejoice	
variety	monotony	

CHOOSING THE RIGHT SYNONYM

A pair of synonyms will have similar definitions, but each synonym will have a specialized meaning of its own. It has been said that *begin* and *commence* are the most closely related synonyms, but even here differences exist. There are many other synonyms for *begin*; and a good writer will recognize the various shades of meaning, choosing the word that best conveys his thoughts.

adroit	(à droit')	*adj.* Skillful, especially in mental areas.
dexterous	(dĕx' tẽr oŭs)	*adj.* Skillful, especially in physical areas.
annul	(ăn nŭl')	*v.* To cancel as if it never existed.
invalidate	(ĭn văl' ĭ dāte)	*v.* To cancel something that has existed.
contentious	(cŏn tĕn' tious)	*adj.* Prone to controversy and struggle.
quarrelsome	(quăr' rĕl sȯme)	*adj.* Irritable; belligerent.
delete	(dĕ lēte')	*v.* To eliminate; erase.
obliterate	(ŏb lĭt' ẽr āte)	*v.* To remove all traces of.
frugal	(frṳ' găl)	*adj.* Economical; thrifty.
parsimonious	(pär' sĭ mō' nĭ ous)	*adj.* Miserly; stingy.
lethargy	(lĕth' ăr ġў)	*n.* Inaction or indifference.
stupor	(stū' pȯr)	*n.* State of shock; loss of senses.
leverage	(lē' vẽr ăġe)	*n.* Advantage through action.
influence	(ĭn' flṳ ençe)	*n.* Ability to sway without force.
mandatory	(măn' dā tō' rў)	*adj.* Demanded by obligation.
necessary	(neç' ĕs săr' ў)	*adj.* Inescapable.
preclude	(prĕ clṳde')	*v.* To prevent; impede.
obviate	(ŏb' vĭ āte)	*v.* To anticipate and dispose of.
retrieve	(rĕ triēve')	*v.* To rediscover; recall.
revive	(rĕ vīve')	*v.* To restore to former condition.

Assignment

Write a sentence for each word in five sets of synonyms from the above list. Try to make your sentences convey the exact meaning of each word.

MEANING OF SYNONYMS

As you have seen, each word has a specific meaning that is similar but not identical to its synonym. In Lesson 81, you saw how antonyms aid in vocabulary building; synonyms can help too. You will better understand the meaning of a new word if you are already familiar with one of its synonyms. Suppose you come across an unfamiliar word such as *condone*. Learning that one of its synonyms is *excuse* will help you to incorporate the new word into your vocabulary.

affable	(ăf′ fȧ ble)	*adj.* Courteous; easy to talk to.
amiable	(ā′ mĭ ȧ ble)	*adj.* Friendly; agreeable.
chronic	(chrŏn′ ĭc)	*adj.* Long-lasting.
continuous	(cŏn tĭn′ ú oŭs)	*adj.* Without interruption.
circumscribe	(çĭr′ cŭm scrībe′)	*v.* To restrict within limits.
encompass	(ĕn cȯm′ pàss)	*v.* To enclose; include.
disparage	(dĭs păr′ ăġe)	*v.* To degrade.
depreciate	(dḗ prē′ çĭ āte)	*v.* To lessen in value; belittle.
expedite	(ĕx′ pḗ dīte)	*v.* To accelerate; remove obstacles.
facilitate	(fȧ çĭl′ ĭ tāte)	*v.* To make less difficult; assist.
irony	(ī′ rṓ nў)	*n.* Feigned ignorance to confound or provoke.
sarcasm	(sär′ că s̬m)	*n.* Ridicule; satire.
malaise	(mă lāi s̬e′)	*n.* Feeling of discomfort.
malady	(măl′ ȧ dў)	*n.* Ailment; sickness.
mien	(miēn)	*n.* Appearance; manner.
demeanor	(dḗ mēan′ ŏr)	*n.* Behavior; bearing.
obsolete	(ŏb′ sṓ lēte)	*adj.* No longer in use.
antiquated	(ăn′ tĭ quắt′ ĕd)	*adj.* Old-fashioned.
pernicious	(pẽr nĭ′ cioŭs)	*adj.* Deadly; injurious.
ruinous	(ru′ i noŭs)	*adj.* Destructive.
	ro͞o	

Assignment

Underscore the word or phrase in parentheses that is most closely related to the word outside the parentheses. Then use each "outside word" in a sentence.

1. affability (sense of humor, pretense, sociability, credulity)
2. chronic (timely, continuous, diseased; elusive)
3. expedite (explain; walk; rush; pretend)
4. mien (bearing; nastiness; smallness; middle)
5. pernicious (stingy; sarcasm; injurious; helpful)

95

VOCABULARY ENRICHMENT

Have you wondered why one word may have numerous synonyms? The answer lies in the many sources of English; words of German, Latin and Greek origin have resulted in a rich and varied language.

You should make use of this variety to increase your vocabulary. As you study the following words, list two synonyms and two antonyms for each one.

abeyance	(à bey′ ănçe)	*n.* Temporarily inactive.
acrimony	(ăc′ rĭ mō′ nў)	*n.* Sharpness of temper.
alleviate	(ȧl lē′ vĭ āte)	*v.* To relieve pain or suffering.
antagonistic	(ăn tăg′ ŏ nĭs′ tĭc)	*adj.* Hostile.
arid	(ăr′ ĭd)	*adj.* Without moisture.
contend	(cŏn tĕnd′)	*v.* To compete.
defray	(dĕ frāy′)	*v.* To ward off; satisfy.
delusion	(dĕ lū şion)	*n.* A false belief.
discrepancy	(dĭs crĕp′ ăn çў)	*n.* Variance.
initiate	(ĭn ĭ′ ti āte)	*v.* To introduce; begin.
intrinsic	(ĭn trĭn′ sĭc)	*adj.* Essential nature.
matriculate	(mȧ trĭc′ ú lāte)	*v.* To admit to membership.
mitigate	(mĭt′ ĭ gāte)	*v.* To make less severe.
porous	(pō′ roŭs)	*adj.* Able to absorb moisture.
pragmatism	(prăg′ mȧ tĭşm)	*n.* Practicality.
precarious	(prĕ câr′ ĭ oŭs)	*adj.* Dependent on circumstances.
rescind	(rĕ scĭnd′)	*v.* To cancel.
taciturn	(tăç′ ĭ tûrn)	*adj.* Habitually quiet; reserved.
temerity	(tĕ mĕr′ ĭ tў)	*n.* Unreasonable contempt of danger; rashness.
trivial	(trĭv′ ĭ ăl)	*adj.* Of little importance.

Assignment

Read the following paragraph, looking up those words that are new to you. Then rewrite the paragraph, substituting well-known words for the italicized words. Look up the derivation of the italicized words and the synonyms you used to replace them.

'The accident down by the *quay* was *lamentable*,' he said with a *grimace*. 'The man driving the car was of athletic build but, at the moment, his hold on the wheel must have been *flaccid*, or he might have been suffering from some *inexplicable vagary*. Anyhow, he had a *genuine aversion* to driving a car. In addition he was of an *incomparably mischievous* and *garrulous* type. His record showed that he had previously committed a *heinous* crime.' [1]

[1] Wilfred Funk, *The Reader's Digest Great Encyclopedic Dictionary*, Second Printing, 1967; p. 1948. Published here with permission of The Reader's Digest, Pleasantville, New York.

ABCDEFGHIJKLESSON 85

Section I: Review of Lessons 81-84

A. Make three columns headed, "Words," "Synonyms," and "Antonyms." List the following words in the first column: *abeyance, adroit, circumscribe, confident, intrinsic, mandatory, mundane, obsolete, pernicious, temperate.* Now choose a synonym and antonym for each of the above words from the list below, recording each one in the appropriate column.

expand	restrict	extreme	inept
uncertain	continuation	suspension	nonessential
deadly	outdated	useful	ordinary
assured	inherent	clever	exceptional
helpful	optional	moderate	required

B. Number your paper from 1 to 10. Beside each number write the word from each group that is not a synonym for the others.

1. rescind, reprove, censure, rebuke, reproach
2. delete, delusion, hallucination, illusion, mirage
3. instigate, stimulate, provoke, start, feign
4. castigate, punish, commend, disapprove, criticize
5. abeyance, alleviate, mitigate, lighten, help
6. lethargy, leverage, stupor, shock, inaction
7. apathy, temerity, audacity, presumption, rashness
8. circumscribe, cancel, delete, rescind, revoke
9. eminent, precarious, distinguished, famous, prominent
10. sagacious, sensible, taciturn, shrewd, wise

C. Copy the following sentences, changing any italicized words that are used incorrectly.

1. The child was *castigated* for the window he broke.
2. Mr. James is *parsimonious* but never stingy with his money.
3. Were they ever able to *revive* her watch from the pool?
4. It is an *obsolete* phrase but still used by some people.
5. Is it fair to *disparage* Elaine's artistic efforts by comparing them with an older girl's?
6. This ground is not *porous* and, therefore, tends to be *arid*.
7. Your promise to speak at the banquet makes your presence there *mandatory*.
8. It was a *heterogeneous* group composed exclusively of dentists.
9. The football coach hopes to recruit *dexterous* men for next year's team.
10. The *irony* of the story was Joan's late arrival after warning the others to be on time.

97

Section II: General Review of Lessons 76-84

A. Rewrite the following sentences, replacing the italicized word or phrase with one of the words in parentheses.

1. This is not a religious *ceremony* but part of their cultural tradition. (rite, wright)
2. I will need more *writing paper* to finish the letter. (stationary, stationery)
3. The Beals own a *small island* in the Caribbean. (aisle, isle)
4. Robert needs the *advice* of a more experienced engineer. (council, counsel)
5. Are you *permitted* to use the pool when there is no lifeguard on duty? (allowed, aloud)
6. He claims that the vase is an *authenic* antique. (feigned, genuine)
7. It is an *evident* fact and not very important. (recondite, obvious)
8. Grandmother's *sickness* is more serious than we originally thought. (malaise, malady)
9. Paul's *indifference* resulted from his ignorance of the facts. (lethargy, stupor)
10. Will it be necessary to *change* our plans for the junior prom? (altar, alter)

B. Write one homonym, one synonym, and one antonym for each of the following words.

martial	capital	bolder
principal	vain	meddle
right	steal	minor

C. Copy the words on the right. Beside each word place the number of the answer from the left column that best defines the word.

1. To make less severe.
2. Temporary inactivity.
3. Aversion; incompatibility.
4. Appearance; manner.
5. Habitually silent; reserved.
6. Of little importance.
7. Advantage through action.
8. Sharpness of temper.
9. Preface.
10. A meeting or series of meetings.
11. Courteous; easy to talk to.
12. Unreasonable contempt of danger.
13. Prone to controversy and struggle.
14. To anticipate and dispose of.
15. Practicality.

session
foreword
mitigate
leverage
temerity
acrimony
mien
abeyance
contentious
antipathy
trivial
obviate
pragmatism
affable
taciturn

86
WORDS OFTEN MISUSED

The next four lessons concentrate on words that are frequently confused because of similar pronunciation or spelling. Observe these words carefully, using them in sentences that reinforce their individual meanings.

advice	(ăd vīçe′)	*n.*	Recommendation.
advise	(ăd vīṣe′)	*v.*	To give counsel.
allusion	(ăl lū′ sion)	*n.*	Indirect reference.
elusion	(ė́ lū′ sion)	*n.*	Evasion.
illusion	(ĭl lū′ sion)	*n.*	Unreal image.
commence	(cŏm měnçe′)	*v.*	To begin.
comments	(cŏm′ měnts)	*n.*	Remarks; criticisms.
cooperation	(cō ŏp′ ēr ā′ tion)	*n.*	Collective action.
corporation	(côr′ pŏ rā′ tion)	*n.*	A body of persons.
decease	(dė́ çēase′)	*n.*	Death. *v.* To die.
disease	(dĭ ṣease′)	*n.*	Illness.
deference	(děf′ ēr ĕnçe)	*n.*	Courteous yielding.
difference	(dĭf′ fēr ĕnçe)	*n.*	State of being unlike.
eminent	(ĕm′ ĭ něnt)	*adj.*	Prominent.
imminent	(ĭm′ mĭ něnt)	*adj.*	Threatening to occur.
incite	(ĭn çīte′)	*v.*	To arouse; to provoke.
insight	(ĭn′ sīght′)	*n.*	Understanding.
persecute	(pēr′ sė́ cūte)	*v.*	To annoy; to afflict.
prosecute	(prŏs′ ė́ cūte)	*v.*	To carry on; to sue.
prophecy	(prŏph′ ė́ çў̄)	*n.*	Prediction.
prophesy	(prŏph′ ė́ sў̄)	*v.*	To foretell.

Assignment

Copy the following sentences, underscoring the words in parentheses that correctly complete the sentences.

1. A mirage is an (allusion, illusion, elusion).
2. The leader attempted to (insight, incite) the mob to violence.
3. It is wrong to (prosecute, persecute) a man because of his religion.
4. What do you (advise, advice) me to do?
5. It is difficult to (prophecy, prophesy) the outcome.
6. Dr. Nolan is an (imminent, eminent) educator.
7. The (decease, disease) finally caused his death.
8. There was splendid (cooperation, corporation) among the members.
9. Students wrote (commence, comments) in their notebooks.
10. The clerks showed (deference, difference) to their employer's wishes.

WORDS WHICH SOUND ALIKE

The following pairs of words are often misspelled because their pronunciations are similar. Note the differences in spelling and meaning.

accede	(ăc çēde′)	v. To attain; to agree to.
exceed	(ĕx çēed′)	v. To go beyond.
accept	(ăc çĕpt′)	v. To receive; approve.
except	(ĕx çĕpt′)	prep. With the exclusion of.
access	(ăc′ çĕss)	n. Means of approach; admission.
excess	(ĕx çĕss′)	n. Surplus; superabundance.
anecdote	(ăn′ ĕc dōte)	n. Brief, amusing story.
antidote	(ăn′ tĭ dōte)	n. Remedy.
formally	(fôr′ măl lў)	adv. Ceremonially.
formerly	(fôr′ mĕr lў)	adv. In time past.
personal	(pēr′ sȯn ăl)	adj. Pertaining to a person; private.
personnel	(pĕr′ sȯn nĕl′)	n. A body of persons.
practicable	(prăc′ tĭ cȧ ble)	adj. Capable of being done.
practical	(prăc′ tĭ căl)	adj. Not theoretical; useful.
precede	(prḗ çēde′)	v. To go before.
proceed	(prṓ çēed′)	v. To advance.
quiet	(quī′ ĕt)	adj. Still; hushed. n. Silence.
quite	(quīte)	adv. Completely; exactly.
respectfully	(rḗ spĕct′ fụl lў)	adv. With regard for.
respectively	(rḗ spĕc′ tĭve lў)	adv. As relating to each in turn.

Assignment

Copy the following sentences, choosing the correct word in parentheses to complete each one.

1. Jewelry is considered (personal, personnel) property.
2. Superintendent Halle will (formally, formerly) resign from the Board of Education this week.
3. I am glad to (accept, except) your offer.
4. Students have (access, excess) to the library.
5. He (respectfully, respectively) deferred to the judgment of his elders.
6. Do you believe that the institute should (accede, exceed) last year's budget?
7. Dr. Evans' amusing (anecdotes, antidotes) are better than medicine.
8. Please (precede, proceed) with your part of the program.
9. Jane felt that something was not (quite, quiet) right.
10. Is your plan (practicable, practical) or is it a prediction?

100

88

WORDS WHICH SOUND AND LOOK ALIKE

The following pairs of words resemble each other in spelling and pronunciation, but differ in meaning. Study spelling, meaning, and pronunciation carefully.

adapted	(à dăpt′ ĕd)	*adj.* Made suitable; adjusted.
adopted	(à dŏpt′ ĕd)	*adj.* Chosen; accepted.
adverse	(ăd vẽrse′)	*adj.* Opposed; contrary.
averse	(à vẽrse′)	*adj.* Reluctant; disliking.
affect	(ăf fĕct′)	*v.* To influence.
effect	(ĕf fĕct′)	*n.* Result. *v.* To accomplish.
appraise	(ăp prāise′)	*v.* To evaluate.
apprise	(ăp prīse′)	*v.* To inform.
command	(cŏm mànd′)	*v.* To order.
commend	(cŏm mĕnd′)	*v.* To praise; recommend.
contest	(cŏn′ tĕst)	*n.* Competition.
context	(cŏn′ tĕxt)	*n.* Interrelated material or conditions.
farther	(fär′ thẽr)	*adj.* Greater distance (in space).
further	(fûr′ thẽr)	*adj.* Additional; greater distance (in time or quantity).
human	(hū′ măn)	*adj.* Pertaining to man.
humane	(hú māne′)	*adj.* Benevolent.
loose	(lōōse)	*adj.* Not fastened firmly.
lose	(lọṣe)	*v.* To mislay something; suffer defeat.
ordinance	(ôr′ dĭ nănçe)	*n.* Rule; law.
ordnance	(ôrd′ nănçe)	*n.* Military supplies.

Assignment

Copy the words on the right. Beside each word place the number of the answer from the left column that best defines the word.

1. To praise.
2. Interrelated facts.
3. To inform.
4. Military equipment.
5. Competition.
6. Untied.
7. To order.
8. To judge as to quality.
9. To influence.
10. A regulation.

2 context
8 appraise
7 command
6 loose
10 ordinance
9 affect
5 contest
4 ordnance
1 commend
3 apprise

101

WORDS OFTEN MISUSED

Learn the meaning and pronunciation of the following words. Note differences in spelling.

addition	(ăd dĭ′ tion)	n. Increase; increment.
edition	(é dĭ′ tion)	n. One issue of a publication.
censor	(çĕn′ sŏr)	n. Overseer of morals.
censure	(çĕn′ sure) shĕr	n. Adverse criticism.
complement	(cŏm′ plé mĕnt)	n. Related supplement.
compliment	(cŏm′ plĭ mĕnt)	n. Flattering remark.
credible	(crĕd′ ĭ ble)	adj. Believable.
creditable	(crĕd′ ĭt à ble)	adj. Praiseworthy.
emigrant	(ĕm′ ĭ grănt)	n. Person leaving one country for another.
immigrant	(ĭm′ mĭ grănt)	n. Person coming into one country from another.
immoral	(ĭm mŏr′ àl)	adj. Corrupt; indecent.
immortal	(ĭm mŏr′ tăl)	adj. Everlasting.
ingenious	(ĭn ġĕn′ ioŭs)	adj. Inventive; clever.
ingenuous	(ĭn ġĕn′ ŭ oŭs)	adj. Frank; sincere.
moral	(mŏr′ ăl)	n. Lesson to be drawn from a story.
morale	(mŏr àle′)	n. Spirit of cooperation.
plaintiff	(plāin′ tĭff)	n. Initiator of legal action.
plaintive	(plāin′ tĭve)	adj. Sorrowful.
weather	(wĕath′ ĕr)	n. State of atmosphere.
whether	(whĕth′ ĕr)	conj. Indication of choice or doubt.

Assignment

Correct any errors in the following paragraph:

Michael's pleasant habit of giving complements to the ladies has not been too successful because the complements aren't credible. The strictest censure would have approved, however, for the complements were creditable. In short, Michael's words might not have been immoral but on the other hand, they weren't immoral. In any case, his habit of complementing people is ingenious and ingenuous. He has used it to advantage in his law practice, particularly when talking with plaintives. He helps the morale of others and, in addition, promotes a morale point of view.

A. Copy the words on the right. Beside each word place the number of the answer from the left column that best defines the word.

1. To arouse; to provoke.	imminent
2. Benevolent.	loose
3. Not fastened.	averse
4. To foretell.	emigrant
5. Person leaving one country for another.	humane
6. Threatening to occur.	incite
7. Brief, amusing story.	anecdote
8. To mislay.	lose
9. To go before.	precede
10. Unwilling.	prophesy

B. Copy the following sentences, selecting the appropriate word shown in parentheses:

1. The (deference, difference) between Roman (morals, morales) and our own is not great.
2. The (personal, personnel) director is (quiet, quite) a (practical, practicable) man.
3. Mrs. Brewer has been suffering for months under the (allusion, illusion) that her friends are trying to (prosecute, persecute) her.
4. I must (command, commend) you on your excellent performance in the (contest, context).
5. The (affect, effect) of his criticism was deadly; she made no (farther, further) effort to improve.
6. I am happy to (except, accept) your invitation.
7. The colonel's task was to (censure, censor) the private who unofficially left the base.
8. I must (appraise, apprise) you of the fact that we must have this property (appraised, apprised).
9. This (decease, disease) seems to flourish in certain (weather, whether) conditions.
10. Before our club (adapted, adopted) its revised constitution, many of the rules had to be (adapted, adopted) to the recent changes in organization.
11. Mr. Price will (advice, advise) you to finish high school.
12. Dale was (formally, formerly) a member of the drama club.

C. You are a patient and admirer of Dr. Evans, a young physician recently graduated from medical school. Using at least ten words from Lessons 86-89, describe Dr. Evans and your reaction to him. Underline each of the ten words from the lessons.

103

ABCDEFGHIJKLESSON **91**

WORDS OFTEN MISUSED

The words in Lessons 91 through 94 are paired according to misuse. Some of the following pairs are unrelated in meaning, while others have the same *general* definitions. Caution should be exercised in using these words interchangeably. Each one has a distinct meaning and is the appropriate choice only when expressing that specific idea.

adjacent	(ăd jā′ çĕnt)	*adj.* Near.
adjoining	(ăd join′ ĭng)	*adj.* Touching.
allude	(ăl lūde′)	*v.* To refer to indirectly.
elude	(ė lūde′)	*v.* To avoid; escape.
apparent	(ăp păr′ ĕnt)	*adj.* Seeming to be so.
evident	(ĕv′ ĭ dĕnt)	*adj.* Obviously so.
cite	(çīte)	*v.* To mention as an authoritative source.
quote	(quōte)	*v.* To repeat the exact words used by another.
crime	(crīme)	*n.* Serious violation of the law.
sin	(sĭn)	*n.* Transgression of a religious code.
eligible	(ĕl′ ĭ ġĭ ble)	*adj.* Qualified.
legible	(lĕġ′ ĭ ble)	*adj.* Clearly written; readable.
famous	(fā′ moŭs)	*adj.* Celebrated; renowned.
infamous	(ĭn′ fȧ moŭs)	*adj.* Of very bad reputation.
imply	(ĭm plȳ′)	*v.* To hint; suggest.
infer	(ĭn fĕr′)	*v.* To surmise; read into.
last	(lăst)	*adj.* Final.
latest	(lāt′ ĕst)	*adj.* Most recent.
marital	(măr′ ĭ tăl)	*adj.* Pertaining to marriage.
martial	(mär′ tial) shăl	*adj.* Pertaining to war.

Assignment

Copy the following sentences. Select the best synonyms from the list to replace the underlined words.

1. Tonight's speaker is an economist whose most recent book deals with foreign aid. *latest*
2. His neglect of himself is a transgression, but his neglect of his children is a felony. *sin* *crime*
3. Gene checked his marriage status as "single." *marital*
4. Bill recites long passages from Sandburg verbatim. *quotes*
5. In some religions, the material world is believed to be observable but not real. *apparent*

104

CHOOSING APPROPRIATE WORDS

Many persons use words that do not convey the intended meaning. As you study the words in this lesson, note those that you have been using inappropriately.

aggravate	(ăg′ grà vāte)	*v.* To worsen; intensify.
exasperate	(ex as′ pẽr āte) ĕg zăs′	*v.* To arouse the anger of.
answer	(ȧn′ swẽr)	*n.* A response. *v.* To respond.
reply	(rḗ plȳ′)	*n.* A formal response, as in a debate. *v.* To respond formally.
continual	(cŏn tĭn′ ú ăl)	*adj.* Occurring in rapid succession.
continuous	(cŏn tĭn′ ú oŭs)	*adj.* Occurring without break.
envious	(ĕn′ vĭ oŭs)	*adj.* Desirous of another's achievements or property.
jealous	(jĕal′ oŭs)	*adj.* Intolerant of rivalry in matters of affection.
ignorant	(ĭg′ nṓ rănt)	*adj.* Lacking knowledge.
illiterate	(ĭl lĭt′ ẽr āte)	*adj.* Unable to read or write.
majority	(mȧ jŏr′ ĭ tȳ)	*n.* More than half.
plurality	(plu̧ răl′ ĭ tȳ)	*n.* More than any other part, but less than half.
noted	(nōt′ ĕd)	*adj.* Eminent; famous.
notorious	(nṓ tō′ rĭ oŭs)	*adj.* Unfavorably known.
perquisite	(pẽr′ qui ṣite)	*n.* An added advantage.
prerequisite	(prḗ rĕq′ u̧ĭ ṣite)	*n.* Preliminary requirement.
perspective	(pẽr spĕc′ tĭve)	*n.* View in correct proportion.
prospective	(prṓ spĕc′ tĭve)	*adj.* Expected.
surprise	(sûr prīṣe′)	*v.* To startle. *n.* Unexpected event.
astonish	(ăs tŏn′ ĭsh)	*v.* To amaze; overwhelm.

Assignment

Copy the following sentences, selecting the best words in parentheses to complete the sentences.

1. Your letter will (aggravate, exasperate) Mr. Austin.
2. Senator Reed made the (answer, reply) to the charge.
3. Since the boy was (ignorant, illiterate), he could not read.
4. Ronald is (jealous, envious) of his brother's success.
5. Have you met your (prospective, perspective) father-in-law?

105

ABCDEFGHIJKLESSON 93

CORRECT WORD USAGE

You are probably familiar with the spelling of the words in the following list. You should also be aware of the distinctions in meaning.

accelerate	(ăc çĕl′ ẽr āte)	*v.*	To hasten; quicken.
exhilarate	(ex hil′ à rāte) ĕg zĭl′	*v.*	To enliven.
compensate	(cŏm′ pĕn sāte)	*v.*	To pay for loss or injury.
remunerate	(rĕ̇ mū′ nẽr āte)	*v.*	To pay for services.
credible	(crĕd′ ĭ ble)	*adj.*	Worthy of belief.
credulous	(crĕd′ ú loŭs)	*adj.*	Believing too readily.
elicit	(é̇ lĭç′ ĭt)	*v.*	To draw forth.
illicit	(ĭl lĭç′ ĭt)	*adj.*	Unlawful.
feasible	(fēa′ ş̣ĭ ble)	*adj.*	Capable of being done.
plausible	(pḷau′ ş̣ĭ ble)	*adj.*	Apparently true.
later	(lāt′ ẽr)	*adj.*	Subsequently.
latter	(lăt′ *t*ẽr)	*adj.*	More recent; the second to be mentioned.
luxuriant	(lŭx ū′ rī ănt)	*adj.*	Showing profuse growth.
luxurious	(lŭx ū′ rĭ oŭs)	*adj.*	Pertaining to material wealth and comfort.
momentary	(mō mĕn tăr′ ў̆)	*adj.*	Short-lived.
momentous	(mŏ́ mĕn′ toŭs)	*adj.*	Important; weighty.
restful	(rĕst′ fụl)	*adj.*	Quiet; relaxed.
restive	(rĕs′ tĭve)	*adj.*	Restless; uneasy.
stature	(stăt′ ú́re)	*n.*	Height; status.
statute	(stăt′ ūte)	*n.*	A law.

Assignment

Copy the words on the right. Beside each word place the number of the answer from the left column that best defines the word.

1. To pay for services.
2. Important; weighty.
3. Apparently true.
4. Gullible; believing readily.
5. To draw forth.
6. Capable of being done; practicable.
7. Restless; uneasy.
8. Unlawful.
9. Showing profuse growth.
10. Believable; worthy of belief.

10 credible
2 momentous
7 restive
3 plausible
8 illicit
5 elicit
9 luxuriant
4 credulous
6 feasible
1 remunerate

106

94

CORRECT WORD USAGE

Develop word awareness. Sharpen your language by adding synonyms to your vocabulary. Learn the precise meaning of the following synonyms and then make sure that you use them appropriately.

among	(á mòng′)	*prep.* Associated with more than two persons or things.
between	(bě twēēn′)	*prep.* In the space that separates two persons or things.
arbitrate	(ár′ bǐ trāte)	*v.* To act as a judge.
conciliate	(cŏn çǐl′ ǐ āte)	*v.* To cause to agree.
character	(chăr′ ăc tēr)	*n.* One's real nature.
reputation	(rěp′ ů tā′ tion)	*n.* One's supposed nature.
compare	(cŏm pâre′)	*v.* To examine for resemblances.
contrast	(cŏn trăst′)	*v.* To examine for differences.
custom	(cŭs′ tŏm)	*n.* A cultural tradition.
habit	(hăb′ ĭt)	*n.* Settled action of one person in relation to circumstances.
discover	(dǐs cóv′ ēr)	*v.* To learn something for the first time.
invent	(ĭn vĕnt′)	*v.* To make for the first time.
educated	(ĕd′ ů cāt′ ĕd)	*adj.* Enlightened through systematic instruction.
intelligent	(ĭn tĕl′ *lĭ* ġĕnt)	*adj.* Having a great capacity to learn.
evidence	(ĕv′ ĭ dĕnçe)	*n.* Facts submitted as proof.
testimony	(tĕs′ tĭ mō′ nў)	*n.* Declaration of a witness.
hardly	(härd′ lў)	*adv.* With difficulty; barely.
scarcely	(scârçe′ lў)	*adv.* By a narrow margin.
partner	(pärt′ nēr)	*n.* A legal associate as in marriage or business.
colleague	(cŏl lēague′)	*n.* An associate in social or professional life.

Assignment

Copy the following sentences, choosing the correct words in parentheses to complete the sentences.

1. There was a warm friendship (among, between) the three students.
2. He had a (character, reputation) that could not be corrupted.
3. (Compare, contrast) the temperature of the equatorial region with that of the arctic region.
4. It was his (custom, habit) to arise at six o'clock.
5. Many attempts were made to (discover, invent) a better engine.

A. Correct the following paragraph, changing words that have been used inappropriately.

Although we knew Henry was an educated speaker, we were aggravated by his surprising inferences about faculty members in his address to the PTA. Of course, he has a notorious character for his restful rhetoric, not for his sound ideas. Nevertheless, he should not have continuously drawn comparisons between the differences in the three local colleges. Henry's colleagues do not correct him about his attitude, for he does not illicit helpful criticism. In fact, he has the annoying custom of accusing all his critics of being jealous of him.

B. The following sentences contain words from Lessons 91-94. Number your paper from 1 to 10. If a sentence contains words appropriately used, write *correct* beside its number. If a word is misused in a sentence, rewrite the sentence, substituting a more suitable word from the preceding four lessons.

1. The railroad company will *compensate* Gerald for the loss of his leg.
2. Vergil told a *credible* story about a four-car accident.
3. Elizabeth is so *credulous* that she believes everything.
4. Do you think that building a new bridge here is *plausible*?
5. The meadow was covered with a *luxurious* growth of grass.
6. *Accelerated* training has an *exhilarating* effect upon superior students.
7. Do you think that we shall be able to *illicit* the facts that we need?
8. By the time I had arrived, there was *hardly* any food left.
9. Marty will provide her with a *luxuriant* life.
10. The sudden rise in the stock market *surprised* the investors.

C. Copy the words on the right. Beside each word place the number of the answer from the left column that best defines the word.

1. Status.	adjacent
2. Short-lived.	apparent
3. To avoid; escape.	illiterate
4. To view in proportion.	prospective
5. Obviously so.	momentary
6. To refer to indirectly.	stature
7. Seeming to be so.	elude
8. Expected.	perspective
9. Near.	evident
10. Can't read or write.	allude

SPECIFIC WORDS
VS. GENERAL WORDS

Inexactness in speaking and writing may result from the overuse of general terms. Only specific words give definite mental images. Instead of an *awful* lecture, you heard a *boring* lecture, or a *monotonous* lecture, or an *inaccurate* lecture, or an *inaudible* lecture (in which case you were subjected to the lecture but did not hear it). In short, the word *awful* is too general to indicate the trouble.

Following are three lists of more specific words for the general terms *awful, nice,* and *make.* Can you think of more synonyms for each word?

awful	nice	make
disgusting	comfortable	compose
fatal	exciting	construct
frightening	exotic	create
grinding	fastidious	develop
nauseating	genial	erect
terrifying	loyal	generate
tiring	luscious	manufacture
ugly	luxurious	originate
unappetizing	pleasant	produce
weird	refreshing	sew

Assignments

A. Copy the following phrases, replacing the adjectives *awful* and *nice* with more descriptive words. Do not use a synonym more than once.

awful day	awful music	nice game
awful dream	awful sensation	nice luncheon
awful accident	awful film	nice fragrance
awful battle	nice chair	nice party
awful food	nice housekeeper	nice apartment
awful hat	nice evening	nice friends

B. Complete the sentences below by inserting a synonym of the verb *to make.* Do not use a synonym more than once.

1. In colonial days, clothing was (*sewn*) in homes.
2. My teacher has (*composed*) several songs.
3. Improved methods of physical training should (*produce*) a nation of athletes.
4. The grandstand was (*constructed*) by a reliable lumber company.
5. John is a skilled draftsman who (*originates*) accurate blueprints.

109

SPECIFIC WORDS
VS. GENERAL WORDS

The synonyms below are more descriptive than the general words for which they may be substituted. Note the emotional overtone of *appeal*, rather then *ask*; *slash*, instead of *cut*; and *escape*, in place of *go*.

However, be careful not to overuse these more "exciting" verbs. At times, *ask, cut,* or *go* may be the most appropriate words; in that case do not hesitate to use them.

ask	cut	go
apply for	carve	chase
beseech	divide	climb
demand	eliminate	fly
implore	mow	race
plead	trim	ride
request	mutilate	run
solicit	reduce	spin
urge	skip	swim
invite	slice	travel
require	avoid	walk

Assignments

A. Write five more synonyms for *ask, cut,* and *go* and use each new word in a sentence.

B. Copy the following sentences, replacing the underlined word or phrase with a more descriptive one. Do not use a synonym more than once.

invited 1. The Harrisons have asked us to spend the weekend with them.
apply for 2. Joe is going to ask for the job of assistant engineer.
beseech 3. As a true friend, I ask you not to make this serious mistake.
solicit 4. I ask for your support in this campaign for funds.
request 5. We ask that you fill out this form before paying the fee.
carve 6. Will you please cut this meat for me?
trim 7. Be sure to cut all the fat from the meat.
reduce 8. I am trying to cut my weight.
skipped 9. Yesterday I cut two classes because I had to cut the lawn.
eliminate 10. We are going to cut this item out of the budget.
run 11. You'd better go to the market before it closes.
climbed 12. While in Switzerland, we went up one mountain in the Alps.
chase, runs 13. I will go after him if he goes across our lawn once more.
traveling 14. Sharon and Eleanor are going to Europe this summer.
spin 15. How fast can you make that wheel go?

110

98

USING APPROPRIATE WORDS

Words should be appropriate to both the subject-matter and the situation. Following are synonyms for the word *bunch: assembly, gang,* and *group.* These words are not interchangeable, however. In informal speaking or writing, a slang term such as *gang* may be acceptable, but in formal useage *group* or *assembly* is more appropriate.

bunch	large	see
bouquet	abundant	discover
bundle	ample	gaze
collection	broad	interview
crowd	gigantic	observe
drove	extensive	peek
flock	extravagant	recognize
herd	generous	stare
pack	lavish	understand
swarm	plentiful	visualize
throng	tremendous	watch

Assignments

A. Write five more synonyms for *bunch, large,* and *see* and use each new word in a sentence.

B. Copy the following sentences, replacing the italicized word or phrase with a more descriptive one. Do not use a synonym more than once.

1. We have a *bunch* of old coins. *collection*
2. A *bunch* of locusts destroyed our crops. *swarm*
3. This *bunch* of flowers is pretty. *boquet*
4. A *bunch* of dogs were after our chickens last night. *pack*
5. A *bunch* of people were headed for the ball park. *throng*
6. Our ranch has a *bunch* of cattle and a *bunch* of turkeys too. *herd, flock*
7. We found a *bunch* of firewood beside the patio. *bundle*
8. David is very tall with *large* shoulders. *broad*
9. At 300 pounds, his figure was *quite large. abundant*
10. We will need a lot of help in moving this *large* rock. *gigantic*
11. The harvest this year was *large. abundant*
12. The company does not favor *large* expense accounts. *extravagant*
13. His father provides him with a *large* allowance. *ample*
14. It is a *large* communications network spanning two continents. *extensive*
15. Do you *see* what I'm talking about? *understand*
16. I can *see* the similarity between the two cultures. ~~reco~~ *observe*
17. Can you *see* what is causing the problem? *recognize*
18. Adam is hoping that the personnel manager will *see* him today. *interview*
19. She *saw* us through the window. *watched*
20. We *saw* the operation on this closed circuit television. *watched*

111

USING TECHNICAL WORDS

In general, it is best to avoid long words which may be unfamiliar to the reader or listener. Your choice of synonyms should not reflect a desire to impress others with your knowledge of words.

However, there are times when only a long or a technical word will convey your meaning. When such a word is needed, do not hesitate to use it. The following list contains synonyms, some of them difficult, for the overworked adjectives *good, bad,* and *funny.*

good	bad	funny
auspicious	deleterious	amusing
benign	faulty	comic
bountiful	flagrant	diverting
copious	immoral	hilarious
estimable	inferior	laughable .
favorable	iniquitous	ludicrous
gratifying	injurious	silly
pleasurable	inopportune	trifling
salutary	tainted	unusual
suitable	wicked	uproarious

Assignments

A. Copy the following phrases, replacing the adjectives *good, bad,* and *funny* with more descriptive words. Do not use a synonym more than once.

good occasion	bad effect	funny anecdote
good experience	bad brakes	funny situation
good harvest	bad conduct	funny behavior

B. Copy the following sentences, substituting a synonym from the above list or one of your own for each italicized word or phrase.

inopportune 1. It is *a bad time* to take a vacation because of our heavy work load.
amusing 2. Ed's *funny* remarks made people question his ability.
suitable 3. Is this a *good* outfit to wear skiing?
pleasurable 4. Doris has a *good* personality; she is gentle and kind towards others.
flagrant 5. The team's actions constituted a *bad* violation of the rules.
injurious 6. Obesity is *bad for* your health.
hilarious 7. We saw a *very funny* comedy last night.
silly 8. The boys created a scene with their *funny* antics.
copious 9. Our university was awarded a *good* amount of money to carry on its research projects.
tainted 10. The criminal's actions demonstrated his *bad* character.

112

A. Copy the following sentences, substituting the most suitable word from those suggested.

1. My car made an awful noise after that recent overhaul.
   (a) grinding (b) fatal (c) vivid (d) frightening

2. Goya painted nice pictures of foreign lands.
   (a) fastidious (b) genial (c) exotic (d) luscious

3. Grandfather cut the turkey.
   (a) divided (b) sliced (c) carved (d) trimmed

4. He always insists on giving people large, expensive gifts.
   (a) ample (b) extravagant (c) abundant (d) generous.

5. It was a funny set of circumstances that don't often occur.
   (a) trifling (b) diverting (c) silly (d) unusual

B. Copy the following sentences, selecting the better word to complete each one.

1. I (demand, request) that he be given a fair trial!
2. Our senior class will (visit, tour) the Capitol Building.
3. Can you (visualize, see) the way the house will look when it's finished?
4. How much electricity can this power plant (produce, generate)?
5. The geese tended to (flock, crowd) together.
6. (Faulty, Injurious) construction resulted in the collapse of the building.
7. The (salutary, benign) effects of exercise are often overlooked.
8. It is impolite to (stare, look) at people in the street.
9. The hotel accommodations are (luxurious, luscious).
10. Hot, humid climates have a (deleterious, iniquitous) effect on her health.

C. Copy the following paragraph, replacing the italicized words with the most appropriate synonyms from the preceding four lessons.

Bob and I *went* to the movies even though it was a *nice* day. It turned out to be a *bad time to go* since there was a *large bunch* of people waiting in line. I was trying to *cut down* my weight but I *saw* Bob eat at least three bags of popcorn. We thought that the picture was *awful* but others thought it was *good*. We were about to *ask* for our money back when the story became more interesting and quite *funny*. The sets took four months to *make* and were *nice*. Our final judgment was that the movie would have been *funnier* if some of the *awful* dialogue had been *cut*.

113

ABCDEFGHIJKLESSON 101

"IE" AND "EI" COMBINATIONS

Lessons 101-104 present commonly misspelled words. The first two lessons cover words with "ie" and "ei" combinations that often cause trouble. Study the two rules below and their application in the following word list.

Rule 1: When "e" has the long "ē" sound following the letter "c," the "e" usually precedes the "i": *receive, ceiling, deceit.*

Rule 2: When "e" has the long "ē" sound and follows letters other than "c," the "i" precedes the "e": *piece, niece, grief.*

achieve	(à chiēve′)	v. To accomplish.
believe	(bĕ liēve′)	v. To trust; accept.
chieftain	(chiēf′ taĭn)	n. Leader of a group.
conceit	(cŏn çeit′)	n. Egotism.
conceive	(cŏn çeive′)	v. To think or suppose.
field	(fiēld)	n. Open country; cleared land.
fiend	(fiēnd)	n. A demon; a wicked person.
grievous	(griēv′ oŭs)	adj. Burdensome; distressing.
perceive	(pĕr çeive′)	v. To comprehend.
pier	(piĕr)	n. A dock.
pierce	(piĕrçe)	v. To puncture.
priest	(priēst)	n. An ordained religious man.
receipt	(rĕ çeĭpt′)	n. A written acknowledgment of something received.
relieve	(rĕ liēve′)	v. To ease; remove.
shriek	(shriēk)	n. Shrill sound; scream.
siege	(siēġe)	n. A blockade.
species	(spē′ çīeṣ)	n. Category of biological classification.
thief	(thiēf)	n. One who steals.
wield	(wiēld)	v. To handle; manipulate.
yield	(yiēld)	v. To submit.

Assignment

Copy the following sentences, correcting any misspelled words.

1. Mrs. Jones always keeps her reciepts.
2. I was deceived by his masquerade.
3. We believed that our football team would win.
4. Eloise recieved three handbags for her birthday.
5. Will you be able to achieve the necessary results with your new method?
6. The thief yeilded after the policemen's siege of his house.
7. The brakes shreiked as the train ground to a halt.
8. Our luggage was unloaded onto the pier.
9. Can you concieve of a more greivous situation?
10. George's fencing lessons have enabled him to wield his sword in a professional manner.

114

"IE" AND "EI" COMBINATIONS

Rule 3: When "e" has the short "ĕ" sound following a consonant, the "i" precedes the "e": *deficient, efficiency, proficient.*

Rule 4: The "e" precedes the "i," following consonants other than "c," when the "ei" combination is sounded like "ā": *weight, veil, neighbor.*

Exceptions: There are many exceptions to these rules: *either, neither, weird, seize, forfeit, counterfeit,* and *leisure,* for example. *Either, neither,* and *leisure* were at one time pronounced with the "ā" sound; the pronunciation of the words changed, but the spelling remained the same.

client	(clī′ ĕnt)	*n.* Patron; customer.
conscience	(cŏn′ sciĕnçe) shĕns	*n.* Awareness of one's conduct.
diet	(dī′ ĕt)	*n.* Eating habits.
eight	(eight) ā	*n.* Number between seven and nine.
experience	(ĕx pē′ rĭ ençe)	*n.* Living through events.
feigned	(feigned) ā	*adj.* Pretended; false.
fiery	(fī′ ĕr ў)	*adj.* Inflamed; passionate.
foreign	(fŏr′ eign)	*adj.* Alien in character.
freight	(freight) ā	*n.* Cargo.
height	(heīght)	*n.* Elevation.
heir	(heir) â	*n.* One who inherits.
patient	(pā′ tient) shĕnt	*adj.* Showing forbearance. *n.* One under a physician's care.
quiet	(quī′ ĕt)	*adj.* Tranquil.
reins	(reins) ā	*n.* Straps to control an animal.
sleigh	(sleigh) ā	*n.* A vehicle that travels on snow or ice.
society	(sŏ çī′ ĕ tў)	*n.* A culture; association.
sufficient	(sŭf fī′ ciĕnt)	*adj.* Adequate.
variety	(và rī′ ĕ tў)	*n.* Diversity.
vein	(vein) ā	*n.* A channel.
weigh	(weigh) ā	*v.* Examine; measure on a scale.

Assignment

Copy the words listed below, correcting any errors in spelling. Write the number of the rule that applies, or the word "exception" next to each one. Use each word in a sentence.

riens *ei*	feigned	soceity *society*
foreign	eight	quiet
variety	hier *heir*	conscience

WORDS WITH DOUBLE LETTERS

Words that contain double letters often cause spelling problems. Study the following list of words carefully, noting the placement of the double letters in each word.

accessory	(ăc çĕs' sŏ rў)	*adj.* Supplementary.
all right	(all rīght)	*adj.* Correct. *adv.* Certainly.
assimilate	(äs sĭm' ĭ lāte)	*v.* Adapt; absorb.
beginning	(bĕ gĭn' nĭng)	*v.* Commencing; starting.
bulletin	(bu̧l' lĕ tĭn)	*n.* A public announcement; a periodical.
collateral	(cŏl lăt' ĕr ăl)	*adj.* Subordinate. *n.* Property used as security for a loan.
colossal	(cŏ lŏs' săl)	*adj.* Gigantic; monstrous.
commitment	(cŏm mĭt' mĕnt)	*n.* A promise or pledge.
corollary	(cŏr' ŏl lăr' ў)	*n.* A consequence; thesis.
dissipate	(dĭs' sĭ pāte)	*v.* To disperse; consume.
embarrass	(ĕm băr' răss)	*v.* To disconcert; confound.
erratic	(ĕr răt' ĭc)	*adj.* Wandering; strange.
garrulous	(găr' ru̧ lŏus)	*adj.* Talkative.
incidentally	(ĭn' çĭ dĕn' tăl lў)	*adv.* By chance.
incorrigible	(ĭn cŏr' rĭ g̈ĭ ble)	*adj.* Incapable of being corrected.
occasional	(ŏc cā' șiŏn ăl)	*adj.* Infrequent.
occurrence	(ŏc cûr' rĕnçe)	*n.* Event.
parallel	(păr' ăl lĕl)	*adj.* Equally distant at all points.
recommend	(rĕc' ŏm mĕnd')	*v.* To praise; advise.
symmetry	(sў̆m' mĕ trў)	*n.* Mutual relationship of parts; balanced proportions.

Assignment

Copy the following sentences, selecting the correctly spelled word in parentheses to complete each one.

1. Bill Allen is (garulous, garrulous) and sometimes quarrelsome.
2. Do you (reccomend, recommend) Pat McGilvrey for this job?
3. Two children in this class are (incorrigible, incorigible).
4. Have you made any (commitments, committments) for next week?
5. (Incidently, Incidentally), we have not (assessed, assesed) members for the June dance.
6. Do you have a copy of last week's (bullettin, bulletin)?
7. Edward's behavior was so (errattic, erratic) that I thought he was ill.
8. What did you give as (collateral, colatteral) for the loan?
9. I'm sorry to cause you (embarrassment, embarassment), but I cannot overlook this (ocurrence, occurrence).
10. These (paralell, parallel) cases have been on four tests.

ABCDEFGHIJKLESSON 104
WORDS FREQUENTLY MISSPELLED
Below is an additional list of words that often present spelling problems. Study them carefully, paying special attention to the syllables likely to cause you trouble.
Word	Pronunciation	Definition
business	(busi′ něss) bĭz′	n. Commercial enterprise.
calendar	(căl′ ĕn där)	n. A schedule.
congratulate	(cŏn grăt′ ú lāte)	v. To wish joy.
convenient	(cŏn vēn iĕnt)	adj. Suitable; handy.
correspondence	(cŏr′ rĕ spŏnd′ ĕnçe)	n. Written communication.
corrupt	(cŏr rŭpt′)	adj. Dishonest; adulterated.
✗ endeavor	(ĕn dĕav′ ŏr)	v. To strive to achieve. n. A determined effort.
epoch	(ĕp′ ŏch)	n. A period of time; an era.
especially	(ĕs pe′ cĭăl lў)	adv. Particularly.
indefinitely	(ĭn dĕf′ ĭ nĭte lў)	adv. Vaguely; limitlessly.
infinity	(ĭn fĭn′ ĭ tў)	n. Unlimited extent of time, space, or quantity.
laboratory	(lăb′ ŏ rȧ tō′ rў)	n. A place devoted to experimental study.
omission	(ŏ mĭs′ sion)	n. Something neglected or left undone.
perpetual	(pĕr pĕt′ ú ăl)	adj. Continuing forever.
prior	(prī ŏr)	adj. Preceding in time.
rhythm	(rhўthm)	n. Ordered pattern of strong and weak elements in sound.
subsequent	(sŭb′ sĕ quĕnt)	adj. Following in time.
transient	(trăn′ sient) shĕnt	adj. Of short duration; brief; passing through.
ultimately	(ŭl′ tĭ măte lў)	adv. Finally.
vicissitude	(vĭ çĭs′ sĭ tūde)	n. Change; difficulty.
Assignments
A. Explain the relationship of the following words in terms of word structure:
finite . . . definite . . . definitely . . . indefinitely . . . infinity
B. Copy the following sentences, correcting any italicized words that are misspelled.
1. The many *vicissitudes* Alex has experienced in his life have made him very nervous.
2. The *ommision* of Harriet's name from the list was a mistake. *omission*
3. Did you *congradulate* our debating team on their latest victory? *congratulate*
4. We will *endeavor* to improve our financial situation.
5. *Prior* to last night's encounter, I had never met Mr. Jacobson.

A. In the following sentences, insert the letters *ie* or *ei* to complete the appropriate words correctly.

1. After a br––f but f––rce battle, the enemy y––lded.
2. Your n––ghbors are rel––ved to know that you have overcome your gr––f.
3. To ach––ve your objective, you must first gain rel––f from self-doubt.
4. During the s––ge, ––ght of our officers were captured.
5. We perc––ved the th––ves as they approached the house.
6. They were for––gners and they shr––ked strange words.
7. Testimony revealed that they had f––gned illness and had dec––ved the pr––sts called to aid them.
8. My n––ce is an effic––nt girl who bel––ves in working hard to ach––ve her goals.
9. Bill is h––r to the Carmody fortune, but he is a pat––nt teacher with no wish for a l––surely life.
10. This spec––s likes to live in open f––lds and its d––t consists mostly of grass.

B. Choose the correct words in parentheses as you copy the following sentences:

1. President Hardesty has conservative ideas about (buisness, business).
2. Such (collosal, colossal) egotism defies belief.
3. When John becomes (garulous, garrulous) at parties, his wife is embarrassed.
4. In the (begining, beginning) you may advise me, but (ultimitly, ultimately) the decision must be mine.
5. Which pin will be a better accessory for my blue dress?
6. You must pull on the (reins, riens) or the horse will not stop pulling the (sleigh, sliegh).
7. What will you use as (colataral, collateral) in securing the loan?
8. I am (especialy, especially) fond of this (rhythm, rythm).
9. The sculpture exhibits approach perfect (symmetry, symetry).
10. Have you made a (committment, commitment) to support his candidacy yet?
11. They seem to be (all right, alright).
12. It will be (convenient, convient) to have supplies on the second floor.
13. Our overcrowded classes are without (paralell, parallel) in our local schools.
14. In our (correspondance, correspondence) we (recommended, reccomended) separate (labratory, laboratory) facilities.
15. We couldn't (asimmilate, assimilate) five new (assistants, asistants) under present conditions.

ABCDEFGHIJKLESSON 106

STATES AND THEIR CAPITALS

The next four lessons are helpful as a reference source for states, their major cities and common abbreviations.

In the following list, two abbreviations are given for each state. One is the standard abbreviation and the other is the two-letter abbreviation authorized for use with zip codes.

States	Standard Abbreviation	Two-Letter Abbreviation	Capital
Alabama	Ala.	AL	Montgomery
Alaska	Alaska	AK	Juneau
Arizona	Ariz.	AZ	Phoenix
Arkansas	Ark.	AR	Little Rock
California	Calif.	CA	Sacramento
Colorado	Colo.	CO	Denver
Connecticut	Conn.	CT	Hartford
Delaware	Del.	DE	Dover
Florida	Fla.	FL	Tallahassee
Georgia	Ga.	GA	Atlanta
Hawaii	Hawaii	HI	Honolulu
Idaho	Idaho	ID	Boise
Illinois	Ill.	IL	Springfield
Indiana	Ind.	IN	Indianapolis
Iowa	Iowa	IA	Des Moines
Kansas	Kans.	KS	Topeka
Kentucky	Ky.	KY	Frankfort
Louisiana	La.	LA	Baton Rouge
Maine	Maine	ME	Augusta
Maryland	Md.	MD	Annapolis
Massachusetts	Mass.	MA	Boston
Michigan	Mich.	MI	Lansing
Minnesota	Minn.	MN	St. Paul
Mississippi	Miss.	MS	Jackson
Missouri	Mo.	MO	Jefferson City

Assignment

Copy the names of the states on the right. Beside the name of each state, place the number of the state capital.

1. Montgomery
2. Juneau
3. Jefferson City
4. Denver
5. Lansing

2 Alaska
4 Colorado
5 Michigan
3 Missouri
1 Alabama

119

STATES AND THEIR CAPITALS

The name of a state should never be abbreviated unless it is used in connection with the name of a city. Learn the spelling of the following states, their abbreviations and their capitals.

States	Standard Abbreviation	Two-Letter Abbreviation	Capital
Montana	Mont.	MT	Helena
Nebraska	Nebr.	NB	Lincoln
Nevada	Nev.	NV	Carson City
New Hampshire	N. H.	NH	Concord
New Jersey	N. J.	NJ	Trenton
New Mexico	N. Mex.	NM	Santa Fe
New York	N. Y.	NY	Albany
North Carolina	N. C.	NC	Raleigh
North Dakota	N. Dak.	ND	Bismarck
Ohio	Ohio	OH	Columbus
Oklahoma	Okla.	OK	Oklahoma City
Oregon	Oreg.	OR	Salem
Pennsylvania	Pa.	PA	Harrisburg
Rhode Island	R. I.	RI	Providence
South Carolina	S. C.	SC	Columbia
South Dakota	S. Dak.	SD	Pierre
Tennessee	Tenn.	TN	Nashville
Texas	Tex.	TX	Austin
Utah	Utah	UT	Salt Lake City
Vermont	Vt.	VT	Montpelier
Virginia	Va.	VA	Richmond
Washington	Wash.	WA	Olympia
West Virginia	W. Va.	WV	Charleston
Wisconsin	Wis.	WI	Madison
Wyoming	Wyo.	WY	Cheyenne

Washington, D.C. (District of Columbia) is the capital of the United States and the only American city that is not part of any state.

Assignment

Match states with capitals.

1. Wyoming
2. New Hampshire
3. New Mexico
4. North Carolina
5. Utah .

2 Concord
4 Raleigh
5 Salt Lake City
1 Cheyenne
3 Santa Fe

MAJOR CITIES IN THE UNITED STATES

Listed below are the names of some major American cities that are difficult to spell and/or pronounce.

Albuquerque	(Ăl′ bŭ quêr′quĕ)	New Mexico
Baltimore	(Bạl′ tĭ mōre)	Maryland
Bayonne	(Bā yōnne′)	New Jersey
Chattanooga	(Chăt′ tȧ nōō′ gȧ)	Tennessee
Chicago	(Chĭ cä′ gō)	Illinois
Cincinnati	(Çĭn′ çĭn nắt′ ĭ)	Ohio
Detroit	(Dĕ troit′)	Michigan
Las Vegas	(Läs Ve′ gȧs) Vā	Nevada
Los Angeles	(Lŏs Ăn′ ġĕ lĕs)	California
Louisville	(Loụ′ ĭs vĭlle)	Kentucky
Memphis	(Mĕm′ phĭs)	Tennessee
Miami	(Mī ăm′ ĭ)	Florida
Milwaukee	(Mĭl wạu′ kĕe)	Wisconsin
Minneapolis	(Mĭn′ nĕ ăp′ ŏ lĭs)	Minnesota
Pittsburgh	(Pĭtts′ bûrgh)	Pennsylvania
San Francisco	(Săn′ Frăn çis′ cō)	California
Schenectady	(Schĕ nĕc′ tȧ dў)	New York
Spokane	(Spŏ kăne′)	Washington
Tacoma	(Tȧ cō′ mà)	Washington
Terre Haute	(Tĕr′ rĕ Haute′) Hōt	Indiana

Assignments

A. Be prepared to dictate the above list to the class. Study the pronunciation guides to help you master the correct spelling.

B. Copy the following paragraphs, correcting any misspellings. Also correct any mistakes in the location of cities.

We left our home in Bayonne, New Jersey, on a windy March day looking forward to sunny days in Los Angeles and Los Vegas. We had friends in Albuqurque, Arizona, who told us not to miss the beautiful Southwest. We planned to first visit some relatives in Detriot and Minneapoles, Minessota, and then proceed west. However, our plane was delayed in Pittsburg, Pennsylvania, and we missed our connecting flight.

We enjoyed ourselves so much in Las Angeles, California, that we decided to see San Francisco as well. Our vacation was memorable but hectic. We agreed that it would have been more restful if we had spent two weeks in Miamia instead.

COMMON ABBREVIATIONS

We use few abbreviations in general writing, but some are commonly used in business correspondence or technical writing. Consult your dictionary if you encounter abbreviations unfamiliar to you. The following list includes some of the most widely used abbreviations.

Abbreviation	Meaning
A.B.	Bachelor of Arts
A.D.	in the year of our Lord
A.R.C.	American Red Cross
B.C.	before Christ
B.S.	Bachelor of Science
C.O.D.	collect on delivery
C.P.A.	Certified Public Accountant
C.S.T.	Central Standard Time
D.D.	Doctor of Divinity
D.D.S.	Doctor of Dental Surgery
e.g.	for example
E.S.T.	Eastern Standard Time
et al.	and others (persons)
etc.	and so forth
i.e.	that is
I.Q.	intelligence quotient
M.D.	Doctor of Medicine
M.S.T.	Mountain Standard Time
Ph.D.	Doctor of Philosophy
P.S.T.	Pacific Standard Time
R.&D.	Research and Development
R.S.V.P.	Please reply
U.N.	United Nations
U.S.S.R.	Union of Soviet Socialist Republics
vs.	against

Assignment

Copy the abbreviations on the right. Beside each abbreviation place the number of the appropriate definition from the left column.

1. Intelligence quotient.
2. And others.
3. Collect on delivery.
4. Eastern Standard Time.
5. That is.
6. For example.
7. Research and Development.
8. United Nations.
9. Please reply.
10. Union of Soviet Socialist Republics.

7 R.&D.
2 et al.
6 e.g.
5 i.e.
4 E.S.T.
3 C.O.D.
8 U.N.
9 R.S.V.P.
10 U.S.S.R.
1 I.Q.

122

ABCDEFGHIJK LESSON # 110

GENERAL REVIEW

Section I: Review of Lessons 106-109

A. Correct all misspelled words in the following sentences.

1. Lansing, the capital city of Michigan, is the home of Michigan State University.
2. Massachusetts has many visitors each summer, especially on Cape Cod.
3. New Mexico is a colorful state; and Santa Fe, its capital, is the second oldest city in the United States.
4. North Carolina is a beautiful state and during the summer it is beseiged by travelers who enjoy its scenery.
5. Virginia is the birthplace of eight presidents.
6. Rhode Island is our smallest state, but it is distinguished historically for its battle for freedom of conscience and action.
7. Pitsburgh is named after William Pitt, founder of Pennsylvania.
8. Cincinnati, Ohio, is known as the Queen City.
9. Chicago, Illinois, is the meat-packing capital of the United States.
10. The Kentucky Derby takes place in Louiville, Kentucky, each spring.

B. Copy the names of the states on the right. Place beside the name of each state the appropriate number from the left column of capital cities.

1. Columbus	3 North Dakota
2. Dover	1 Ohio
3. Bismark	4 Vermont
4. Montpelier	5 Oregon
5. Salem	7 New Mexico
6. St. Paul	2 Delaware
7. Santa Fe	6 Minnesota
8. Carson City	9 Nebraska
9. Lincoln	8 Nevada
10. Annapolis	10 Maryland

C. Copy the following phrases giving the correct abbreviation for each one.

Pacific Standard Time P.S.T.
collect on delivery C.O.D.
please reply R.S.V.P.
against vs.
in the year of our Lord A.D.

and so forth etc.
American Red Cross A.R.C.
Doctor of Medicine M.D.
Doctor of Philosophy Ph.D.
for example e.g.

123

Section II: General Review of Lessons 86-109

A. Copy the following sentences, choosing the correctly spelled word in parentheses to complete each one.

1. Was the (prophecy, prophesy) a happy one?
2. Mr. Holmes will (accede, exceed) to your request.
3. Did you (apprise, appraise) Bonnie of the situation?
4. Dick's (moral, morale) is low and he has been very (plaintiff, plaintive) lately.
5. To what are you (alluding, eluding) in your speech?
6. Tom can read and write but is (ignorant, illiterate) in many areas.
7. It was a (momentary, momentous) occasion and will be remembered for many years.
8. Andy is (educated, intelligent) but has not had the benefit of formal schooling.
9. Does this explanation give you any more (incite, insight) into the problem?
10. We tried to (elicit, illicit) a response from the Senator, but he refused to be quoted.

B. Using the synonyms you studied in Lessons 96-99, substitute a more specific and descriptive term for each italicized word.

1. Smoking is an *awful* habit that you should not develop.
2. I received a *nice* letter from Aunt Bertha.
3. We were able to *make* new plans from the old ones.
4. Harold *asked* the Lawrences to our party, but they were going out of town.
5. Is it warm enough to *go* in the lake today?

C. Copy the following sentences, correcting any misspelled words in italics.

1. My *conscience* will not allow me to *yeild*.
2. I was *embarassed* by his *erattic* behavior.
3. Our teacher described the *epoc* during which the Roman Empire was at its height.
4. Can two *parallel* lines ever cross one another?
5. Is there *sufficient vareity* in this menu?

D. After each state's postal abbreviation, write the name of the state, its standard abbreviation, and the name of a city in the state.

Example: IL . . . Illinois . . . Ill. . . . Chicago

NV	AL	MT	MI	LA	KY	IA	ID
nevada	Alabama	Montana	Michigan	Louisiana	Kentucky	Iowa	Idaho
CO	CT	AR	AK	SC	TN	WA	HI
Colorado	Connecticut	Arizona	Alaska	South Carolina	Tennessee	Washington	Hawaii

124

Part 4

ABCDE FGHIJKLMNO

Enriching Your Vocabulary

We live in a world of change and discovery. It is difficult to keep up with developments in science, economics and culture. Part Four emphasizes vocabulary building in these areas.

Lessons 111-130 cover fields of knowledge from literature to space exploration.

Lessons 131-145 present words related to entertainment, hobbies, and pastimes.

Lessons 145-160 introduce basic business vocabularies in areas such as banking, labor relations, and transportation.

ABCDEFGHIJKLESSON 111
LAW

Following are words relating to various phases of law. Be prepared to dictate the list to the class and to use the words in sentences.

acquittal	(ăc quĭt′ tăl)	n. Verdict of innocence.
adjudicate	(ăd jụ′ dĭ cāte)	v. To settle by judicial decision.
affidavit	(ăf′ fĭ dā′ vĭt)	n. A sworn statement in writing.
alias	(ā′ lĭ ăs)	n. An assumed name.
apprehend	(ăp′ prḗ hĕnd′)	v. To lay hold of; to arrest.
attest	(ăt tĕst′)	v. To bear witness to.
claimant	(clāim′ ănt)	n. One who asserts a right to something.
clemency	(clĕm′ ĕn cў)	n. Leniency; mildness.
deposition	(dĕp′ ố sĭ′ tion)	n. Written testimony.
executor	(ĕx ĕc′ ụ̍ tŏr)	n. One who carries out a will.
felony	(fĕl′ ố nў)	n. A serious violation of the law.
guardian	(guărd′ ĭ ăn)	n. Protector; legal custodian.
incriminate	(ĭn crĭm′ ĭ nāte)	v. To charge with or involve in a crime.
indictment	(ĭn dīct′ mĕnt)	n. Written statement charging a person with an offense.
legacy	(lĕg′ ȧ çў)	n. Gift of property by will.
libel	(lī′ bĕl)	n. A defamatory statement in writing.
misdemeanor	(mĭs′ dḗ mēan′ ŏr)	n. A minor violation of the law.
slander	(slăn′ dẽr)	n. Untrue oral accusation.
subpoena	(sŭb poē′ nȧ)	n. Writ summoning a witness.
warrant	(wạr′ rănt)	n. An authorization.

Assignment

Copy the words on the right. Beside each word place the number of the appropriate definition from the left column.

1. To arrest.
2. Writ summoning a witness.
3. A defamatory statement in writing.
4. To involve in a crime.
5. Gift of property by will.
6. Grave crime.
7. Written testimony.
8. Misdeed.
9. An authorization.
10. Untrue oral accusation.

6 felony
3 libel
7 deposition
8 misdemeanor
2 subpoena
4 incriminate
10 slander
1 apprehend
5 legacy
9 warrant

127

112

GOVERNMENT

Following are some general terms relating to governmental processes. Be sure that you know how to use them correctly.

autocracy	(au tŏc′ rȧ çў)	n. Rule by an individual.
ballot	(băl′ lŏt)	n. Ticket used in voting.
citizenship	(çĭt′ ĭ zĕn shĭp′)	n. Membership in a nation.
communism	(cŏm′ mú nĭșm)	n. System in which goods are owned in common.
constitutional	(cŏn′ stĭ tū′ tion ăl)	adj. Relating to the structure of government.
democracy	(dẽ mŏc′ rȧ çў)	n. Government by the people.
dictator	(dĭc tā′ tŏr)	n. Head of state with absolute authority.
diplomacy	(dĭ plō′ mȧ çў)	n. Conducting international relations.
disfranchise	(dĭs frăn′ chīșe)	v. To deprive of the rights of citizenship.
enfranchise	(ĕn frăn′ chīșe)	v. To give the rights of citizenship.
incumbent	(ĭn cŭm′ bĕnt)	n. Holder of an office.
injunction	(ĭn jŭnc′ tion)	n. Court order directing or prohibiting.
legislator	(lĕġ′ ĭs lā′ tŏr)	n. Member of a law-making body.
mandate	(măn′ dāte)	n. Order; command.
oligarchy	(ŏl′ ĭ gär chў)	n. Government by a few.
propaganda	(prŏp′ ȧ găn′ dȧ)	n. Doctrine spread to further one's own ideas.
protocol	(prō′ tŏ cŏl)	n. A code of diplomatic or military etiquette.
representative	(rĕp′ rẽ șĕnt′ ȧ tĭve)	n. One who is chosen to speak for others.
republic	(rẽ pŭb′ lĭc)	n. State in which the power resides in the electorate.
unanimous	(ú năn′ ĭ moŭs)	adj. Being of one mind.

Assignment

Rewrite the following paragraph, substituting appropriate terms for any words used incorrectly.

In our political science class, we learned the differences between an oligarchy, rule by one man; an autocracy, rule by a small group; and a democracy, rule by the people. In a democracy, most adults are disfranchised. The people hear propaganda from all sides and then elect legislators. Governments have varying constitutional frameworks but all observe injunctions when dealing with one another.

ABCDEFGHIJKLESSON 113

GOVERNMENT

This lesson contains terms related to the three levels of government in the United States: local, state and federal.

alderman	(ạl′ dẽr măn)	*n.*	Member of the city council.
appropriation	(ăp prō′ prĭ ā′ tion)	*n.*	Money delegated for a specific use.
assessor	(ăs sĕs′ õr)	*n.*	One who evaluates property.
bureaucracy	(bū reạuc′ rȧ çў)	*n.*	Government conducted by numerous departments.
candidate	(căn′ dĭ dāte)	*n.*	One who aspires to office.
caucus	(cau′ cŭs)	*n.*	Policy meeting of political leaders.
coroner	(cŏr′ ό nẽr)	*n.*	Official who investigates unusual deaths.
embassy	(ĕm′ băs sў)	*n.*	Ambassador's residence.
envoy	(ĕn′ voy)	*n.*	One sent on a mission.
governor	(gȯv′ ẽr nõr)	*n.*	Chief officer of a state.
impeach	(ĭm pēach′)	*v.*	To accuse an official of misconduct.
indemnity	(ĭn dĕm′ nĭ tў)	*n.*	Protection from loss.
judicial	(jụ di′ cĭal) dĭsh	*adj.*	Relating to the administration of justice.
mayor	(māy′ õr)	*n.*	Head official of a city.
municipal	(mứ nĭç′ ĭ păl)	*adj.*	Pertaining to local government.
naturalization	(năt′ ứ răl ĭ zā′ tion)	*n.*	Act of conferring citizenship rights.
precinct	(prē′ cĭnct)	*n.*	Election district.
presidential	(prĕṣ′ ĭ dĕn′ tiăl)	*adj.*	Pertaining to the chief officer.
quorum	(quō′ rŭm)	*n.*	Number of members needed to transact business.
senator	(sĕn′ ȧ tõr)	*n.*	Member of the Senate.

Assignment

Copy the following sentences, substituting synonyms from the above list for italicized words.

1. *Enfranchisement* is available to women as well as men. naturalization
2. My *election district* favors the incumbent. precinct
3. The *residence of the ambassador* is being redecorated. embassy
4. The *amount of money allowed* for education is inadequate. appropriation
5. Our state will have a new *top man* in 1974. governor

129

ABCDEFGHIJKLESSON 114

POLITICS

The following terms describe the political process in the United States. You should become familiar with all of these words.

bipartisan	(bī pär′ tĭ şăn)	adj.	Representing two parties.
campaign	(căm pāign′)	n.	Drive to influence voters.
census	(çĕn′ sŭs)	n.	Official count of the population.
constituent	(cŏn stĭt′ ú ĕnt)	n.	Voter in a representative's district.
convention	(cŏn vĕn′ tion)	n.	Formal political meeting.
electorate	(é lĕc′ tŏr ăte)	n.	Body of voters.
filibuster	(fĭl′ ĭ bŭs′ tĕr)	n.	Obstructive action to delay legislation.
gerrymander	(ġĕr′ rў măn′ dĕr)	n.	Redistricting for unfair political advantage.
initiative	(ĭ nit′ ĭ ā tĭve) nĭsh	n.	Right of voters to introduce legislation.
lobbying	(lŏb′ bў ĭng)	v.	Influencing a legislator.
nominee	(nŏm′ ĭ nēe′)	n.	One named as a candidate.
ordinance	(ôr′ dĭ nănçe)	n.	A local law or regulation.
patronage	(pā′ trọn age) ĭj	n.	Jobs bestowed as political favors.
platform	(plăt′ fôrm′)	n.	Declaration of principles.
prerogative	(pré rŏg′ à tĭve)	n.	Exclusive right or privilege.
proxy	(prŏx′ ў)	n.	One who acts for another.
recall	(ré′ cạll)	n.	Removal of an official by popular vote.
reciprocity	(rĕç′ ĭ prŏç′ ĭ tў)	n.	Mutual recognition of rights.
referendum	(rĕf′ ĕr ĕn′ dŭm)	n.	Process of submitting a measure to popular vote.
urban	(ûr′ băn)	adj.	Pertaining to the city.

Assignment

Number your paper from 1 to 10. Beside each number write the word from the list that relates to each of the statements below.

1. Is it illegal to block action by speaking to consume time?
2. Senator Halverson receives many letters from his followers.
3. Governor Gerry, of Massachusetts, caused his state to be divided in order to give unfair advantage to one political party.
4. The voters in my state want the right to introduce legislation.
5. The meeting had representatives from both political factions.
6. Next Tuesday the public is voting on the proposed ouster of our tax assessor.
7. The Democrats and Republicans always announce a set of principles on which their candidates will run.
8. An official count of the population is taken every ten years.
9. Speed regulations are strictly enforced within the city limits.
10. The appointment of judges is the right of the governor.

A. Underline the word in parentheses most closely related to the word outside parentheses:

1. alias (immigrant, assumed name, estrangement)
2. felony (covey of birds, downfall, crime)
3. apprehend (understand, notify, arrest)
4. incriminate (distinguish between like objects, involve in a crime, explain)
5. indictment (formal accusation, oration, invitation)
6. urban (sophisticated, outside the city, in the city)
7. bipartisan (divided in two parts, happy-go-lucky, representing two parties)
8. prerogative (questioning, requirement, exclusive privilege)
9. proxy (president, substitute, knowledge)
10. ordinance (military supplies, patience, law or regulation)

B. Reword the following sentences to show that you understand the meaning of the italicized words.

1. Mr. X's record revealed a number of youthful *misdemeanors* but no *felonies*.
2. We did not *apprehend* him because we had no proof of his guilt.
3. We had Mr. X make a *deposition* concerning his relationship to the deceased.
4. The committee *unanimously* voted to drop the matter in spite of the *coroner's* suspicions.
5. *Affidavits* from every member of our group completed the official papers turned over to the police.
6. Even so, we may be *subpoenaed* to testify in this case, since Mr. X's correspondence has *incriminated* us in this incredible situation.
7. Because of political *patronage*, some judges may hold positions of trust for which they are not qualified.
8. Since the police had no *warrant* to search our premises, we refused to admit them.
9. The defendant's record revealed weaknesses that caused the judge to recommend *clemency*.
10. The executor of the estate could not find the *codicil* to the will which the deceased man's widow said she had witnessed.
11. In my opinion, the *incumbent* will win the campaign.
12. Some people feel that the *judicial* branch of the government has the most power.
13. Denise's uncle has been appointed her *guardian*.
14. The successful conduct of *diplomacy* is important to any nation.
15. Mr. Josephson is the *nominee* of our party for governor.

SPACE EXPLORATION

Space exploration has expanded our vocabulary. Words that predate space exploration have been given new meanings, and new words have been created to describe objects and procedures previously nonexistent.

acceleration	(ăc cĕl' ẽr ā' tion)	*n.* The time rate of change of velocity.
astronaut	(ăs' trō naut)	*n.* Space traveler.
booster	(bōost' ẽr)	*n.* Auxiliary propulsion system.
capsule	(căp' sūle)	*n.* Pressurized compartment for astronauts.
centrifuge	(çĕn' trĭ fuġe)	*n.* A machine that produces gravitational effects.
free fall	(frēē fạll)	*n.* Weightlessness.
gravity	(grăv' ĭ tỹ)	*n.* Attraction of a greater mass for a lesser one.
gyroscope	(ġỹ' rṓ scōpe)	*n.* Navigational device.
hydrogen	(hỹ' drō ġĕn)	*n.* The simplest element.
inertia	(ĭn ẽr' tiạ shạ)	*n.* Tendency of matter to remain at rest or in uniform motion.
interplanetary	(ĭn' tẽr plăn' ḗ tãr' ỹ)	*adj.* Between planets.
jettison	(jĕt' tĭ sȯn)	*n.* Elimination of cargo.
missile	(mĭs' sĭle)	*n.* A rocket.
orbit	(ôr' bĭt)	*n.* Path of one body around another.
planet	(plăn' ĕt)	*n.* Celestial body that revolves around a star.
propellant	(prō pĕl' lănt)	*n.* Fuel mixture.
reentry	(rē ĕn' trỹ)	*n.* Return into earth's atmosphere from space.
satellite	(săt' ĕl līte)	*n.* A secondary planet; a man-made space vehicle.
staging	(stāġ' ĭng)	*n.* Successive separation of spacecraft's units.
thrust	(thrŭst)	*n.* Forward force.

Assignment

Copy the words on the right. Beside each word place the number of the appropriate definition from the left column.

1. Forward force.
2. Return into earth's atmosphere.
3. Celestial body revolving around a star.
4. Attraction of mass for lesser bodies.
5. Tendency of matter to remain at rest or in uniform motion.

4 gravity
5 inertia
3 planet
2 reentry
1 thrust

132

NUCLEAR ENERGY

Nuclear energy has been adapted for the generation of electric power, medical and agricultural research, and industrial testing. Following are some basic terms related to these fields.

alpha particle	(ăl′ phȧ pär′ tĭ cle)	*n.*	Nuclear particle ejected in some atomic reactions.
atom	(ăt′ ȯm)	*n.*	Smallest particle of an element.
bombard	(bŏm bärd′)	*v.*	To subject to the impact of high velocity atomic particles.
breeder	(brēēd′ ĕr)	*n.*	Atomic reactor.
cloud chamber	(cloud chăm′ ber)	*n.*	Vaporized chamber showing paths of atomic particles.
cyclotron	(çy̆′ clō trŏn)	*n.*	An accelerator giving particles a spiral path.
electron	(ḗ lĕc′ trŏn)	*n.*	Most elementary charge of negative electricity.
element	(ĕl′ ḗ mĕnt)	*n.*	A fundamental substance of like atoms, indivisible by ordinary means.
fission	(fĭs′ ſion)	*n.*	Splitting atomic nuclei.
fusion	(fū′ ṣion)	*n.*	Union of atomic nuclei.
ion	(ī′ ŏn)	*n.*	Electrically charged atoms.
isotope	(ī′ sō tōpe)	*n.*	One of a species of atoms differing only in atomic mass number.
lead	(lĕad)	*n.*	Metal that shields against radioactivity.
neutron	(neū′ trŏn)	*n.*	Uncharged atomic particle.
nucleus	(nū′ clḗ ŭs)	*n.*	Central part of an atom.
plutonium	(plu̟ tō′ nĭ ŭm)	*n.*	A fissionable, radioactive metallic element.
proton	(prō′ tŏn)	*n.*	Positively charged particle of the nucleus.
radioactivity	(rā′ dĭ ȯ̇ ăc tĭv′ ĭ ty̆)	*n.*	The spontaneous emission of nuclear energy.
tracer	(trā′ çĕr)	*n.*	An atom used to track a chemical process.
uranium	(u̇ rā′ nĭ ŭm)	*n.*	A fissionable, radioactive metallic element.

Assignment

Write a paragraph on the peaceful uses of the atom, using any references available to you. Try to include some of the above terms. Underline each term as you use it.

ABCDEFGHIJKLESSON **118**

**AUTOMATION AND
DATA PROCESSING**

This lesson presents some of the specialized terminology associated with automation and data processing.

automation	*n.* A process of mechanization; a self-regulating process.
central processing unit	*n.* A unit that directs the input, processing, and output of data.
collator	*n.* A machine that will combine two decks of punched cards in sequence.
data processing	*n.* The recording, classifying, and computing of information.
electronic computer system	*n.* System in which both numeric and alphabetic data are processed in the form of electrical pulses.
flow chart	*n.* Diagram showing the sequence of operations in a data processing system.
hardware	*n.* The physical equipment or devices making up a data-processing system.
input	*n.* Data to be processed.
machine language	*n.* Any one of several computer languages for writing operation codes.
magnetic tape	*n.* Tape on which data are recorded in the form of magnetized spots.
numerical	*adj.* Expressed by numbers rather than letters.
optical scanner	*n.* A device that speed-reads data from a page into a computer.
output	*n.* Data that have been processed.
program	*n.* A group of related routines fed into a computer to process data.
programmer	*n.* Technician who plans the steps necessary to produce the desired information.
punched card	*n.* Card punched with a pattern of holes to represent data to be recorded.
real-time	*n.* Actual time taken by a computer to process data.
software	*n.* Collection of programs and routines used with a computer.
storage	*n.* A device into which data can be entered and retrieved at a later time.
verifier	*n.* A machine used to check the accuracy of card punching.

Assignment

Write a short paragraph about automation and the changes it has made in our lives.

MODERN TECHNOLOGY

This lesson contains a sampling of terms from three specialized fields: medical technology, oceanography, and pollution control.

Medical terms

allergen	(ăl′ lĕr ġĕn)	n. Allergy-inducing substance.
antigen	(ăn′ tĭ ġĕn)	n. Foreign substance causing the production of an antibody.
biopsy	(bī′ ŏp sў)	n. Removal of tissue from a living body for examination.
disinfectant	(dĭs′ ĭn fĕc′ tănt)	n. Chemical destroyer of germs.
ligature	(lĭg′ à tŭre)	n. Thread to tie blood vessels.
suture	(sū′ tŭre)	v. Joining edges of a wound.

Oceanography

aquanaut	(ăq′ uȧ näut)	n. An underwater scientist.
aquatic	(à quät′ ĭc)	adj. Pertaining to water.
decompression	(dē′ cŏm prĕs′ sion)	n. Gradual lessening of pressure exerted on a diver.
hydrophone	(hў′ drŏ phōne)	n. Underwater microphone.
plankton	(plănk′ tŏn)	n. Minute marine life.
scuba	(scụ′ bȧ)	n. Underwater breathing apparatus.
sonar	(sō′ när)	n. Device for locating underwater objects.

Pollution Control

abatement	(à bāte′ mĕnt)	n. Decrease in amount of pollutants.
chlorine	(chlō′ rĭne)	n. Disinfectant for water.
contamination	(cŏn tăm′ ĭ nā′ tion)	v. Pollution.
dispersal	(dĭs pĕr′ săl)	n. Distribution of pollutants.
ecology	(ĕ cŏl′ ŏ ġў)	n. The interrelationship of organisms and their environment.
effluent	(ĕf′ flú ĕnt)	n. Outflow of liquid waste.
emission	(ē mĭs′ sion)	n. Discharge of pollutants into the air or water.

Assignment

Copy the following sentences, filling in the blanks with words from the above list.

1. S cuba diving is popular.
2. A biopsy revealed that the tumor was malignant.
3. Industrial waste is causing contamin of our water supply.
4. Chlorine helps to counteract some of this c ontamination
5. The aquanaut reported his underwater observations.

135

ABCDEFGHIJKLESSON 120
REVIEW

A. Explain the structure of the following words in terms of prefixes, word roots, and suffixes:

astronaut
hydrophone
aquanaut
interplanetary
reentry

decompression
disinfectant
input
propellant
radioactivity

B. Copy the words in the right column. Beside each word, place the number of the appropriate definition.

1. Device to locate underwater objects.
2. Underwater breathing apparatus.
3. Joining the edges of a wound.
4. Thread used to tie off blood vessels.
5. A machine that checks the accuracy of card punching.
6. An accelerator giving particles a circular path.
7. Minute plant and animal life of the sea.
8. Removal of tissue from a living body for examination.
9. Liquid waste; outflow.
10. A fundamental substance consisting of like atoms.

6 cyclotron
7 plankton
8 biopsy
4 ligature
3 suture
1 sonar
9 effluent
2 scuba
10 element
5 verifier

C. Complete the following sentences with words from the previous four lessons.

1. E _mission_ of smoke and _effluent_ wastes from factories and mills will have to be controlled.
2. O _utput_ refers to data that have been fed into a computer and processed.
3. An _electronic computer system_ processes both numeric and alphabetic data as electrical pulses.
4. To b _ombard_ a substance is to subject it to the impact of high velocity atomic particles.
5. H _elium_ is the simplest and lightest of all elements.
6. The path of one body around another is known as its o _rbit_.
7. A sequence of operation instructions in diagram form is called a f _low_ c _hart_.
8. A _batement_ of air pollution has been hastened by the use of lead-free gasoline.
9. The c _entral processing unit_ is the controlling unit in a computer system.
10. A s _atellite_ is a man-made object designed to orbit in space.

136

LITERATURE

The term "literature" covers many different forms of writing. This lesson presents some of the major types of literature.

allegory	(ăl′ lḗ gō′ rў)	*n.* A story in which the true meaning is symbolized.
author	(au′ thŏr)	*n.* One who writes a book.
ballad	(băl′ lăd)	*n.* A popular short poem, usually founded on folklore.
biography	(bī ŏg′ rȧ phў)	*n.* The written history of a person's life.
chronicle	(chrŏn′ ĭ cle)	*n.* An account of events; a history.
classics	(clăs′ sĭcs)	*n.* Ancient Greek and Roman literature.
description	(dḗ scrĭp′ tion)	*n.* A depicting; an account.
drama	(drä′ mȧ)	*n.* A play.
epic	(ĕp′ ĭc)	*n.* A long formal poem describing a heroic figure.
epigram	(ĕp′ ĭ grăm)	*n.* Witty expression or inscription.
essay	(ĕs sāy)	*n.* A literary composition, analytical in nature.
fable	(fā′ ble)	*n.* A story of supernatural happenings with a moral.
fiction	(fĭc′ tion)	*n.* An imagined story.
legend	(lĕǵ′ ĕnd)	*n.* A story retold from the past.
narrative	(năr′ rȧ tĭve)	*n.* The recital of a story. *adj.* Pertaining to a story.
novel	(nŏv′ ĕl)	*n.* Fictitious story.
poetry	(pō′ ĕt rў)	*n.* Verse; poetic works collectively.
saga	(sä′ gȧ)	*n.* A story of Icelandic heroic adventure.
sonnet	(sŏn′ nĕt)	*n.* A fixed verse form of fourteen lines.
treatise	(trēat′ ĭse)	*n.* A systematic argument.

Assignment

Copy the words on the right. Beside each word place the number of the answer from the left column which best defines the word.

1. *Beowulf* is a narrative poem of heroic action.
2. A history of Lincoln's life.
3. An account of events of the Civil War.
4. This book is filled with witty expressions.
5. A novel.
6. A story from long ago.
7. A poem taken from folklore.
8. A fixed verse form of fourteen lines.
9. The *Kalevala* is a story of a Finnish hero.
10. *Pilgrim's Progress* symbolized Bunyan's life.

epigrams
epic
chronicle
fiction
biography
saga
allegory
sonnet
legend
ballad

122
LITERATURE

The field of literature, like those scientific fields discussed earlier, has its own technical vocabulary. The following list contains terms that should become part of your vocabulary.

alliteration	(ăl lĭt' ĕr ā' tion)	*n.*	Repetition of an initial sound in consecutive words.
blank verse	(blănk vērse)	*n.*	Unrhymed verse with regular rhythm.
climax	(clī' măx)	*n.*	Peak of dramatic tension.
couplet	(coŭp' lĕt)	*n.*	Two successive lines of closely related verse.
denouement	(de noᵤe ment') dá män	*n.*	The final occurrence which clarifies the plot.
dialogue	(dī' à lŏgᵤe)	*n.*	A written conversation.
didacticism	(dī dăc' tĭ çĭṣm)	*n.*	Writing to instruct.
free verse	(frēē vērse)	*n.*	Verse with no regular rhythm or rhyme.
historian	(hĭs tō' rĭ ăn)	*n.*	Writer of history.
manuscript	(măn' ú scrĭpt)	*n.*	An unpublished work.
metaphor	(mĕt' à phôr)	*n.*	A term used in place of another to suggest a likeness between them.
naturalism	(năt' ú răl ĭṣm)	*n.*	Realism in literature.
novelist	(nŏv' ĕl ĭst)	*n.*	Writer of novels.
plagiarize	(plā' ġĭ à rīze)	*v.*	To pass off as one's own the writings of another.
pun	(pŭn)	*n.*	A play on words of the same sound but different meanings with humorous effect.
satire	(săt' īre)	*n.*	Literature used to ridicule.
sequel	(sē' quĕl)	*n.*	Continuation of something published before.
simile	(sĭm' ĭ lē)	*n.*	A figure of speech comparing two unlike things using words such as "like," or "as."
soliloquy	(só lĭl' ó quȳ)	*n.*	Monologue.
trilogy	(trĭl' ó ġȳ)	*n.*	Three related tales.

Assignment

Copy the following sentences, substituting the best synonym from the list above for each italicized word or word group.

1. He is the *author* who wrote ten volumes on the Roman Empire.
2. He also wrote an *essay that ridiculed* the ruling class.
3. Dean wrote a *second book*, a continuation of his first novel.
4. Smith wrote *three novels* about the adventurous Jackson family.
5. *To pass off as one's own the writings of another* is a crime.

138

123

ART AND THE DANCE

The classification of art includes many related areas such as painting, sculpture, and ceramics. This lesson outlines two areas which might be classified as art, and defines terms related to them.

Art

classical	(clăs′ sĭ căl)	*adj.* Conforming to an established art form.
cubism	(cūb′ iṣm)	*n.* Abstract painting stressing geometric shapes.
culture	(cŭl′ tŭre)	*n.* Enlightenment and refinement of taste.
decorative	(děc′ ŏ rā′ tĭve)	*adj.* Ornamental.
impressionism	(ĭm prěs′ sion ĭṣm)	*n.* School of painting using dots of primary colors to represent reflected light.
motif	(mō tĭf′)	*n.* Theme or dominant feature.
pointillism	(poin′ tĭl lĭsm) pwăn	*n.* Neoimpressionism; colors dotted on a white canvass.
realism	(rē′ ăl ĭṣm)	*n.* Exact representation of nature.
tempera	(těm′ pěr à)	*n.* Painting medium of an eggwhite base rather than oil.
virtuoso	(vir′ tŭ ō′ sō) vûr′	*n.* Master artist or performer.

Dance

audition	(au dĭ′ tion)	*n.* A tryout.
auditorium	(au′ dĭ tō′ rĭ ŭm)	*n.* Public room for audiences.
ballerina	(băl′ lĕ rĭ′ nà)	*n.* A female ballet dancer.
ballet	(băl′ let) lā	*n.* A classical dance form; a story told through dance.
choreographer	(chō′ rē ŏg′ rà phěr)	*n.* Dance arranger or director.
minuet	(mĭn′ ŭ ět′)	*n.* A slow, graceful dance.
pantomime	(păn′ tŏ mime)	*n.* Action expressed by bodily and facial movements.
pas de deux	(päs dē deûx′)	*n.* Dance for two.
pirouette	(pĭr′ oụ ette′)	*n.* A full turn in ballet.
rehearsal	(rḗ hĕar′ săl)	*n.* Practice session.

Assignment

Copy the following sentences, selecting the correct words from the above list to complete the sentences.

1. A female ballet dancer is a *ballerina*
2. A director of movements of a ballet is a *choreographer*
3. A master artist is called a *virtuoso*
4. A show acted without spoken words is a *pantomime*
5. The theme of a work of art is the *motif*.

ABCDEFGHIJKLESSON 124
MUSIC

The fine arts also include music. The words below describe various types of musical composition, as well as terms related to the field of music. This lesson provides a basis for your understanding of the musical terminology you may encounter in reading or conversation.

adagio	(à dä′ ġiō)	*adv.* Slowly.
alto	(ăl′ tō)	*n.* Part sung by highest male or lowest female voice.
anthem	(ăn′ thĕm)	*n.* A song of praise or gladness.
aria	(ä′ rĭ à)	*n.* A solo part for the voice.
baritone	(băr′ ĭ tōne)	*n.* Male voice between bass and tenor.
bass	(bāss)	*n.* Part sung by lowest male voice.
carol	(căr′ ól)	*n.* A song of praise or joy.
contralto	(cŏn trăl′ tō)	*n.* A part sung by the lowest female or highest male voice.
dissonance	(dĭs′ só nănçe)	*n.* Mingling of discordant sounds.
encore	(en′ cōre) äng′	*n.* Additional music played in response to applause.
modulation	(mŏd′ ú lā′ tion)	*n.* Changing from one key to another.
nocturne	(nŏc′ tûrne)	*n.* A dreamy, night serenade.
opera	(ŏp′ ẽr à)	*n.* A drama mostly sung.
operetta	(ŏp′ ẽr ĕt′ tà)	*n.* A light musical drama.
oratorio	(ŏr′ à tō′ rĭ ō)	*n.* A Biblical drama set to music.
philharmonic	(phĭl′ hăr mŏn′ ĭc)	*adj.* Pertaining to music.
quartet	(quạr tĕt′)	*n.* A group of four performers.
recital	(ré çĭt′ ăl)	*n.* A performance.
rhapsody	(rhăp′ só dў)	*n.* A musical composition of irregular form.
symphony	(sўm′ phó nў)	*n.* A composition for a full orchestra.

Assignment

Copy the following paragraphs, correcting any words from the list above which are misspelled. Underline each word you correct.

During Christmas week we heard the oretorio "The Messiah," the Boston Symphony, and a recital of anthens and carols at the auditorium.

After Dr. Paul returned from Vienna, he composed a rapsody, a nocterne, and an operatta called "Song of the Rose." Martha said she meant to try out for the contralo part, and Mr. Barazon said he would try out for the part of the baretone.

Tomorrow Bob and I are going to the opara. Usually, Bob enjoys the music from the philearmonic orchestra more than the singing. However, there is an airea in this opara that he especially likes.

140

A. Rewrite the following sentences, correcting misspelled words.

   1. The soliloquey was very moving.
   2. John's narattive of the accident was confused.
   3. Howard is a writer of boring novils and dull epigrammes.
   4. It is unethical to plagerize.
   5. Some people think that sattire is more amusing than commedy.
   6. The disonnance of some modern music reflects the conflicts and tensions of modern life.
   7. For her appearance with the phillharmonic orchestra, the opera singer selected an arria from *Aida*.
   8. The quartet sang a medley of Christmas carrols.
   9. Degas' paintings of ballerenas are favorites at exhibits.
   10. The sponsors of the show insisted on choosing the canvasses to be displayed.

B. Copy the words in the right column. Beside each word, write the number of the appropriate definition.

   1. Song of praise or gladness.   motif
   2. Relating to music.   aria
   3. Tryout.   audition
   4. Theme or dominant feature.   nocturne
   5. Solo part for the voice.   philharmonic
   6. Night serenade.   symphony
   7. Composition for a full orchestra.   anthem
   8. Action expressed by gestures.   encore
   9. Additional performance.   opera
   10. Drama sung rather than spoken.   pantomime

C. In the following statements, mark similes *S*, metaphors *M*, and epigrams *E*. (Consult your dictionary for more detailed definitions, if necessary.)

   1. Her tears are like the summer rain, soon to be followed by the sunshine of her smile.
   2. On this New Year's Day, Old Father Time reminds us that it is later than we think.
   3. "A little knowledge is a dangerous thing."
   4. He watches his flock like a good shepherd.
   5. Like a great, translucent balloon, the moon sails along in the star-studded heavens, unaware of our special concern.

D. Give examples that illustrate the meaning of the following words: author, biography, historian, anthem, operetta.

Example: Allegory—*Pilgrim's Progress*, by John Bunyan.

ABCDEFGHIJKLESSON 126
EDUCATION

The following list of words covers some of the procedures, titles and terminology related to the various levels of education.

academic	(ăc′ à dĕm′ ĭc)	*adj.*	Pertaining to the study of general subjects.
administration	(ăd mĭn′ ĭs trā′ tion)	*n.*	Governing body of an educational institution.
campus	(căm′ pŭs)	*n.*	The grounds of a school.
coeducation	(cō′ ĕd′ ủ cā′ tion)	*n.*	The education of both sexes at the same school.
diploma	(dĭ plō′ mȧ)	*n.*	Document certifying graduation.
examination	(ex am′ ĭ nā′ tion) ĕg zăm	*n.*	A testing of knowledge.
extracurricular	(ĕx′ trȧ cŭr rĭc′ ủ lȧr)	*adj.*	Not in the regular course of study.
forum	(fō′ rŭm)	*n.*	A place for discussion.
gymnasium	(ġўm nā′ ṣĭ ŭm)	*n.*	A place where physical exercises are performed.
intramural	(ĭn′ trȧ mū′ răl)	*adj.*	Confined to members of the college.
kindergarten	(kĭn′ dẽr gär′ tĕn)	*n.*	School for small children.
matriculate	(mä trĭc′ ủ lāte)	*v.*	To enroll.
pedagogue	(pĕd′ ȧ gŏg*ue*)	*n.*	A teacher; schoolmaster.
prerequisite	(pré rĕq′ ui ṣĭte) wĭ	*n.*	A preliminary requirement.
semester	(sé mĕs′ tẽr)	*n.*	Half a school year.
syllabus	(sўl′ *l*ȧ bŭs)	*n.*	A summary outline of the course.
technical	(tĕc*h*′ nĭ căl)	*adj.*	Pertaining to a scientific field.
thesis	(thē′ sĭs)	*n.*	A theme involving research.
valedictorian	(văl′ é dĭc tō′ rĭ ăn)	*n.*	Top scholar in graduating class who gives the farewell address.
vocational	(vó cā′ tion ăl)	*adj.*	Pertaining to skills or trade to be used in a career.

Assignment

Copy the following sentences, correcting any words which are misused or misspelled.

1. Dave was valetudinarian of his class.
2. Martha's tmesis on plant ecology was brilliant.
3. He lacked the prerogatives to marginate.
4. We attended the dance in the school gynaisum.
5. She participated in intramural, extracuricular activities.

142

EDUCATION

There are many fields of study at both the elementary and secondary levels, as well as at the undergraduate and postgraduate levels in college. The following list contains a sampling of these fields.

agronomy	(à grŏn′ ŏ mў)	n.	Science of soil management.
algebra	(ăl′ ġĕ brà)	n.	The use of symbols in computations for unknown quantities.
anthropology	(ăn′ thrŏ pŏl′ ŏ ġў)	n.	Study of man in various cultures.
archaeology	(är′ chaĕ ŏl′ ŏ ġў)	n.	Study of man's past cultures through material remains.
arithmetic	(à rĭth′ mĕ tĭc)	n.	Computation by numbers.
botany	(bŏt′ à nў)	n.	Study of plant life.
chemistry	(chĕm′ ĭs trў)	n.	Science dealing with the composition of substances.
economics	(ē′ cŏ nŏm′ ĭcs)	n.	Study of factors affecting production and distribution of wealth.
geography	(ġĕ ŏg′ rà phў)	n.	Study of the earth in its present state.
geology	(ġĕ ŏl′ ŏ ġў)	n.	Study of the physical history of the earth.
grammar	(grăm′ *m*är)	n.	The rules governing speech and writing.
language	(lăn′ guage) gwĭj	n.	Speech and writing.
meteorology	(mē′ tĕ ŏr ŏl′ ŏ ġў)	n.	Study of the atmosphere.
physics	(phў*s*′ ĭcs)	n.	Study of the interaction of matter and energy.
physiology	(phўs′ ĭ ŏl′ ŏ ġў)	n.	Branch of biology dealing with life processes.
psychology	(*p*sў chŏl′ ŏ ġў)	n.	Study of the mind and behavior.
rhetoric	(r*h*ĕt′ ŏ rĭc)	n.	The art of expressive speech.
science	(s*c*ī′ ĕnçe)	n.	Systematized knowledge.
sociology	(sō′ çĭ ŏl′ ŏ ġў)	n.	Study of social institutions.
statistics	(stà tĭs′ tĭcs)	n.	The collection and analysis of numerical data.

Assignment

Copy the following statements. If a statement is true, write "true" after its number. If a statement is false, rewrite it, substituting words from the above list.

1. The study of plant life is physiology.
2. Chemistry deals with the composition of substances.
3. Botany is the study of the origin of man.
4. Geography is the science of the earth.
5. The study of the atmosphere and its phenomena is meteorology.

ABCDEFGHIJKLESSON 128
EDUCATION

Colleges and universities have a specialized vocabulary of their own. This lesson gives an overview of some of these terms.

accredited	(ăc crĕd′ ĭt ĕd)	*adj.* Meets prescribed requirements.
alma mater	(äl′ må mä′ tẽr)	*n.* One's school.
alumni	(å lŭm′ nī)	*n.* Graduates of a school.
bursar	(bûr′ sår)	*n.* Treasurer of the school.
calculus	(căl′ cú lŭs)	*n.* Advanced mathematics.
chancellor	(chàn′ çel lõr)	*n.* The president of a college.
curriculum	(cŭr rĭc′ ú lŭm)	*n.* The courses offered by an educational institution.
dean	(dēan)	*n.* An administrative officer of a college.
dissertation	(dĭs′ sẽr tä′ tion)	*n.* Presentation of the results of extended research into a subject.
doctorate	(dŏc′ tõr åte)	*n.* Highest academic degree.
emeritus	(é mĕr′ ĭ tŭs)	*adj.* Designating an honorary title equivalent to the one held before retirement.
faculty	(făc′ ŭl tў)	*n.* The teaching and administrative staff of a school.
fellowship	(fĕl′ lŏw shĭp)	*n.* Stipend for graduate studies.
humanities	(hú măn′ ĭ tĭes)	*n.* Areas of learning regarded as cultural; the liberal arts.
professor	(prŏ fĕs′ sõr)	*n.* A college teacher of the highest rank.
registrar	(rĕġ′ ĭs trär)	*n.* An official keeper of records at a college.
scholarship	(schŏl′ år shĭp)	*n.* Fund for the support of a student.
seminar	(sĕm′ ĭ när′)	*n.* A group of students engaged in original research.
tuition	(tú ĭ′ tion)	*n.* Fee charged for instruction.
university	(ū nĭ vẽr′ sĭ tў)	*n.* An institution of colleges and/or graduate schools.

Assignment

Number your paper from 1 to 5. Beside each number write the word from the list above which best answers each question below.

1. What title is given to a college teacher of highest rank?
2. What title is given the official keeper of records?
3. What is an institution consisting of several colleges called?
4. By what other name are the graduates of a college known?
5. What is the collective term for the teaching and administrative staff of a college?

ABCDEFGHIJKLESSON 129

RELIGION

Religion may be defined as man's belief in the existence of a supreme being, or in the existence of supernatural influences which control his life. This lesson gives an overview of the common terms associated with the major religions.

agnostic	(ăg nŏs' tĭc)	n. One who believes that the existence of a Supreme Being is unknowable.
atheist	(ā' thḗ ĭst)	n. One who does not believe in a Supreme Being.
benediction	(bĕn' ḗ dĭc' tion)	n. A blessing.
blasphemy	(blăs' phḗ mў)	n. Irreverence toward something sacred.
catechism	(căt' ḗ chĭ̦sm)	n. Religious doctrine in the form of questions and answers.
confirmation	(cŏn' fĭr mā' tion)	n. A church rite.
congregation	(con' grḗ gā' tion) cŏng	n. An assembly for worship.
deacon	(dēa' cŏn)	n. Officer of a church.
disciple	(dĭs çī' ple)	n. A follower.
dogma	(dŏg' mà)	n. Body of doctrines.
ecumenical	(ĕc' ū̇ mĕn' ĭ căl)	adj. Worldwide.
hymn	(hўmn)	n. A song of praise.
missionary	(mĭs' sion ār' ў) mĭsh'	n. One sent to spread religion.
mosque	(mŏsque)	n. Place of Muslim worship.
orthodox	(ôr' thŏ́ dŏx)	adj. Conforming to doctrine and standardized practices.
pagoda	(på gō' dà)	n. Buddhist or Hindu temple of worship.
scriptures	(scrĭp' túres)	n. Sacred writings.
sermon	(sēr' mŏn)	n. A public religious discourse.
synagogue	(sўn' à gŏgue)	n. Place of Jewish worship.
theology	(thḗ ŏl' ṓ ġў)	n. The study of religion.

Assignment

Copy the following sentences, selecting the correct words from the above list to fill in each blank.

1. At the end of the service the chaplain pronounced the _____.
2. The children memorized the _____.
3. The nations united in an _____ day of prayer.
4. He said he was an _____ in his beliefs.
5. A _____ is a Jewish temple of worship.
6. The pastor rebuked the stranger who uttered _____.
7. The _____ went to Africa to convert the natives.
8. Buddhists worship in tower-like structures known as _____.
9. The _____ accepted the instructions of the missionary.
10. _____ is the study of religion.

145

Section I: Review of Lessons 126-129

A. Copy the words in the right-hand column. Beside each word write the number of the appropriate definition.

1. Top scholar in the graduating class.   bursar
2. Course of study.   chancellor
3. Place of open discussion.   forum
4. A follower.   pedagogue
5. A song of praise.   orthodox
6. Worldwide.   valedictorian
7. Treasurer, or cash keeper.   ecumenical
8. Head of a university.   syllabus
9. Teacher of children.   hymn
10. Conforming to doctrines or practices.   disciple

B. Copy the following paragraphs, completing unfinished words.

Today we live in an era of technology. The life sciences of biology, b———, and p——— have made great advances. They have been supplemented by other sciences such as p———, the study of man's mental and emotional makeup, and s——— the study of social institutions. All these fields use s——— to substantiate their research with numerical data.

Space feats have aroused interest in earth s———. M——— covers the atmosphere and its phenomena. G——— is concerned with the earth and its life, particularly with distribution of animals and plant life. G——— on the other hand, is concerned with the history of the earth and its life, especially as recorded in rocks.

C. Explain the structure of the following words in terms of prefixes, word roots, and suffixes:

benediction   accredited   prerequisite   intramural
coeducation   anthropology   theology   administration

D. The following sentences contain italicized words that may be misused. Rewrite the incorrect sentences so that these words are used properly.

1. *Grammar* is the art of speaking expressively.
2. Scientific management of the land is *agronomy.*
3. Mrs. Lowe's long teaching career demonstrates her success as a *syllabus.*
4. A *professor* is a university teacher of the highest rank.
5. Synagogue, pagoda, and mosque are the names of *scriptures.*

Section II: General Review of Lessons 111-129

A. Copy the words on the left, selecting the best definition for each one from the choices given in parentheses.

1. warrant   (authorization, slander, subpoena, ballot)
2. mandate   (caucus, envoy, order, proxy)
3. ion   (element, atomic fuel, tracer, charged atom)
4. novel   (epic, fiction, classic, treatise)
5. tempera   (marine life, paint, satire, opera)
6. motif   (theme, solo, temple, hymn)
7. rhetoric   (language, religious doctrine, essay, speech)
8. reciprocity   (popular vote, mutual recognition, diplomacy, protocol)
9. census   (policy meeting, program, population count, restriction)
10. contaminate   (pollute, abate, disperse, compute)

B. Copy the following sentences, correcting any italicized words that are misspelled or misused.

1. An *allergen* is a foreign substance causing the production of antibodies in our systems.
2. To *disenfranchise* is to deprive a citizen of his rights.
3. An *epogramm* is a witty expression or inscription.
4. A *verifier* is used in data processing to combine two decks of punched cards in sequence.
5. *Plutonium* is a metallic element that is both fissionable and radioactive.
6. A verdict of innocence is known as an *acquitel*.
7. A *congragation* is an assembly of people gathered to worship.
8. Jean's *diplommer* certified that she had graduated.
9. An *affidavit* is a sworn statement in writing.
10. "Blue bells bring beauty . . ." is an example of *alitteration*.

C. Copy the words on the right. Beside each word place the number of the answer from the left column that best defines the word.

1. Present holder of an office.   clemency
2. Exact representation of nature.   incumbent
3. Uncharged atomic particle.   quorum
4. Elimination of cargo.   jettison
5. Leniency; mildness.   neutron
6. Master performer.   automation
7. Summary outline of a course.   aquatic
8. Required attendance to conduct business.   realism
9. Pertaining to water.   virtuoso
10. Mechanization.   syllabus

131
THEATER

Millions of Americans each year are entertained, amused, and sometimes shocked by plays and movies. This lesson contains some of the common terms associated with this branch of entertainment.

actor	(ăc′ tŏr)	*n.* Male theatrical performer.
actress	(ăc′ trĕss)	*n.* Female theatrical performer.
animation	(ăn′ ĭ mā′ tion)	*n.* The process of effecting lifelike movement.
articulation	(är tĭc′ ŭ lā′ tion)	*n.* Speaking in distinct syllables and words.
camera	(căm′ ẽr à)	*n.* Instrument recording images.
censor	(çĕn′ sõr)	*v.* To subject to examination and possible repression.
cinema	(çĭn′ é mà)	*n.* Motion picture or movie theater.
comedian	(cố mē′ dĭ ăn)	*n.* An actor who plays amusing roles.
comedienne	(cố mē′ dĭ ĕn*ne*′)	*n.* Actress who plays amusing roles.
comedy	(cŏm′ ĕ dў)	*n.* A light and amusing drama.
director	(dī rĕc′ tŏr)	*n.* One who supervises the production of a play or movie.
documentary	(dŏc′ ŭ mĕn′ tà rў)	*n.* A factual film.
ingenue	(in′ ge′ nüe′) ăn zhá	*n.* An actress representing a naive girl.
photogenic	(phŏ′ tố ġĕn′ ĭc)	*adj.* Suitable for being photographed.
playwright	(plāy′ *wr*īght′)	*n.* One who writes plays.
revue	(rế vüe′)	*n.* A medley of songs, dances, and skits.
scenario	(sćế nä′ rĭ ō′)	*n.* Screenplay, script.
technicolor	(tĕc*h* nĭ cŏl′ ŏr)	*n.* Color motion pictures.
theater	(thē′ à tẽr)	*n.* An edifice for dramatic performances.
tragedy	(trăġ ĕ dў)	*n.* A serious drama with a catastrophic ending.

Assignment

Copy the following sentences, substituting the best synonym from the above list for each italicized word or word group.

1. Are you going to the *movies* this evening?
2. This *factual film* was made in Italy.
3. The producer said the aging *star* could not play the part of a *naive girl*.
4. There are still viewers who prefer black and white films to *colored motion pictures*.
5. The audience enjoyed the *medley of songs and skits*.

FOOD AND DINING

Both the gourmet (one who appreciates fine food) and the gourmand (one who is a glutton for food) find pleasure in dining at a good restaurant. The following words refer to various methods of preparing foods, and various types of dishes you may encounter when dining out.

appetizer	(ăp′ pé tīz′ ẽr)	*n.* Small portion of food served before a meal.
artichoke	(är′ tĭ chōke)	*n.* An herb with coarse leaves.
au gratin	(au′ grå′ tin′) tăn	*adj.* Crusted with browned bread crumbs or cheese.
barbecue	(bär′ bé cūe)	*v.* To cook over an open fire. *n.* An outdoor meal so cooked.
café au lait	(cå′ fé′ au lāit) fä	*n.* Coffee with milk in equal parts.
coleslaw	(cōle slaw)	*n.* A salad made of cabbage.
consommé	(cŏn′ sŏm mé′) mä	*n.* A clear soup.
delicatessen	(dĕl′ ĭ cå tĕs′ sĕn)	*n.* A store selling cold meat, preserves, and relishes.
goulash	(gou′ läsh)	*n.* A stew of beef or veal with vegetables and paprika.
hibachi	(hĭ bä′ chi) chē	*n.* A Japanese grill.
marinate	(mär′ ĭ nāte)	*v.* To soak meat before cooking.
mince	(mĭnçe)	*v.* To chop very fine.
ragout	(rä gout′)	*n.* A highly seasoned meat stew.
sauerkraut	(sauer′ kraut′) sour krout	*n.* Cabbage fermented in brine.
sauté	(sau té′) tā	*adj.* Fried lightly and quickly.
smorgasbord	(smôr′ găs bôrd′)	*n.* Swedish dishes served buffet style.
soufflé	(souf′ flé′) flä	*n.* A light, fluffy baked dish.
spaghetti	(spå ghĕt′ tĭ)	*n.* Long strings of flour paste.
table d'hote	(tå blē d'hōte′)	*n.* A meal for which one pays a fixed price irrespective of what one orders.
torte	(tȯrte)	*n.* A rich cake made with many eggs and little flour.

Assignment

Copy the words on the left, selecting the word that best matches it from the three choices given.

1. smorgasbord (a) Swedish buffet (b) appetizer (c) a thick soup
2. au gratin (a) spoiled (b) with cheese (c) shredded
3. café au lait (a) pudding (b) pastry (c) coffee with milk
4. mince (a) spice (b) chop fine (c) broil
5. consommé (a) clear soup (b) combination (c) parfait

133
HEALTH

The language of medicine is often confusing. This lesson defines some common terms which should become familiar to you.

anesthesia	(ăn′ ĕs thē′ sĭ à)	*n.* Loss of sensation.
calorie	(căl′ ố rĭe)	*n.* Unit of food energy.
congenital	(cŏn ġĕn′ ĭ tăl)	*adj.* Existing at birth.
corpuscle	(côr′ pŭs cle)	*n.* A body cell.
dermatologist	(dēr′ mà tŏl′ ố ġĭst)	*n.* A doctor who specializes in diseases of the skin.
diagnosis	(dī′ ăg nō′ sĭs)	*n.* Analysis of the cause or nature of a condition.
diathermy	(dī′ à thĕr′ mў)	*n.* Heat used in treatment.
geriatrics	(ġĕr′ ĭ ăt′ rĭcs)	*n.* Science of medicine concerned with old age.
healthful	(hĕalth′ fu̟l)	*adj.* Physically or mentally beneficial.
hemoglobin	(hē′ mố glō′ bĭn)	*n.* Protein matter in red corpuscles.
insulin	(ĭn′ sú lĭn)	*n.* Substance aiding utilization of sugar in the body.
isometrics	(ī′ số mĕt′ rĭcs)	*n.* Muscle-strengthening exercises.
oculist	(ŏc′ ú lĭst)	*n.* A doctor who specializes in diseases of the eye.
optometrist	(ŏp tŏm′ ḗ trĭst)	*n.* One who examines eyes and prescribes eye glasses.
orthodontist	(ôr′ thố dŏn′ tĭst)	*n.* A dental specialist in straightening teeth.
physician	(phў sĭç ĭan)	*n.* A medical doctor.
podiatrist	(pố dī′ à trĭst)	*n.* One who treats minor disorders of the feet.
psychiatrist	(*p*sў chī′ à trĭst)	*n.* A doctor who treats mental disorders.
psychologist	(*p*sў chŏl′ ố ġĭst)	*n.* One who studies the mind.
ptomaine	(*p*tō māine)	*n.* Poisonous substance coming from spoiled food.

Assignment

Copy the following paragraphs, correcting any misspelled words from the above list. Underline each word you correct.

Just a month after Mary had ptomain poisoning from eating salad at a picnic, a rash appeared on her face. She was so upset that her dermetologist suggested she see a psychietrist.

To reduce weight, you should limit your calory intake; and it is well to have your physican check your hemoglobin. You might also look into the benefits of isemetrics.

LESSON # 134
CLOTHING AND FASHION

The world of fashion has an interesting vocabulary, with a large number of French words. The following words describe various types of apparel.

ascot	(ăs′ cŏt)	n.	A broad neck scarf.
beret	(bē ret′)	n.	A round, flat cap.
	rā		
bolero	(bó lê′ rō)	n.	A short jacket, usually open at the front.
cardigan	(cär′ dĭ găn)	n.	A collarless sweater opening ing down the front.
cashmere	(căsh′ mēre)	n.	A fine wool.
culotte	(cú lŏtte′)	n.	A divided skirt.
cummerbund	(cŭm′ mẽr bŭnd′)	n.	Broad fitted sash often arranged in overlapping folds.
dacron	(dā′ cron)	n.	A synthetic fabric.
	crän		
embroidery	(ĕm broi′ dẽr ў)	n.	The art of ornamenting cloth with needlework.
ensemble	(en sem′ ble)	n.	A costume of two or more pieces.
	än sŏm		
haberdashery	(hăb′ ẽr dăsh′ ẽr ў)	n.	Men's furnishings.
mackinaw	(măck′ ĭ naw)	n.	A short, heavy coat.
millinery	(mil′ lĭ nẽr ў)	n.	Hats for women.
negligee	(nĕg′ lĭ geé)	n.	Woman's dressing gown.
	zhā		
stole	(stōle)	n.	A long, narrow shoulder scarf, often of fur.
suede	(suede)	n.	A tanned skin rubbed into a nap.
	swād		
topcoat	(tŏp′ cōat′)	n.	A lightweight outer coat.
trousseau	(troṵs seau′)	n.	The personal outfit of a bride.
	sō		
tuxedo	(tŭx ē′ dō)	n.	A semi-formal evening suit for men.
worsted	(wọrs′ tĕd)	n.	A smooth-surfaced woolen cloth.

Assignment

Copy the words on the right. Beside each word place the number of the answer from the left column which best defines the word.

1. Costume of two or more pieces.	cummerbund
2. Long narrow shoulder scarf.	tuxedo
3. Broad fitted sash.	ensemble
4. Divided skirt.	stole
5. Semi-formal evening suit.	culotte

A. Copy the words in the right column. Beside each word place the number of the appropriate definition in the left column.

   1. Small Japanese stove for cooking.   ingenue
   2. Truthful; certified in writing.   ascot
   3. A broad neck scarf.   cinema
   4. Actress representing a naive girl.   gourmand
   5. Stew of meat and vegetables.   negligee
   6. Connoisseur of foods and beverages.   documentary
   7. Coffee with milk in equal amounts.   hibachi
   8. Motion picture or movie theater.   ragout
   9. A woman's dressing gown.   gourmet
   10. Glutton for food.   café au lait

B. Copy the following sentences, correcting any italicized words that are misspelled or misused.

   1. Maryanne is going to see an *orthodontist* to have a corn removed from her foot.
   2. This restaurant makes delicious potatoes *au gratan.*
   3. How expensive is this blue *cashemere cardigan?*
   4. Ira was the star of the *review;* he is a very funny comedian.
   5. *Embroodiery* is Dorothy's hobby.
   6. The Tarnows are having a *barbecue* next Saturday afternoon.
   7. Was Joel's heart murmur a *congenidle* defect.
   8. Peggy bought a coat and dress *ensomble* for her *truseau.*
   9. Harvey's *tuxedo* still fits him but the *cumerbund* is too tight.
   10. *Censership* restrictions on motion pictures have been relaxed.

C. Complete the following sentences by completing words taken from Lessons 131-134.

   1. C_____ is amusing drama where man is usually able to triumph over his problems, whereas in t_____, man is defeated.
   2. Cartoon characters come to life through the process of a_____.
   3. The d_____ requested another c_____ to cover the distant shots.
   4. The d_____ cleared Louise's skin of a rash.
   5. His d_____ was that her skin trouble was related to diet.
   6. Her p_____, however, believes that her various skin disorders develop from emotional stress.
   7. P_____, as well as physicians, are busy trying to understand and prevent mental and emotional disorders.
   8. P_____ and o_____ often find that patients have unknowingly abused their feet and their teeth.
   9. Even o_____ have patients with eye trouble chiefly emotional in nature.
   10. At long last the general public seems to be aware of the relationship of a h_____ environment to healthy people.

ABCDEFGHIJK LESSON **136**
HOBBIES

In this lesson on hobbies, pastimes ranging from sports to stamps are covered. Perhaps you will become interested in one of the hobbies described here.

astrology	(ăs trŏl′ ŏ̇ ġy̆)	n.	Study of the supposed influences of stars on humans.
ceramics	(çé răm′ ĭcs)	n.	The art of making pottery.
entomology	(ĕn tŏ mŏl′ ŏ̇ ġy̆)	n.	The study of insects.
etymology	(ĕt y̆ mŏl′ ŏ̇ ġy̆)	n.	The history of words, showing source and development.
fencing	(fĕn′ çĭng)	n.	The art of attack and defense with the sword.
floriculture	(flō′ rĭ cŭl′ tŭre)	n.	The cultivation of ornamental flowering plants.
graphology	(grăph ŏl′ ŏ̇ ġy̆)	n.	The study of handwriting.
gymnastics	(ġy̆m năs′ tĭcs)	n.	Bodily exercises demonstrating muscle control.
jogging	(jŏg′ gĭng)	v.	Moving at a slow pace with marked beats.
karate	(kă rät′ ē)	n.	Japanese art of self-defense.
numismatist	(nŭ mĭṣ′ mà tĭst)	n.	A specialist in coins and medals.
ornithologist	(ôr′ nĭ thŏl′ ŏ̇ ġĭst)	n.	Student of birds.
palette	(păl′ ĕtte)	n.	A painter's color board.
philatelist	(phĭ lăt′ ĕ lĭst)	n.	One who collects and studies postage stamps.
photography	(phŏ̇ tŏg′ rà phy̆)	n.	The art of taking pictures with a camera.
sculpture	(scŭlp′ tŭre)	n.	Art of carving or cutting wood, stone or metal.
skeet	(skēēt)	n.	A form of trapshooting using clay targets.
skiing	(ski′ ĭng) skē	n.	The sport of gliding on skis over snow.
weaving	(wēav′ ĭng)	n.	To interlace yarns into fabric.
wrestling	(wrĕs′ tlĭng)	n.	Sport of hand to hand combat.

Assignment

Number your paper from 1 to 5. Beside each number write the word from the list above which best describes the activity defined below.

1. The study of the influence of stars on human beings.
2. Science of growing ornamental flowering plants.
3. Study of handwriting.
4. The study of the history of words.
5. The study of insects.

ATHLETICS

Team sports such as baseball, basketball, football and hockey are becoming increasingly popular at both the amateur and professional levels. A knowledge of the following terms will increase your interest in these sports.

battery	(băt′ tĕr y̆)	n.	Pitcher and catcher.
champion	(chăm′ pĭ ȯn)	n.	One acknowledged supreme.
diamond	(dī′ à mȯnd)	n.	The infield of a baseball park.
dribble	(drĭb′ ble)	v.	To move the ball by successive taps or kicks.
foul	(foul)	n.	Violation of the rules.
fumble	(fŭm′ ble)	v.	To fail to hold onto the ball.
gridiron	(grĭd′ ī ron) ẽrn	n.	A football field.
hockey	(hŏck′ ēy)	n.	A game played with a ball and curved sticks.
inning	(ĭn′ nĭng)	n.	A division in baseball; a turn at bat for each team.
javelin	(jăve′ lĭn)	n.	A spear-like pole thrown for distance.
Olympics	(Ō ly̆m′ pĭcs)	n.	International athletic games held once every four years.
polo	(pō′ lō)	n.	Game played with a wooden ball and mallets, on horseback.
quarterback	(qua̧r′ tĕr băck′)	n.	Key football player on the offensive team.
referee	(rĕf ĕr ēē′)	n.	Judge in athletic games.
scrimmage	(scrĭm′ mage) ĭj	n.	Practice play in football; interplay of teams during the game.
slalom	(slä′ lȯm)	n.	Skiing a zigzag down-hill course.
soccer	(sŏc′ cĕr)	n.	A game in which the hands and arms cannot be used to move the ball.
stadium	(stā′ dĭ ŭm)	n.	An open air arena for sports events.
trophy	(trō′ phy̆)	n.	Award for victory.
umpire	(ŭm′pīre)	n.	An official who rules on plays.

Assignment

Copy each of the following statements. Number your paper from 1 to 5. If a statement is true, write true after its number. If a statement is false, rewrite it.

1. A battery is a storage place for baseball equipment.
2. The Olympic games are held once every four years.
3. A foul is an act contrary to the rules.
4. A quarterback is a kind of molding used in building.
5. A trophy is a memorial of a victory.

There are many other types of team and individual sports, some of which are listed below. How many of the terms and names of sports which follow are familiar to you?

angling	(an′ gling)	*n.*	Fishing with hook and line.
backgammon	(băck′ găm′ mŏn)	*n.*	Board game of chance and skill.
badminton	(băd′ mĭn′ tŏn)	*n.*	A game using light rackets to volley shuttlecocks over a net.
billiards	(bĭl liards) yĕrdz	*n.*	A game where balls are hit into pockets of a table with cues.
caddie	(căd′ *d*ĭe)	*n.*	One who carries golf clubs.
canoeing	(cȧ n*o*e′ ĭng)	*v.*	Art of managing a canoe.
chess	(chĕs*s*)	*n.*	A game of strategy and skill played on a board.
croquet	(crȯ́ quet′) kā	*n.*	A game using mallets to drive wooden balls through hoops.
handball	(hănd′ bạ*ll*)	*n.*	A game using the hands to hit balls off the walls.
jai alai	(jai ä laī′) hī	*n.*	A game using a basket strapped to the wrist to play a ball off the walls.
la crosse	(lȧ crȯsse′)	*n.*	A field game where the ball must be carried with a racket.
motorcycle	(mō′ tŏr çȳ′ cle)	*n.*	An automotive bicycle.
racquet	(răc′ quĕt)	*n.*	A game played with ball and rackets in a walled court.
shot-put	(shŏt′ pụt′)	*n.*	Throwing a spherical weight for distance.
skin diving	(skĭn dīv′ ĭng)	*n.*	Swimming under water.
snorkel	(snôr′ kĕl)	*n.*	An air tube protruding above the water.
surf-riding	(sûrf′ rīd′ ĭng)	*n.*	Skimming waves on a long board.
tennis	(tĕn′ *n*ĭs)	*n.*	A game in which the ball is hit over a low net.
tournament	(tọur′ nȧ mĕnt)	*n.*	A series of contests.
volleyball	(vŏl′ *l*ey bạ*ll*′)	*n.*	A game of hitting a ball with the hands over a net.

Assignment

Copy the following sentences, selecting the correct word in parentheses to complete each one.

1. While playing (chess, croquet), Pat broke a mallet.
2. The (volleyball, canoe) flew over the net.
3. She dropped her (snorkel, racket) and lost the tennis game.
4. He lost the trophy for (jai alai, chess) because he sprained his ankle.
5. (Chess, Racquet) is a game calling for speed.

TRAVEL

This lesson summarizes the general terminology and specific procedures related to long-distance travel.

ballast	(băl′ lȧst)	*n.* Heavy substance used to improve a ship's stability.
bow	(bow)	*n.* Forward part of a ship.
buoy	(bu̦o′ y̆)	*n.* A float to mark something beneath the water.
compass	(cȯm′ pȧss)	*n.* Device for determining directions.
detour	(dḗ tour′)	*n.* Deviation in course.
en route	(en ro̦u̦te′) än	*n.* On the way.
excursion	(ĕx cûr′ sion)	*n.* A pleasure trip.
freighter	(freight′ ēr) frāt	*n.* Ship that transports cargo.
gyroscope	(g̈ȳ′ rṓ scōpe)	*n.* Leveling device on ships.
interstate	(ĭn′ tēr stāte′)	*adj.* Between states.
intrastate	(ĭn′ trä stāte′)	*adj.* Within a state.
passport	(pȧss′ pōrt)	*n.* A document of permission to leave and reenter one's country.
purser	(pûr′ sēr)	*n.* A ship official who keeps the financial records.
sextant	(sĕx′ tănt)	*n.* Instrument used to determine latitude and longitude.
steerage	(stēer′ age) ij	*n.* Section of ship used by low-fare passengers.
stern	(stērn)	*n.* The rear end of a ship.
steward	(stew′ ārd) stū	*n.* Employee who attends to passengers' wants.
tourist	(tour′ ĭst)	*n.* One who travels for pleasure.
transoceanic	(trăns′ ō ç̆ĕ ăn′ ĭc)	*adj.* Across the ocean.
visa	(vi șȧ) vē	*n.* An endorsement on a passport denoting that it has been examined and that the bearer may proceed.

Assignment

Copy the words in the first column below. Beside each word write the synonym which best matches it from the three given.

1. **gyroscope** (a) balancing device (b) telephoto lens (c) kite
2. **detour** (a) sailboat (b) deviation in course (c) group rate
3. **buoy** (a) an urchin (b) a float (c) a swimmer
4. **freighter** (a) cargo vessel (b) box car (c) deck hand
5. **purser** (a) a pocketbook (b) grimace (c) ship official

ABCDEFGHIJK LESSON 140

REVIEW

A. Copy the words in the right column. Beside each word place the number of the appropriate definition from the left column.

1. A pleasure trip.	entomology
2. History of words.	ornithologist
3. Student of birds.	philatelist
4. Stamp collector; one knowl- edgeable about postage stamps.	excursion etymology
5. Cultivation of ornamental plants.	floriculture
6. Painter's color board.	palette
7. Endorsement on a passport.	scrimmage
8. Skiing in a zigzag downhill course between upright obstacles.	visa slalom
9. Study of insects.	
10. Practice football game.	

B. Complete the following sentences by completing words from Lessons 136-139:

1. When we were t_____ in Europe, we found that we did not have a v_____ for Russia in our p_____.
2. We used delay time to study Italian s_____ in Florence and Rome.
3. Our youngsters went s_____ d_____ off the coast.
4. To don a face mask, flippers, and s_____ for deep-sea exploration must be a thrill.
5. We "oldsters" preferred a bridge t_____ and b_____ games, but the young folks practiced water s_____.
6. Our hotel hostess believed in a_____, and she cast horoscopes for all of us.
7. Some of the guests tried to interest us in bird watching, but unfortunately we are not o_____.
8. From Italy we proceeded to the O_____ games, and there we especially enjoyed the s_____ events and the h_____ games.
9. I myself never played any games more strenuous than c_____, but as a p_____ buff, I was at all the athletic events with my camera.
10. We have excellent pictures of many of the winners receiving their t_____.

C. Write a sentence for each of the following words:

buoy	sextant
gyroscope	transoceanic
interstate	tournament
intrastate	en route

157

COMMUNICATIONS

Modern methods of communication are both varied and specialized. The following words are related to oral and written communication.

airmail	(âir′ māil)	*n.*	Mail sent by aircraft.
bulletin	(bul′ *lĕ* tĭn)	*n.*	Brief statement to public; a periodical.
cablegram	(cā′ bl*e* grăm)	*n.*	A message sent by telegraphic cable.
cipher	(çī′ phẽr)	*n.*	Method of writing in code.
connotation	(cŏn′ nŏ *tā*′ tion)	*n.*	Implied meaning.
correspondence	(cŏr′ *rĕ* spŏnd′ ĕnçe)	*n.*	Communication by letter.
directory	(dĭ rĕc′ tŏ rў)	*n.*	Listing of names, addresses and telephone numbers.
enclosure	(ĕn clō′ sure)	*n.*	Material sent with a letter.
envelope	zhẽr (ĕn′ vĕ lōpe)	*n.*	Paper folded to enclose a letter.
inference	(ĭn′ fẽr ĕnce)	*n.*	Deduction; conclusion.
letterhead	(lĕt′ *tĕ*r hĕad′)	*n.*	Stationery with a printed heading.
memorandum	(mĕm′ ŏ răn′ dŭm)	*n.*	Informal message; reminder.
pronunciation	(prŏ nŭn′ çĭ ā′ tion)	*n.*	Manner of articulating words.
questionnaire	(quĕs′ tion nâire′)	*n.*	Set of questions submitted to a group of people.
radiogram	(rā′ dĭ ŏ grăm′)	*n.*	Message transmitted over radio waves.
semantics	(sĕ măn′ tĭcs)	*n.*	Study of word meanings.
telegram	(tĕl′ ĕ grăm)	*n.*	Electrically transmitted message.
telephone	(tĕl′ ĕ phōne)	*n.*	Instrument that reproduces sounds at a distance through electrical impulses.
vocabulary	(vŏ căb′ ŭ lăr′ ў)	*n.*	Stock of words and phrases.
ZIP Code	(zĭp cōde)	*n.*	Figures indicating a mail zone.

Assignment

Copy the words on the right. Beside each word place the number of the appropriate definition.

1. Method of secret writing.
2. Implied meaning.
3. Deduction; conclusion.
4. Communication by letter.
5. Material sent with a letter.

cipher
correspondence
inference
enclosure
connotation

RADIO AND TELEVISION

Radio and television have similar vocabularies. They both inform and entertain. Listed below are familiar words that relate to these media.

announcer	(ăn noun' çẽr)	n. One who introduces a broadcast.
antenna	(ăn tĕn' nȧ)	n. Rod for radiating or receiving radio waves.
audio	(au' dĭ ō)	adj. Pertaining to sound.
broadcast	(brôad' càst')	v. Act of transmitting sound or images.
commentator	(cŏm' mĕn tā' tŏr)	n. One who analyzes news events.
commercial	(cŏm mẽr' çial)	n. Paid advertisement.
emcee	(ĕm' çēe')	n. Master of ceremonies; host of a program.
microphone	(mī' crō phōne)	n. Instrument for transmitting sound.
network	(nĕt' wõrk)	n. A group of stations owned by a broadcasting company.
newscaster	(news̯' căs' tẽr)	n. One who broadcasts news.
panelist	(păn' ĕl ĭst)	n. Member of a discussion group.
script	(scrĭpt)	n. Written text of a play.
sponsor	(spŏn' sõr)	n. Person or organization paying for a program.
stereophonic	(stĕr' ē ố phŏn' ĭc)	adj. Three-dimensional sound.
telecast	(tĕl' ế càst')	v. To broadcast by television.
telegenic	(tĕl' ế ġĕn' ĭc)	adj. Suitable for television.
teleplay	(tĕl' ế plāy')	n. A play written for television.
transistor	(trăns̯ ĭs' tŏr)	n. An electronic device for amplification.
transmitter	(trăns mĭt' tẽr)	n. Sending station.
video	(vĭd' ế ō)	adj. Pertaining to the image.

Assignment

Copy the following sentences, substituting synonyms from the above list for italicized words.

1. Kevin is one of the *persons paying* for the Dick Alden show.
2. Eloise has mislaid the *copy of the play*.
3. Have you seen any *advertisements* for our products on television?
4. Politicians who are *attractive on television* have a great advantage.
5. The *picture projection* equipment of my new color television set is defective.

NEWSPAPERS AND MAGAZINES

This lesson contains a sampling of the language of the professional journalist.

banner	(băn′ nẽr)	n. Headline extending across the entire page.
boilerplate	(boil ẽr plāte)	n. Plates of news articles sold to small newspapers.
by-line	(bȳ′ līne)	n. Line giving the writer's name.
caption	(căp′ tion)	n. Headline; subtitle.
columnist	(cŏl′ ŭm nĭst)	n. One who writes continuing comment on daily affairs.
copy	(cŏp′ ў)	n. Manuscript; written material.
copyright	(cŏp′ ў rīght)	n. Exclusive right to publish.
dateline	(dāte′ līne)	n. The city from which a news dispatch comes and its date.
deadline	(dĕad′ līne′)	n. Hour after which no copy can be inserted.
delete	(dḗ lēte′)	v. Printing term meaning "omit."
dummy	(dŭm′ mў)	n. Model copy in proposed form.
editorial	(ĕd′ ĭ tō′ rĭ ăl)	n. Column expressing the editor's views.
format	(fôr′ măt)	n. Shape, size and general style of a publication.
journalism	(joûr′ năl ĭṣm)	n. Managing, editing, or writing for periodicals.
masthead	(màst′ hĕad′)	n. Printed matter including the title, ownership, and rates.
monograph	(mŏn′ ố grȧph)	n. Treatise on a limited topic.
newsprint	(newṣ′ prĭnt′)	n. Cheap grade of paper from wood pulp.
pamphlet	(păm′ phlĕt)	n. Booklet with a paper cover.
release	(rḗ lēase′)	v. To approve for publication.
scoop	(scōōp)	v. To beat a rival in reporting a story.

Assignment

Copy the words in the left column. Beside each word indicate by the letter a, b, or c the closest synonym.

1. copyright   (a) errorless (b) right to publish (c) directions
2. caption   (a) heading (b) correction (c) cartoon
3. dummy   (a) useless writeup (b) model layout (c) mistake
4. format   (a) page style (b) per-page cost (c) schedule
5. delete   (a) headline (b) weather report (c) omit
6. copy   (a) manuscript (b) publish (c) plates
7. editorial   (a) journalism (b) editor's column (c) critical
8. banner   (a) headline (b) masthead (c) dateline
9. pamphlet   (a) newspaper (b) monograph (c) booklet
10. by-line   (a) title (b) credit line (c) brief comment

PRINTING AND PUBLISHING

Some terms common to the publishing world are presented below. They describe the technical aspects of preparing and printing manuscript.

boldface	(bōld' fāçe)	*adj.*	Heavy-faced type.
edit	(ĕd' ĭt)	*v.*	To revise and prepare for publication.
electrotype	(ḗ lĕc' trṓ tȳpe)	*n.*	Plate of type used in printing.
folio	(fō' lĭ ō)	*n.*	Page of a book; page number.
font	(fŏnt)	*n.*	Size and style of typeface.
galley	(găl' leў)	*n.*	Printed copy before it is divided into pages.
halftone	(hä*l*f' tōne)	*n.*	A middle tint, neither dark nor light.
layout	(lāy' out')	*n.*	Arrangement of copy on a page.
leading	(lĕad' ĭng)	*n.*	Space between lines of print.
linotype	(līn' ṓ tȳpe)	*n.*	Machine that casts solid lines of type.
lower case	(lōw' ẽr cāse')	*n.*	Small letters.
monotype	(mŏn' ṓ tȳpe)	*n.*	Machine that casts each letter on an individual body.
pica	(pī' cȧ)	*n.*	Printing measurement; one-sixth of an inch.
proof	(prōōf)	*n.*	Impression taken from type for examination.
prospectus	(prṓ spĕc' tŭs)	*n.*	Booklet describing a forthcoming edition.
royalty	(roy' ăl tў)	*n.*	Payment to an author based on the sale of his books.
signature	(sĭg' nȧ tūre)	*n.*	One of several units to be bound into a book.
stet	(stĕt)	*v.*	Symbol indicating that something erased is to remain.
typographical	(tȳ' pṓ grăph' ĭ căl)	*adj.*	Pertaining to printing.
upper case	(ŭp' *p*ẽr cāse')	*n.*	Capital letters.

Assignment

Copy the following paragraph, changing any words that are misspelled or misused.

Our class toured a printing plant. We saw examples of editted manuscript. The publisher had planned the layout of each page, marking folioes, and how many pacas of leading to leave. The desired font was indicated, as were those words to be printed in boldcase. This book was to be set on a linotype machine which would cast each character separately. After the publisher corrected the proofs, the text would be printed. The final procedure was to fold and bind the siganttures.

ABCDEFGHIJK LESSON 145

GENERAL REVIEW

Section I: Review of Lessons 141-144

A. Complete the following paragraphs by filling in the unfinished words.

I received an a_____ letter containing comments and i_____ that I did not like about my most recent business venture. Instead of answering by t_____ or t_____, I wrote a rather hot reply on stationery with my business l_____ and sent it in a stamped e_____ complete with z_____ c_____ number. I did not realize that my language with its unmistakable c_____, placed under a U.S. stamp, would subject me to the charge of libel.

I sent a r_____ to my lawyer, on vacation in London, and he replied by c_____. He sometimes sends messages in c_____, but in this message he used strong words from his everyday v_____. A m_____ arrived two days later, telling me the legal steps to take before his arrival and warning me to be more prudent in future c_____.

B. Copy the words in the right column. Beside each word place the number of the appropriate definition from the left column.

1. Capital letters.	newsprint
2. Payment made to author on the sale of his book.	prospectus
	upper case
3. Model layout used by a printer.	royalty
4. Cheap paper from wood pulp.	proof
5. Headline across the page.	copyright
6. Heading.	banner
7. Booklet describing a forthcoming edition.	caption
	dummy
8. Exclusive right to publish.	delete
9. To omit; remove.	
10. Impression taken from type for examination.	

C. Rewrite the following paragraphs, correcting all misspelled words:

As a sponser of radeo programs, we are thinking of trying television commericals to promote our health foods. Our advertising agency had first sent us a dummy copy of a full-page ad for two weekly magazines. In reading this copy, it occurred to us that the money might better be spent on telavision commericals.

We have asked the agency to submit some plans for telacasts. A questionaire is being circulated to determine people's preferences before a skript is written.

Section II: General Review of Lessons 131-144

A. Copy the words in the right column. Beside each word place the number of the appropriate definition from the left column.

1. A factual film.	appetizer
2. Ornamental needlework.	isometrics
3. Small portion of food served before a meal.	tournament
	en route
4. Carving or cutting materials into works of art.	documentary
	video
5. A series of contests.	sculpture
6. Pertaining to sound.	audio
7. Judge in athletic games.	embroidery
8. Muscle-strengthening exercises.	referee
9. Pertaining to the image.	
10. On the way.	

B. Copy the following sentences, selecting the correct word in parentheses to fill in the blanks.

1. Richard has the sense of humor of a _____ (comedian, comedienne).
2. The _____ (numismatist, philatelist) showed us his collection of early Spanish coins.
3. The exclusive right to publish something is known as the _____ (release, copyright).
4. Ships are kept balanced and level through the use of a _____ (gyroscope, sextant).
5. This topcoat is made out of _____ (ascotted, worsted) wool.
6. Mrs. Maclin receives a _____ (royalty, pica) for each copy of her book that is sold.
7. The _____ (oculist, diathermy) treatments made the strained muscle stop aching.
8. A _____ (psychiatrist, psychologist) is a physician who treats people with mental disorders.
9. Some painters like to mix and blend colors on their _____ (skeet, palette).
10. Do you _____ (marinate, sauté) the roast in tomato sauce before cooking it?

C. Copy the words on the left, selecting the definition that best matches it from the three choices given.

1. cinema   (a) technicolor (b) movie theater (c) scenario
2. corpuscle   (a) hemoglobin (b) blood (c) body cell
3. battery   (a) pitcher and catcher (b) racket (c) scrimmage
4. ptomaine   (a) pastry (b) food poisoning (c) vegetable
5. dacron   (a) beef stew (b) animal hide (c) fabric

This list briefly defines some of the occupations related to the business world. You should be able to use each title exactly.

accountant	(ăc count' ănt)	*n.*	One who prepares financial reports.
analyst	(ăn' á lўst)	*n.*	One who systematically separates and studies a complex situation.
appraiser	(ăp prāiṣ' ẽr)	*n.*	One who evaluates property.
auditor	(au' dĭ tõr)	*n.*	Person authorized to examine another's accounts.
bookkeeper	(bŏŏk' kēēp' ẽr)	*n.*	One who keeps accounts.
broker	(brō' kẽr)	*n.*	Dealer in money, stocks, or other goods.
consultant	(cŏn sŭl' tănt)	*n.*	One who gives professional advice or service.
economist	(é cŏn' ó mĭst)	*n.*	One who studies and directs the use of resources.
engineer	(ĕn ġĭ nēer')	*n.*	One who designs new systems or products.
entrepreneur	(en' trẽ prẽ neûr') än	*n.*	Organizer of business enterprises.
financier	(fĭn' ăn çiẽr')	*n.*	Investor on a large scale.
industrialist	(ĭn dŭs' trĭ ăl ĭst)	*n.*	One owning or managing an industry.
manufacturer	(măn' ú făc' tŭr ẽr)	*n.*	One who produces goods.
machinist	(má çhĭn' ĭst)	*n.*	One skilled in the use of machine tools.
merchant	(mẽr' chănt)	*n.*	Retailer; storekeeper.
programmer	(prŏ' grăm mẽr)	*n.*	One who writes a computer program.
realtor	(rē' ăl tõr)	*n.*	Real estate broker.
salesman	(sāles' măn)	*n.*	One who sells merchandise, land, or securities.
technician	(tĕch nĭ ciăn)	*n.*	One skilled in technical details of a subject.
underwriter	(ŭn' dẽr writ' ẽr)	*n.*	An insurer.

Assignment

Read the following statements. Copy the sentences, substituting terms from this lesson for any words incorrectly used.

1. You should go to an economist to have your tax return checked.
2. Entrepreneurs manage the business affairs of other people.
3. A broker evaluated our operating procedures at the plant.
4. He suggested that we employ an over-all auditor to tighten our operating schedules and to evaluate performance.
5. The underwriter of our computer program was causing the delay.

164

BOOKKEEPING AND ACCOUNTING

Bookkeeping and accounting are the methods used for recording financial information about a business. A knowledge of accounting principles is valuable for anyone planning a career in business.

account	(ăc count')	*n.*	Financial record.
accrual	(ăc crṳ' ăl)	*n.*	Increase in an asset or a liability.
amortization	(à môr' tǐ zā' tion)	*n.*	Gradual liquidation of a debt.
asset	(ăs' sĕt)	*n.*	A valuable possession.
balance	(băl' ănçe)	*n.*	Difference between two sides of an account.
capital	(căp' ĭ tăl)	*n.*	Excess of assets over liabilities; net worth.
contingent	(cŏn tǐn' ġĕnt)	*adj.*	Dependent on the happening of a future event.
credit	(crĕd' ĭt)	*n.*	Entry on the right-hand side of an account.
debit	(dĕb' ĭt)	*n.*	Entry on the left-hand side of an account.
depreciation	(dḗ prē çǐ ā' tion)	*n.*	A lessening in value.
equity	(ĕq' uǐ tў)	*n.*	Value of property after charges.
expenditure	(ĕx pĕn' dǐ tủre)	*n.*	Outlay of revenue.
inventory	(ĭn' vĕn tō' rў)	*n.*	Value of goods on hand.
journal	(joûr' năl)	*n.*	Book of original entry.
ledger	(lĕdġ' ēr)	*n.*	Book of final entry.
liability	(lǐ à bĭl' ĭ tў)	*n.*	Amount owed.
payable	(pāy' à ble)	*adj.*	Referring to an account owed.
proprietor	(prō prī' ĕ tōr)	*n.*	Owner.
receivable	(rḗ çēiv' à ble)	*adj.*	Referring to an account to be collected.
stockholder	(stŏck' hōl' dēr)	*n.*	One who owns stock.

Assignment

Copy the following sentences, selecting the correct words in parentheses to complete the sentences.

1. Items owned by a business that will be converted into cash in a reasonably short time are known as (liabilities, assets).
2. A company can distort its profits by taking high or low (depreciation, amortization) on assets.
3. Some businesses attempt to keep a perpetual (journal, inventory) of goods on hand.
4. Sums owed on open account are called accounts (payable, receivable).
5. A statement of the financial condition of a business on a specific date is called a (balance sheet, ledger).

165

148
AGRICULTURE

Modern farming has become increasingly specialized, with the development of scientific methods and products. Some common terms related to the various activities of agriculture are listed below.

alfalfa	(ăl făl′ fà)	*n.*	Deep-rooted plant; ·hay.
alkali	(ăl′ kà lĭ)	*n.*	Salts detrimental to soil fertility.
barley	(bär′ lĕy̆)	*n.*	Cereal grass.
citrus	(çĭt′ rŭs)	*adj.*	Pertaining to type of fruit such as the lemon.
cultivate	(cŭl′ tĭ vāte)	*v.*	To till the soil.
fallow	(făl′ lōw)	*adj.*	Untilled; uncultivated.
fertile	(fĕr′ tĭle)	*adj.*	Productive; fruitful.
fertilizer	(fĕr′ tĭ līz′ ĕr)	*n.*	Substance to nourish soil.
fodder	(fŏd′ dĕr)	*n.*	Coarse food fed to domestic animals.
forage	(fŏr′ age) ĭj	*n.*	Food eaten by animals when grazing.
horticulture	(hôr′ tĭ cŭl′ túre)	*n.*	Cultivation of a garden or orchard.
husbandry	(hŭṣ′ bănd rỹ)	*n.*	Farming.
insecticide	(ĭn sĕc′ tĭ çĭde)	*n.*	Insect killer.
irrigate	(ĭr′ rĭ gāte)	*v.*	To supply land with water through canals.
legume	(lĕg′ ūme)	*n.*	Any edible vegetable.
mulch	(mŭlch)	*n.*	Substance used to protect plant roots.
orchard	(ôr′ chărd)	*n.*	Group of fruit trees.
pasture	(pàs′ túre)	*n.*	Grassland used for feeding animals.
prairie	(prâir′ ĭe)	*n.*	Level or rolling land.
subsidy	(sŭb′ sĭ dỹ)	*n.*	Government aid to farmers.

Assignment

Number your paper from 1 to 10. Beside each number write the word from the above list that relates to the question.

1. How much land have you left uncultivated?
2. What do you use to kill bugs and insects?
3. Does the government aid wheat farmers?
4. Is it true that this soil contains mineral salt that destroys fertility?
5. Are you going to attend the lectures on gardening?
6. Will you buy some lemons, oranges and grapefruits?
7. When did you acquire this group of apple trees?
8. How many acres of grassland are used for grazing?
9. How much animal feed will you need for the winter?
10. What type of soil is most fruitful?

ABCDEFGHIJK**LESSON** # 149
TEXTILES

The creation of new fabrics is closely related to the new developments in clothing design. The words below cover a few types of fabric, made from both natural and synthetic fibers.

acetate	(ăç' ĕ tāte)	n.	Cellulose fiber.
calico	(căl' ĭ cō)	n.	Cotton cloth printed with a figured pattern.
corduroy	(côr' dŭ roy')	n.	Coarse cotton fabric with piled surface.
cotton	(cŏt' ton)	n.	Fabric made of soft, white fibrous substance.
denier	(dĕn iĕr')	n.	Unit expressing the fineness of yarns.
denim	(dĕn' ĭm)	n.	Coarse cotton twill.
eiderdown	(eī' dĕr down')	n.	Feathers from the eider duck.
flannel	(flăn' nĕl)	n.	Soft woolen cloth.
gingham	(gĭng' hăm)	n.	Cotton cloth of dyed yarn.
grosgrain	(grōs' grāin')	n.	Silk fabric having heavy transverse cords.
muslin	(mŭs' lĭn)	n.	Coarse, heavy cotton cloth.
nylon	(nȳ' lŏn')	n.	Synthetic fabric.
percale	(pĕr cāle')	n.	Fine, closely woven cotton fabric.
plaid	(plăid)	adj.	Cross-barred pattern.
rayon	(rāy' ŏn)	n.	Cellulose filament forced through minute holes.
satin	(săt' ĭn)	n.	A silk fabric with a thick texture and glossy surface.
seersucker	(seēr' sŭck' ĕr)	n.	Light linen or cotton fabric of slightly puckered weave.
serge	(sĕrġe)	n.	Twilled worsted fabric.
taffeta	(tăf' fĕ tà)	n.	A fine, glossy silk fabric.
velvet	(vĕl' vĕt)	n.	A soft fabric with thick pile.

Assignment

Copy the words in the right column. Beside each word write the number of the appropriate definition from the left column.

1. Twilled worsted fabric.
2. Soft woolen cloth.
3. Cotton cloth of dyed yarn.
4. Linen fabric of puckered weave.
5. Measurement of the fineness of yarns.
6. Fine, closely woven cotton fabric.
7. Silk with heavy transverse cords.
8. Coarse cotton twill.
9. Down from the body of an eider duck.
10. Cross-barred pattern.

flannel
gingham
seersucker
serge
eiderdown
denim
percale
denier
grosgrain
plaid

167

A. Copy the following sentences, correcting any underlined words that are misspelled or misused.

1. A <u>financier</u> keeps a company's financial records and adjusts the <u>budget</u> accordingly.
2. A <u>programmer</u> prepared their schedule of departmental surveys.
3. The gradual liquidation of a debt is known as <u>ammortization</u>.
4. Most businesses have a <u>contingent</u> fund in case of emergency.
5. Accounts <u>receiveable</u> refers to money owed the corporation.
6. <u>Entreprenors</u> play an important role in capitalism.
7. Arid soil is often <u>alkali</u> and, therefore, difficult to farm even if <u>irrigatted</u>.
8. <u>Muslan</u> and <u>precale</u> are two cotton fabrics used in making bed sheets.
9. <u>Acetate</u> and <u>rayon</u> are both synthetic, cellulose fibers.
10. It is wise to wear <u>demin</u> overalls when working in the <u>orcherds</u>.
11. "<u>Manifacturer</u>" and "<u>industralist</u>" are two titles that may refer to the same person.
12. An <u>expenditure</u> could be defined as the creation of a <u>libility</u> for the purchase of an <u>assest</u>.
13. <u>Satan</u> is a more appropriate fabric for a dress than <u>flannel</u>.
14. The <u>merchent</u> asked the <u>realeter</u> to find a better location for his <u>store</u>.
15. A <u>ledger</u> is a <u>permanant</u> record of a company's financial accounts.

B. Copy the words in the right column. Beside each word write the number of the appropriate definition:

1. Edible vegetable.	husbandry
2. Untilled; uncultivated.	prairie
3. Grassland for feeding animals.	insecticide
4. Cultivation of gardens or orchards.	legume
5. Farming.	subsidy
6. Insect killer.	fallow
7. Food for horses and cattle.	pasture
8. Level or rolling land.	horticulture
9. Substance that protects plant roots.	forage
10. Government grant.	mulch

C. Explain the structure of the following words in terms of prefixes, word roots, and suffixes:

consultant	depreciation	stockholder
contingent	salesman	underwriter

MONEY AND BANKING

The following list of words relates to monetary theories and practices. A familiarity with these words is helpful for personal money management, as well as for business investments.

bimetallic	(bĭ′ mḗ tăl′ lĭc)	*adj.*	Using a double metallic standard for currency.
bullion	(bul′ lion)	*n.*	Uncoined gold or silver.
coinage	(coin′ age) yŭn	*n.*	The act of minting money.
collateral	(cŏl lăt′ ĕr ăl) ĭj	*n.*	Security for payment of debt.
deficit	(dĕf′ ĭ çĭt)	*n.*	Excess of expenditures over income.
deflation	(dḗ flā′ tion)	*n.*	Reduction in the volume of money or credit.
domestic	(dṓ mĕs′ tĭc)	*adj.*	Pertaining to one's own country; internal.
elasticity	(ḗ lăs′ tĭç′ ĭ tў)	*n.*	Degree of variation in supply and demand as related to price.
Eurodollars	(Eū′ rō dŏl′ lārs)	*n.*	U.S. dollars deposited in Europe to finance trade.
fiscal	(fĭs′ căl)	*adj.*	Pertaining to financial matters.
fluctuation	(flŭc′ tú ā′ tion)	*n.*	A temporary or minor change in economic conditions.
inflation	(ĭn flā′ tion)	*n.*	Disproportionate increase in the volume of money or credit.
liquidity	(lĭ quĭd′ ĭ tў)	*n.*	Possession of assets readily convertible to cash.
maturity	(mȧ tū′ rĭ tў)	*n.*	The time fixed for payment.
monetary	(mŏn′ ḗ tȧr ў)	*adj.*	Relating to money.
negotiable	(nḗ gō′ ti ȧ ble) shĭ	*adj.*	Transferable with or without endorsement.
parity	(păr′ ĭ tў)	*n.*	Equality of purchasing power between currencies at a given ratio.
specie	(spḗ′ cie) shĭ	*n.*	Gold or silver coin.
usurious	(ū sur ĭ oŭs)	*adj.*	Charging illegal or exorbitant interest rates.
vault	(vault)	*n.*	A room for safekeeping of valuables.

Assignment

Define the following words and use each one in a sentence.

maturity	collateral	deficit
bullion	fluctuation	parity
vault	monetary	fiscal

169

152

INVESTMENTS

Investments increase the productive ability of an economy. The following list contains many of the terms related to investments.

bankruptcy	(bănk′ rŭpt çў)	*n.*	State of financial ruin.
brokerage	(brō kēr age) ij	*n.*	Firm that buys and sells securities.
capital	(căp′ ĭ tăl)	*n.*	Amount of property owned.
convertible	(cŏn vĕrt′ ĭ ble)	*adj.*	Exchangeable for a different kind of security.
debenture	(dé bĕn′ tŭre)	*n.*	Certificate issued as evidence of debt.
debt	(dĕbt)	*n.*	Financial obligation.
dividends	(dĭv′ ĭ dĕnds)	*n.*	Profits apportioned among stockholders.
investment	(ĭn vĕst′ mĕnt)	*n.*	Use of money to earn more money.
issue	(is′ sūe) ĭsh	*n.*	Securities offered for sale.
margin	(mär′ ġĭn)	*n.*	Percent of total price needed to buy stock.
marketable	(mär′ kĕt à ble)	*adj.*	Fit or able to be sold.
option	(ŏp′ tion)	*n.*	Right to invest at a given price for a given time.
pension	(pĕn′ sion)	*n.*	Payment for past services.
portfolio	(pōrt fō′ lĭ ō)	*n.*	One's total investment.
redemption	(ré dĕmp′ tion)	*n.*	The repurchase of its securities by a corporation.
revenue	(rĕv′ ĕ nūe)	*n.*	The yield on an investment.
security	(sé cū′ rĭ tў)	*n.*	Evidence of debt; a stock or bond certificate.
shareholder	(shăre′ hōl′ dĕr)	*n.*	Owner of shares in a fund, property, or corporation.
solvency	(sŏl′ vĕn çў)	*n.*	Ability to pay all debts.
trust	(trŭst)	*n.*	Corporation issuing trust certificates to replace the stock of its acquired companies.

Assignment

Complete the following paragraph. Then reword the paragraph in terms that indicate your understanding of the words in this lesson.

Mr. Allenby has a p_____ representing his i_____ program. Many of the older i_____ of common stock could be sold at a profit, but the o_____ to exchange c_____ preferred stock for common stock is not appealing in a depressed market. Mr. Allenby is counting on the d_____ from preferred stocks and the i_____ from his d_____ bonds to pay his d_____ to the b_____ house. He has been buying stocks on m_____, but now wishes to pay his account in full.

RISK AND INSURANCE

The main purpose of insurance is the reduction of risk. This lesson defines several types of insurance as well as related terms.

adjuster	(ăd jŭst' ẽr)	*n.*	One who settles differences in claims.
annuity	(ăn nū' ĭ tў)	*n.*	An amount payable yearly.
arson	(är' son)	*n.*	Malicious burning of property.
beneficiary	(bĕn' ḗ fĭ' ci ar' ў) fĭsh ĭ ẽr	*n.*	One designated to receive the proceeds of a policy.
cancellation	(căn' çĕl lā' tion)	*n.*	Termination; revocation.
comprehensive	(cŏm' prḗ hĕn' sĭve)	*adj.*	Covering all but specifically excluded risks.
endowment	(ĕn dow' mĕnt)	*n.*	Insurance claim payable at maturity.
forfeiture	(fôr' feĭ tŭre)	*n.*	Loss of some right; a penalty.
hazard	(hăz' ãrd)	*n.*	A risk; a danger.
indemnity	(ĭn dĕm' nĭ tў)	*n.*	Payment for loss.
insurance	(ĭn sụr' ănce)	*n.*	Coverage against loss.
longevity	(lŏn ģĕv' ĭ tў)	*n.*	Long duration of life.
mutual	(mū' tṹ ăl)	*adj.*	Pertaining to an insurance company owned by its policyholders.
negligence	(nĕg' lĭ ģĕnçe)	*n.*	Failure to exercise care.
policy	(pŏl' ĭ çў)	*n.*	Contract of insurance.
premium	(prē' mĭ ŭm)	*n.*	Sum paid for insurance.
rider	(rīd' ẽr)	*n.*	An additional clause; amendment.
survivor	(sûr vī võr)	*n.*	One who outlives another.
underwriter	(ŭn' dẽr wrīt' ẽr)	*n.*	Company offering the insurance.
waiver	(wāiv' ẽr)	*n.*	Act of giving up a claim.

Assignment

Copy the following paragraphs, correcting misspelled words. Underline each word you correct.

The insurence company canceled the policy when it was discovered that the policyholder was guilty of arsen. In another instance, they determined that a poorly installed electric appliance was a hazerd, that the homeowner was guilty of neglegence, and they refused to pay indemity.

Mr. Dodd had a rider on his homeowner's polisy covering theft and breakage of his collection of rare Egyptian pottery. When he died, the beneficary of his life insurance policy received an annuity.

REAL ESTATE

The construction of business and residential properties is one of America's fastest growing industries. Real estate is also of great importance because of the problem of housing the world's population. The following words relate to real estate terminology.

abstract	(ăb′ străct)	n.	Summary of title to land.
appraisal	(ăp prāiş′ ăl)	n.	A valuation of property.
assessment	(ăs sĕss′ mĕnt)	n.	A tax on property.
dower	(dow′ ĕr)	n.	Share of a husband's estate given by law to his widow.
easement	(ēaşe′ mĕnt)	n.	An acquired right to use another's land.
ejectment	(é jĕct′ mĕnt)	n.	Action to recover property and damages.
encumbrance	(ĕn cŭm′ brănçe)	n.	A claim upon an estate.
escrow	(ĕs′ crōw)	n.	A conditional deed.
eviction	(é vĭc′ tion)	n.	Dispossession of a tenant by his landlord.
foreclose	(fōre clōşe′)	v.	To take over because of default in payment.
freehold	(frēē′ hōld)	n.	An estate held for life.
frontage	(frȯn′ tage)	n.	Front boundary of a lot.
lease	(lēase) tĭj	n.	A real estate contract.
lien	(lien) lēn	n.	Legal claim upon property.
mortgage	(môrt′ gage) gĭj	n.	Loan secured with property.
premises	(prĕm′ ĭs ĕs)	n.	A piece of real estate.
quitclaim	(quĭt clāim)	n.	A deed of release.
realtor	(rē′ ăl tōr)	n.	Real estate broker.
subdivision	(sŭb′ dĭ vĭ′ sion)	n.	A tract of land divided into lots for sale.
sublet	(sŭb lĕt′)	v.	To sublease; a tenant renting to another.

Assignment

Number your paper from 1 to 5. Beside each number write the word from the list above which best relates to each of the following sentences.

1. Mr. Conrory has let his farm land to James Raney.
2. This broker is a member of the National Association of Real Estate Boards.
3. That tract of land is being divided into lots to be sold for home building.
4. Mac, who has a two-year lease on his garage, rented it to Bob.
5. The broker recommended someone authorized to evaluate land.

155
REVIEW

A. Copy the words in the right-hand column. Beside each word write the number of the appropriate definition in the left column.

1. Pertaining to financial matters.
2. An amount payable yearly.
3. Additional clause; amendment.
4. Uncoined gold or silver in the shape of bars or ingots.
5. Legal claim against property.
6. Claim upon an estate.
7. Charging an illegal rate of interest.
8. That which is used as security for the payment of a debt.
9. Possession of assets readily convertible into cash.
10. Gold or silver coin.

liquidity
lien
collateral
specie
bullion
fiscal
rider
annuity
encumbrance
usurious

B. Complete the following paragraph by filling in the incomplete words.

Today variable i____e policies appeal to investors looking for maximum s____y during a period of i____n. Many i____e companies have merged with i____t companies so that the buyer's i____e dollar is in part an i____t dollar. During i____n, the m____y value of these variable p____s should increase. The policyholder has the o____n of taking c____l gains in cash or in more i____e. U____s recommend these combination p____s for young people because p____s are low for young men and women, and c____l from the i____s involved builds substantially over the years.

C. Correct spelling errors:

Marie has just paid her first premium. Her insurence pollicy has convertibel features that appeal to her. After five years, she can change to an annuity or to an endowment pollicy. A rider is attached that guarantees indemnity in case of personal disability.

Marie's brother Bill advised her to buy a variable pollicy with an investment feature. Bill is Marie's chief benefishiary, but the family is famous for longevity and he believes that Marie will live to collect the pollicy at its maturity. Bill himself has a comprahensive pollicy that covers most hazzards to life, limb, and pocketbook.

LABOR AND INDUSTRIAL RELATIONS

Some of the terms involved in the business relationship between employers and their employees are presented in this lesson.

absenteeism	(ăb' sĕn tēē' ĭşm)	n. Continual interruption of attendance at work.
apprentice	(ăp prĕn' tĭçe)	n. One receiving on-the-job training.
arbitration	(är' bĭ trā' tion)	n. Hearing and determining a dispute with the decision binding on both parties.
boycott	(boy' cŏtt)	v. To refrain from using or buying items.
coercion	(cố ẽr çion)	n. Force applied physically, morally, or legally.
compensation	(cŏm' pĕn sā' tion)	n. Payment for services.
demotion	(dế mō' tion)	n. Reduction to a lower rank.
discrimination	(dĭs crĭm' ĭ nā' tion)	n. Unfair distinction in treatment of workers.
exploitation	(ĕx' ploi tā' tion)	n. Using others for one's own benefit.
grievance	(griēv' ănçe)	n. A cause of complaint.
injunction	(ĭn jŭnc' tion)	n. A court order.
mediation	(mē' dĭ ā' tion)	n. Attempt at reconciliation.
mobility	(mố bĭl' ĭ tў)	n. Ease with which a worker can change positions.
motivation	(mố' tĭ vā' tion)	n. Reason for taking action.
negotiation	(nế gō ti ā tion) shĭ	n. Process of bargaining between two parties.
personnel	(pẽr sŏn nĕl')	n. Employees of a business.
picket	(pĭck' ĕt)	n. A striker demonstrating before his place of work.
productivity	(prố' dŭc tĭv' ĭ tў)	n. Output per unit of effort.
vacation	(vā cā' tion)	n. A period of exemption.
vocation	(vố cā' tion)	n. One's occupation.

Assignment

Number your paper from 1 to 5. If a statement is true, write true after its number. If a statement is false, rewrite it, substituting a word from the above list.

1. An apprentice learns a trade through practical experience.
2. Injunction means to constrain by force or law.
3. Productivity is compensation for services.
4. Using others for one's own benefit is exploitation.
5. Mobility is a force that incites to action.

157
MARKETING

Terms relating to the buying, selling, and promotion of goods are included below. These words summarize the process of moving goods from producer to consumer.

auction	(auc′ tion)	n. A public sale of property to the highest bidder.
commodity	(cŏm mŏd′ ĭ tў)	n. An article of commerce.
competition	(cŏm′ pḗ tĭ′ tion)	n. Striving for the same market.
consumer	(cŏn sūm′ ẽr)	n. One who uses goods and services.
discount	(dĭs′ count)	n. A reduction in cost.
distribution	(dĭs trĭ bū′ tion)	n. Transportation and dispersal of goods.
goodwill	(gŏŏd′ wĭll′)	n. Intangible business advantages due to reputation.
innovation	(ĭn′ nố vā′ tion)	n. Introduction of a new idea.
invoice	(ĭn′ voiçe)	n. An itemized statement of shipped goods.
margin	(mär′ ġĭn)	n. The difference between cost and selling price.
markup	(märk′ ŭp′)	n. The percentage of increase in selling price over cost.
merchandise	(mẽr′ chăn dīṣe)	n. Trade goods bought or sold.
middleman	(mĭd′ dle măn′)	n. A dealer between the producer and the consumer.
overhead	(ō′ vẽr hĕad′)	n. General expenses such as rent, taxes, and utilities.
promotion	(prố mō′ tion)	n. Activity to increase sales.
retailer	(rẽ′ tāil ẽr)	n. A merchant who sells directly to the consumer.
trademark	(trāde′ märk)	n. A symbol used to indicate a brand of merchandise.
transaction	(trăns ăc′ tion)	n. An act involving buying and selling.
vendor	(vĕn′ dŏr)	n. A seller.
wholesale	(whōle′ sāle′)	n. Sale of goods in large quantity to retailers.

Assignment

Copy the definitions below. Beside each definition write the word which best matches it from the three words given.

1. competition   (a) demand (b) rivalry (c) award
2. commodities   (a) commerce (b) goods (c) commission
3. goodwill   (a) kindness (b) compliment (c) prestige
4. middleman   (a) soldier (b) dealer (c) buyer
5. overhead   (a) expense (b) gable (c) exchange

TRANSPORTATION

Some words related to air, land and water transportation are listed in this lesson. Included are the names of various types of vehicles, as well as the specific terminology relating to them.

aeronautics	(âer′ ṓ nau′ tĭcs)	*n.* Science dealing with operation of aircraft.
altimeter	(ăl tĭm′ ḗ tẽr)	*n.* Instrument for measuring altitude.
anchor	(an′ chor) ăng′ kẽr	*n.* Device holding a ship in a particular place.
automobile	(au′ tṓ mṓ′ bĭle)	*n.* A motor vehicle.
carburetor	(cär′ bṹ rĕt′ ŏr)	*n.* Mixer for air and gasoline.
ceiling	(çēil′ ĭng)	*n.* Height of a cloud base.
channel	(chăn′ *n*ĕl)	*n.* Deeper part of a river, harbor, or strait.
chassis	(chăs′ *sĭs*)	*n.* Frame under an automobile.
chauffeur	(chauf feûr′) shṓ	*n.* A person employed to drive a car.
commuter	(cŏm mŭt′ ẽr)	*n.* One who travels daily.
diesel	(diē′ ṣĕl)	*n.* Type of internal combustion engine.
dinghy	(dĭng′ *h*ȳ)	*n.* Small boat of various kinds.
fuselage	(fū′ ṣĕ lage′) läzh	*n.* Body of an airplane.
hangar	(hăng′ ãr)	*n.* Housing for airplanes.
helicopter	(hĕl′ ĭ cŏp′ tẽr)	*n.* Aircraft supported by rotors turning on a vertical base.
limousine	(lĭm′ ou ṣīne)	*n.* A large, luxurious sedan.
navigator	(năv′ ĭ gā tŏr)	*n.* One who directs a ship's course.
propeller	(prṓ pĕl′ *l*ẽr)	*n.* Blades mounted on a revolving shaft of an airplane.
radar	(rā′ där)	*n.* Detecting device for aircraft.
stewardess	(stew′ ãr dĕs*s*)	*n.* Airline hostess.

Assignment

The following sentences contain words which are misused. Copy the sentences, replacing each misused word with a more appropriate word from the list above.

1. The diesel broke loose from the pier and floated downstream.
2. Since the fuselage of the old airplane was damaged, it was stored in the harbor.
3. The repairman said the carburetor of the automobile was bent out of alignment.
4. The pilot got a faulty altitude reading because the radar was malfunctioning.
5. The helicopter reported poor visibility due to a low channel.

ABCDEFGHIJKLESSON **159**

TRANSPORTATION

This lesson includes words related to military vehicles. It also contains words which pertain to the shipment of goods.

barge	(bärġe)	*n.*	A large flat boat for moving goods short distances.
boatswain	(bōat′ swain) bō′ s′n	*n.*	Petty officer of a merchant ship.
cruiser	(cruiṣ′ ẽr)	*n.*	Type of war vessel.
embarkation	(ĕm′ bär kā′ tion)	*n.*	Act of boarding a boat.
freighter	(freight′ ẽr) frāt	*n.*	Vessel used mainly to carry cargo.
jetliner	(jĕt′ līn′ ẽr)	*n.*	A jet-propelled airliner.
lading	(lād′ ĭng)	*n.*	Loading; cargo; freight.
nautical	(nau′ tĭ căl)	*adj.*	Pertaining to shipping.
parachute	(păr′ à çhu̱te)	*n.*	Device for making a safe descent from an airplane.
periscope	(pĕr′ ĭ scōpe)	*n.*	Device used on submarines to view the surface.
propulsion	(pró pŭl′ sion)	*n.*	Forward thrust.
subway	(sŭb′ wāy)	*n.*	Underground electric railway.
supersonic	(sū′ pẽr sŏn′ ĭc)	*adj.*	Faster than the speed of sound.
tonnage	(tȯn′ nage) ĭj	*n.*	Carrying capacity of a ship.
truckage	(trŭck′ age) ĭj	*n.*	Movement of goods by truck; the fee charged.
turnpike	(tûrn′ pīke)	*n.*	A toll road.
velocity	(vḗ lŏç′ ĭ tў)	*n.*	Speed; quickness of motion.
via	(vī′ à)	*n.*	By way of.
visibility	(vĭṣ′ ĭ bĭl′ ĭ tў)	*n.*	Range of vision.
waybill	(wāy′ bĭll′)	*n.*	Document identifying a shipment of freight.

Assignment

Copy the following sentences, substituting the best synonym from the list above for each italicized word or word group.

1. He descended from his burning plane in a *device for making a safe landing*.
2. Because the *document describing the machines* was lost, the tractors were switched to a siding.
3. The *forward thrust* produced by a jet engine is the result of the rearward discharge of heated air and exhaust gases.
4. The weather had so curtailed our *range of vision*, that all planes were grounded.
5. We watched the *boats loaded with freight* moving slowly out of the harbor.

177

Section I: Review of Lessons 156-159

A. Complete the following paragraph:

Frank and Edna are going by j_____ to Africa on a v_____. Frank's v_____ as a p_____ director has many c_____ but nevertheless the daily g_____ requiring m_____ add up to trouble-filled days. His success in reducing a_____ during the past year has increased the p_____ of his company.

B. Copy the words in the right-hand column. Beside each word write the number of the appropriate definition from the left column.

1. Small boat.	altimeter
2. Body of an airplane.	hangar
3. Structure for housing airplanes.	dinghy
4. Instrument for measuring altitude.	fuselage
5. Article of commerce.	coercion
6. Itemized statement of shipped goods.	compensation
7. Introduction of something new.	exploitation
8. Constraining by force.	invoice
9. Payment for services.	innovation
10. Using others for one's own benefit.	commodity

C. Copy the following paragraph, substituting words from Lesson 157 for the underlined words.

A store proprietor has many responsibilities. He has to contend with other proprietors in selling goods. Introduction of something new may cause an increase in his general expenses if the customers don't like the goods and his inventory accumulates. Maintenance of public support requires effort and activities that increase the sale of his products and services.

D. Copy the following sentences, choosing the correct word in parentheses to complete each one.

1. In (negotiation, arbitration), a decision by the third party is binding on the other two.
2. The workers threatened to strike and (picket, boycott) the company.
3. A (wholesaler, retailer) sells in larger quantities to smaller businessmen for resale to the public.
4. The percentage of increase between the cost of an item and its selling price is known as the (overhead, margin).
5. The airline pilot checked his (altimeter, periscope) to see how high they were flying.

Section II: General Review of Lessons 146-159

A. Read each of the following sentences. If a statement is true, write true after its number. If a statement is false, substitute the appropriate vocabulary word to make it true.

1. Alfalfa is a nutritious cereal grass.
2. Jerry's suit is made out of a twilled worsted fabric known as serge.
3. A financier is a large-scale investor.
4. Palmer, Inc. issued a portfolio as evidence of their debt.
5. Tom's uncle signed a rider giving up all claims to the family business.
6. A ledger is a book of original entry whose accounts are then recorded in a journal.
7. The loan company put a lease on all income from our property.
8. The union tried to organize a nationwide boycott of Ellwood appliances.
9. An engineer is highly skilled in the use of machine tools.
10. Bullion is minted money in the form of coins.

B. Copy the series of words below, underlining the word in each group which does not relate to the others.

1. bookkeeper; accountant; auditor; financier
2. fodder; mulch; forage; alfalfa
3. gingham; calico; corduroy; flannel
4. dower; specie; bimetallic; monetary
5. revenue; interest; margin; dividend
6. forfeiture; endowment; waiver; cancellation
7. retailer; consumer; vendor; wholesaler
8. barge; freighter; cruiser; helicopter
9. amortization; collateral; receivable; liability
10. cotton; acetate; rayon; nylon

C. Copy the words in the right column. Beside each word write the number of the appropriate definition from the left column.

1. Uncultivated.
2. Pertaining to financial matters.
3. An insurer.
4. Repurchase of securities by a corporation.
5. Value of property after charges.
6. Freedom of movement.
7. Underground electric railway.
8. Unit expressing the fineness of yarns.
9. Equality of purchasing power between currencies.
10. A conditional deed.

underwriter
equity
fallow
denier
fiscal
parity
redemption
escrow
mobility
subway

INDEX

A

A.B., 122
abatement, 135
abeyance, 96
absence, 28
absent, 80
absenteeism, 174
abstract, 172
abundant, 35
academic, 142
accede, 100
accelerate, 39, 106
acceleration, 132
accent, 77
accept, 100
acceptable, 33
acceptance, 28
access, 100
accessible, 33
accessory, 116
accommodate, 39
accomplishment, 30
account, 165
accountant, 164
accredited, 144
accrual, 165
accumulate, 39
acetate, 167
achieve, 114
acquittal, 127
acrimony, 96
actor, 29, 148
actress, 148
A.D., 122
adagio, 139
adapted, 101
addition, 102
address, 80
ad hoc, 85
adjacent, 104
adjoining, 104

adjournment, 30
adjudicate, 127
adjuster, 171
adjustment, 30
administration, 142
administrator, 29
adopted, 101
adroit, 94
adverse, 101
advertise, 38
advice, 99
advise, 99
adviser, 41
aerial, 80
aeronautics, 176
affable, 95
affect, 101
affidavit, 127
afterward, 40
agenda, 69
aggravate, 105
agitation, 31
agnostic, 145
agreement, 30
agronomy, 143
airmail, 158
aisle, 91
Alabama, 119
à la carte, 85
Alamo, 83
Alaska, 119
Albany, 120
Albuquerque, 121
alderman, 129
alfalfa, 166
algebra, 143
alias, 127
alkali, 166
all right, 116
allegory, 137
allergen, 135
alleviate, 96

alliance, 28
alliteration, 138
aloud, 90
allowed, 90
allude, 104
allusion, 31, 99
alma mater, 144
alpha particle, 133
altar, 91
alter, 91
alteration, 31
altimeter, 176
alto, 139
alumni, 144
amateur, 79
amiable, 95
among, 107
amortization, 165
amusement, 30
analogous, 73
analyst, 164
analyze, 38
anchor, 176
ancient, 79
anecdote, 100
anesthesia, 150
angling, 155
angular, 34
animation, 148
Annapolis, 119
annihilate, 39
announcer, 159
annuity, 171
annul, 94
answer, 105
antagonistic, 96
antecedent, 26
antedate, 26
ante meridian, 26
antenna, 159
anteroom, 26
anthem, 140

anthropology, 143
antidote, 100
antigen, 135
antipathy, 93
antiquated, 95
aplomb, 85
apparent, 35, 104
appetizer, 149
applicant, 35
Appomattox, 83
appraisal, 172
appraise, 101
appraiser, 164
appreciate, 39
apprehend, 127
apprentice, 174
apprise, 101
approbation, 93
appropriation, 129
aquanaut, 135
aquatic, 135
arbitrate, 107
arbitration, 174
A.R.C., 122
archaeology, 143
archery, 36
archipelago, 69
architect, 69
archives, 69
aria, 140
arid, 96
Aristotle, 82
arithmetic, 143
Arizona, 119
Arkansas, 119
arson, 171
arctic, 74
artichoke, 149
articulation, 148
ascot, 151
assessment, 172
assessor, 129
asset, 165
assignment, 30
assimilate, 116

assistant, 35
assurance, 28
asthma, 70, 75
astonish, 105
astrology, 153
astronaut, 132
atheist, 145
athletic, 73
Atlanta, 119
atom, 133
attendant, 35
attest, 127
attribute, 78
au gratin, 149
auction, 175
audio, 159
audition, 139
auditor, 164
auditorium, 139
auditory, 36
Augusta, 119
Austin, 120
author, 137
authorize, 38
autocracy, 128
automation, 134
automobile, 176
auxiliary, 74
available, 33
avant-garde, 84
averse, 101
awkwardly, 40

B

backgammon, 155
bachelor, 29
badminton, 155
bail, 89
balance, 165
bale, 89
ballad, 137
ballast, 156
ballerina, 139
ballet, 139

ballot, 128
Baltimore, 121
bankruptcy, 170
banner, 160
barbecue, 149
barge, 177
baritone, 140
barley, 166
bass, 140
Baton Rouge, 119
battery, 154
Bayonne, 121
B.C., 122
beggar, 34
beginning, 116
believe, 114
benediction, 145
beneficiary, 36, 171
benevolence, 28
beret, 151
berth, 91
between, 107
bicuspid, 25
bicycle, 25
biennial, 25
billiards, 155
bimetallic, 169
biography, 137
biopsy, 135
bipartisan, 130
biped, 25
birth, 91
Bismarck, 120
blank verse, 138
blasphemy, 145
boatswain, 177
boilerplate, 160
Boise, 119
boisterous, 74
bolder, 90
boldface, 161
bolero, 151
bombard, 133
bon voyage, 84
bookkeeper, 164

booster, 132
Boston, 119
botany, 143
boulder, 90
boundary, 74
bow, 156
boycott, 174
breeder, 133
brighten, 39
brilliant, 35
broadcast, 159
brochure, 69
broker, 164
brokerage, 170
B.S., 122
buffet, 75
bulletin, 116, 158
bullion, 169
Bunche, Ralph, 82
buoy, 156
bureaucracy, 129
bursar, 144
business, 117
by-line, 160

C

cablegram, 158
caddie, 155
café, 85
café au lait, 149
Cairo, 83
calculate, 39
calculus, 144
calendar, 117
calico, 167
California, 119
calorie, 150
camera, 148
campaign, 130
campus, 142
cancellation, 171
candidate, 129
cannon, 91
canoeing, 155

canon, 91
capital, 79, 165, 170
capsule, 132
caption, 160
carat, 91
carburetor, 176
cardigan, 151
caret, 91
Caribbean, 83
carol, 140
carrot, 91
Carson City, 120
carte blanche, 84
cashmere, 151
castigate, 93
catalog, 80
catalogue, 80
catechism, 145
caucus, 129
cause célèbre, 85
cautiously, 40
cede, 91
ceiling, 176
censor, 102, 148
censure, 102
census, 130
central processing unit,
    134
centrifuge, 132
ceramics, 153
cereal, 89
cession, 89
champion, 154
chancellor, 144
chandelier, 69
channel, 176
character, 69, 107
characterize, 38
Charleston, 120
chassis, 176
chasten, 70
chastise, 38
Chattanooga, 121
chauffeur, 176
chemistry, 143

Chesapeake Bay, 83
chess, 155
chestnut, 70
Cheyenne, 129
Chicago, 121
chieftain, 114
chlorine, 135
choreographer, 139
christen, 70
chronic, 95
chronicle, 137
Cincinnati, 121
cinema, 148
cipher, 158
circular, 34
circumscribe, 95
cite, 90, 104
citizenship, 128
citrus, 166
civilize, 38
claimant, 127
classical, 139
classics, 137
clemency, 127
client, 115
climax, 138
clockwise, 40
cloud chamber, 133
C.O.D., 122
coeducation, 142
coercion, 174
coherent, 18
coinage, 169
coincidence, 18
coleslaw, 149
collateral, 116, 169
collator, 134
colleague, 107
collector, 29
Colorado, 119
colossal, 116
Columbia, 120
Columbus, 120
columnar, 34
columnist, 160

combine, 18
comedian, 148
comedienne, 148
comedy, 148
command, 101
commence, 99
commend, 101
commentator, 159
comments, 99
commercial, 159
commitment, 116
commodity, 175
communicate, 18
communism, 128
commuter, 176
companion, 18
compare, 107
compass, 156
compensate, 106
compensation, 174
competition, 175
compile, 18
complaisant, 93
complement, 102
complicate, 18
compliment, 102
component, 35
compose, 18
compound, 80
comprehensive, 171
comrade, 18
conceit, 114
conceive, 114
conciliate, 18, 39, 107
Concord, 120
condense, 18
conduct, 76
conductor, 29
confer, 18
conference, 28
confidence, 28
confinement, 30
confirmation, 145
conflict, 78
conform, 18

confusion, 31
congenital, 150
congratulate, 69, 116
congregation, 145
connect, 18
Connecticut, 119
connotation, 158
conscience, 115
consensus, 18
consign, 18
consolidate, 18
consommé, 149
constituent, 130
constitutional, 128
construction, 18
consultant, 164
consumer, 175
contaminate, 135
contend, 96
content, 80
contentious, 94
contest, 77, 101
context, 101
contingent, 165
continual, 105
continuous, 95, 105
contralto, 140
contrast, 107
convenient, 35, 117
convention, 130
convertible, 33, 170
convict, 78
cooperation, 99
coordinate, 18
copy, 160
copyright, 160
corduroy, 167
corollary, 116
coroner, 129
corporation, 99
corps, 75
corpuscle, 150
correspondence, 28,
    117, 158
correspondent, 35

corrupt, 117
cotton, 167
council, 91
counsel, 91
coup d'état, 84
couplet, 138
co-workers, 18
C.P.A., 122
credible, 33, 102, 106
credit, 165
creditable, 102
credulous, 106
crime, 104
croquet, 155
cruiser, 177
C.S.T., 122
cubism, 139
cuisine, 84
culotte, 151
cultivate, 166
culture, 139
cummerbund, 151
cupboard, 70, 75
Curie, Marie, 82
curriculum, 144
custom, 107
customer, 41
cyclotron, 133

D

dacron, 151
data processing, 134
dateline, 160
D.D., 122
D.D.S., 122
deacon, 145
deadline, 160
dean, 144
debenture, 170
debonair, 84
debris, 75
debit, 165
debt, 170
decade, 25

184

decathlon, 25
decease, 99
decompression, 135
decorative, 139
decrepit, 19
deduction, 19
deference, 99
defiant, 93
deficit, 169
definitely, 75
deflation, 169
defray, 96
degrade, 19
Delaware, 119
delete, 94, 160
delicatessen, 149
delusion, 96
demeanor, 95
democracy, 128
demotion, 174
denier, 167
denim, 167
denouement, 138
Denver, 119
departure, 19
dependable, 33
deposition, 127
depot, 70
depreciate, 95
depreciation, 19, 165
dermatologist, 150
Des Moines, 119
descend, 19
description, 137
designer, 41
despise, 19, 38
detach, 19
deteriorate, 19
detour, 156
Detroit, 121
development, 30
deviate, 19
dexterous, 94
diagnosis, 150
dialogue, 138

diamond, 154
diathermy, 150
dictator, 128
didacticism, 138
diesel, 176
diet, 115
difference, 99
digest, 77
diligent, 35
dinghy, 176
diphtheria, 69
diploma, 142
diplomacy, 128
director, 148
directory, 158
disability, 23
disappointment, 30
disapproval, 93
disastrous, 73
discernment, 30
disciple, 145
disconnect, 23
discount, 175
discourage, 23
discover, 23, 107
discrepancy, 23, 96
discriminate, 23
discrimination, 174
discuss, 23
discussion, 31
disease, 99
disfranchise, 128
disinfectant, 135
disparage, 95
dispersal, 135
dispose, 23
dispute, 23
dissertation, 144
dissipate, 116
dissonance, 140
distract, 23
distribution, 175
distributor, 29
dividends, 170
doctor, 29

doctorate, 144
documentary, 148
dogma, 145
domestic, 169
Dover, 119
dower, 172
downward, 40
drama, 137
dribble, 154
drowned, 73
dummy, 160

E

earlier, 41
easement, 172
easily, 40
ecology, 135
economics, 143
economist, 164
ecumenical, 145
edible, 33
edit, 161
edition, 102
editor, 29
editorial, 160
educated, 107
effect, 101
effluent, 135
e.g., 122
eiderdown, 167
eight, 115
ejectment, 172
elasticity, 169
electorate, 130
electron, 133
electronic computer
  system, 134
electrotype, 161
element, 133
elevator, 29
elicit, 106
eligible, 104
elm, 73
elude, 104

elusion, 99
embarkation, 177
embarrass, 116
embassy, 129
embroidery, 151
emcee, 159
emeritus, 144
emigrant, 102
eminent, 99
emission, 135
en route, 156
enclosure, 158
encompass, 95
encore, 84, 140
encouragement, 30
encumbrance, 172
endeavor, 73, 117
endowment, 171
endurance, 28
enfranchise, 128
engineer, 164
enlargement, 30
ensemble, 151
entirely, 40
entomology, 153
entrepreneur, 164
envelope, 158
envious, 105
environment, 30
envoy, 129
epic, 137
epigram, 137
epistle, 70
epoch, 117
equity, 165
equivalent, 35
erratic, 116
error, 29
escort, 77
escrow, 172
especially, 117
esprit de corps, 84
essay, 137
E.S.T., 122
establishment, 30

et al., 122
etc., 122
et cetera, 84
etymology, 153
Eurodollars, 169
eviction, 172
evidence, 107
evident, 104
examination, 142
exaggerate, 39
exaggeration, 19
exasperate, 105
exceed, 100
excel, 19
except, 100
exceptional, 19
excess, 100
excessive, 19, 93
excursion, 156
executor, 127
exercise, 38
exhale, 19
exhibition, 31
exhilarate, 106
exile, 19
exorbitant, 19
expedite, 95
expenditure, 165
experience, 28, 115
explode, 19
exploitation, 174
export, 19
exposé, 85
expulsion, 19
extension, 31
extract, 78
extracurricular, 142

F

fable, 137
facilitate, 95
factory, 36
faculty, 144
fait accompli, 84

fallow, 166
familiar, 34
famous, 104
farther, 101
fasten, 39
faster, 41
faux pas, 84
feasible, 33, 106
February, 74
feigned, 93, 115
fellowship, 144
felony, 127
fencing, 153
ferment, 78
fertile, 166
fertilizer, 166
fiction, 137
field, 114
fiend, 114
fiery, 115
filibuster, 130
film, 73
financier, 164
finery, 36
finesse, 85
fiscal, 169
fission, 133
flannel, 167
floriculture, 153
Florida, 119
flow chart, 134
fluctuation, 169
fodder, 166
folio, 161
font, 161
forage, 166
forearm, 26
forebears, 26
foreboding, 26
forecast, 26
foreclose, 26, 172
forefathers, 26
forefinger, 26
foreign, 115
format, 160

foremost, 26
forerunner, 26
foreword, 90
forfeiture, 171
formally, 100
formerly, 100
forth, 89
forum, 142
forward, 40, 90
foul, 154
foundry, 73
fourth, 89
fragrance, 28
Frankfort, 119
free fall, 132
freehold, 172
free verse, 138
freight, 115
freighter, 156, 177
frequently, 40
Freud, Sigmund, 82
friendlier, 41
frontage, 172
frugal, 94
fulfillment, 30
fumble, 154
further, 101
fuselage, 176
fusion, 133

G

galley, 161
Gandhi, Mohandas, 82
garrulous, 116
genre, 85
genuine, 93
geography, 143
geology, 143
Georgia, 119
geriatrics, 150
gerrymander, 130
Gettysburg, 83
gigantic, 69
gilt, 89

gingham, 167
gist, 69
glisten, 70
globular, 34
gnash, 70
goodwill, 175
goulash, 149
government, 30
governor, 29, 129
grammar, 143
granary, 36
graphology, 153
gravity, 132
gridiron, 154
grievance, 174
grievous, 73, 114
grosgrain, 167
guardian, 127
guilt, 89
gymnasium, 142
gymnastics, 153
gyroscope, 132, 156

H

haberdashery, 151
habit, 107
halftone, 161
handball, 155
handkerchief, 70
handling, 73
hangar, 176
happier, 41
harder, 41
hardly, 107
hardware, 134
Harrisburg, 120
Hartford, 119
hasten, 70
Hawaii, 119
hazard, 171
healthful, 150
hear, 90
heartrending, 73
heavenly, 93

heavily, 74
height, 73, 115
heir, 115
Helena, 120
helicopter, 176
hemoglobin, 150
herb, 75
here, 90
heterogenous, 93
hibachi, 149
hindrance, 73
historian, 138
hockey, 154
homeward, 40
homogenous, 93
Honolulu, 119
hors d'oeuvres, 84
horticulture, 166
human, 101
humane, 101
humanities, 144
hungry, 73
husbandry, 166
hydrogen, 132
hydrophone, 135
hymn, 145

I

Idaho, 119
i.e., 122
ignorant, 35, 105
illegible, 20
illicit, 106
Illinois, 119
illiterate, 105
illusion, 99
imminent, 99
immaterial, 20
immigrant, 102
immoral, 102
immortal, 20, 102
impartial, 20
impassable, 20
impeach, 129

imperfect, 20
impersonal, 20
imply, 104
impossible, 20
impressionism, 139
improbable, 20
improvement, 30
inadequate, 20
incapable, 20
incapacitate, 20
incidentally, 116
incite, 99
inconvenient, 20
incorrigible, 116
incriminate, 127
inculcate, 39
incumbent, 128
indefensible, 33
indefinitely, 117
indemnity, 129, 171
independence, 28
independent, 20
indestructible, 33
Indiana, 119
Indianapolis, 119
indication, 31
indict, 70, 75
indictment, 127
indirectly, 20
indistinctly, 40
industrialist, 164
inertia, 132
inevitably, 20
infamous, 104
infer, 104
inference, 158
infinity, 117
inflation, 169
influence, 94
ingenious, 102
ingenue, 148
ingenuous, 102
inhabitant, 35
initiate, 96
initiative, 130

injunction, 128, 174
inning, 154
innocence, 28
innovation, 175
innumerable, 33
input, 134
insecticide, 166
insensible, 20
insert, 78
insight, 99
insignificant, 20
inspector, 29
instigate, 93
insular, 34
insulin, 150
insult, 77
insurance, 28, 171
integral, 73
intelligent, 107
intercede, 21
intercept, 21
intercollegiate, 21
interfere, 21
intermediate, 21
intermingle, 21
international, 21
interplanetary, 132
interrupt, 21
interstate, 156
interval, 21
intervene, 21
intolerant, 20
in toto, 85
intramural, 142
intrastate, 156
intrinsic, 96
invalid, 79
invalidate, 94
invent, 107
inventor, 29
inventory, 165
investment, 170
invisible, 33
invoice, 175
ion, 133

Iowa, 119
ipso facto, 85
I.Q., 122
Iran, 83
Iraq, 83
irony, 95
irregular, 34
irresistible, 33
irresponsible, 20
irrigate, 70, 166
irritate, 39
isle, 91
isometrics, 150
isotope, 133
issue, 170
ivory, 74

J

Jackson, 119
jai alai, 155
javelin, 154
jealous, 105
Jefferson City, 119
jeopardy, 75
jetliner, 177
jettison, 132
jogging, 153
joie de vivre, 85
journal, 165
journalism, 160
judicial, 129
Juneau, 119
juvenile, 79

K

Kansas, 119
karate, 153
Kentucky, 119
Kenya, 83
kindergarten, 69, 142
King, Martin L., 82
Kosygin, Aleksei, 82

L

laboratory, 117
laborer, 41
la crosse, 155
lading, 177
laissez-faire, 84
language, 143
Lansing, 119
Las Vegas, 121
last, 104
later, 41, 106
latest, 104
latter, 106
laudable, 33
laundry, 73
lavatory, 36
layout, 161
lead, 133
lease, 172
ledger, 165
leading, 161
legacy, 127
legend, 137
legible, 104
legislator, 128
legume, 166
leisure, 79
length, 69
lengthwise, 40
lessen, 90
lesson, 90
lethargy, 94
letterhead, 158
leverage, 94
liability, 165
liable, 74
libel, 127
library, 74
licorice, 74
lien, 172
ligature, 135
lightning, 73
likewise, 40
limousine, 176

Lincoln, 120
linear, 34
linotype, 161
liquidity, 169
literature, 74
Little Rock, 119
loan, 90
lobbying, 130
localize, 38
lone, 90
longevity, 171
loose, 101
Los Angeles, 121
lose, 101
Louisiana, 119
Louisville, 121
lower case, 161
lunar, 34
luxuriant, 106
luxurious, 106

M

machine language, 134
machinist, 164
mackinaw, 151
Madison, 120
magician, 31
magnetic tape, 134
Maine, 119
maintenance, 74
majority, 105
malady, 95
malaise, 95
mandate, 128
mandatory, 94
manufacturer, 164
manuscript, 138
Mao Tse-tung, 82
margin, 170, 175
marinate, 149
marital, 104
marketable, 170
markup, 175
marshal, 90

Marshall, John, 82
martial, 90, 104
Maryland, 119
Massachusetts, 119
massacre, 74
masthead, 160
material, 79
matriculate, 96, 142
maturity, 169
mayor, 129
M.D., 122
measurement, 30
medal, 90
meddle, 90
mediation, 174
memorandum, 158
Memphis, 121
merchandise, 175
merchant, 164
metaphor, 138
meteorology, 143
Miami, 121
Michelangelo, 82
Michigan, 119
microphone, 159
middleman, 175
mien, 95
military, 74
millinery, 151
Milwaukee, 121
mince, 149
miner, 91
Minneapolis, 121
Minnesota, 119
minor, 91
minuet, 139
minute, 79
misapplication, 23
misapply, 23
misbehave, 23
misdeed, 23
misdemeanor, 127
misfortune, 23
misgiving, 23
mishandle, 23

misleading, 23
mispronounce, 23
missile, 132
mission, 31
missionary, 145
Mississippi, 119
Missouri, 119
misspell, 23
mitigate, 96
mobility, 174
mobilize, 38
modernize, 38
modulation, 140
moisten, 39, 70
molecular, 34
momentary, 106
momentous, 106
monarch, 25
monastery, 36
monetary, 169
monogamy, 25
monograph, 160
monotony, 25
monotype, 161
Montana, 120
Montgomery, 119
Montpelier, 120
moral, 102
morale, 102
morning, 89
mortgage, 172
mortuary, 36
mosque, 145
motif, 85, 139
motivation, 174
motorcycle, 155
mourning, 89
M.S.T., 122
mulch, 166
mundane, 93
municipal, 129
muslin, 167
mutual, 171

N

naphtha, 69
narrative, 137
Nashville, 120
naturalism, 138
naturalization, 129
nautical, 177
navigator, 176
nearer, 41
Nebraska, 120
necessary, 94
negligee, 151
negligence, 171
negotiable, 169
negotiation, 174
network, 159
neutron, 133
Nevada, 120
New Hampshire, 120
New Jersey, 120
New Mexico, 120
New Orleans, 83
New York, 120
newscaster, 159
newsprint, 160
Niagara Falls, 83
niche, 69
Nobel, Alfred, 82
noblesse oblige, 85
nocturne, 140
nominee, 130
North Carolina, 120
North Dakota, 120
notable, 33
notary, 36
noted, 105
notorious, 105
novel, 137
novelist, 138
nucleus, 133
numerical, 134
numismatist, 153
nylon, 167

O

obedient, 35
object, 77
obliterate, 94
observance, 28
obsolete, 95
obviate, 94
obvious, 93
occasion, 31
occasional, 116
occupant, 35
occurrence, 116
oculist, 150
official, 79
Ohio, 120
Oklahoma, 120
Oklahoma City, 120
oligarchy, 128
Olympia, 120
Olympics, 154
Omar Khayyam, 82
omission, 31, 117
opera, 140
operetta, 140
opponent, 35
optical scanner, 134
option, 170
optometrist, 150
oratorio, 140
orbit, 132
orchard, 166
ordinance, 101, 130
ordnance, 101
Oregon, 120
original, 79
originator, 29
ornithologist, 153
orthodontist, 150
orthodox, 145
otherwise, 40
output, 134
overhead, 175

P

pagoda, 145
palette, 153
pamphlet, 160
panelist, 159
pantomime, 139
parachute, 177
parallel, 116
paralyze, 38
parity, 169
parliament, 75
parsimonious, 94
particular, 34
partner, 107
pas de deux, 139
passable, 33
passport, 156
pasture, 166
patient, 115
patronage, 130
payable, 165
peculiar, 34
pedagogue, 142
Pennsylvania, 120
pension, 170
per annum, 84
percale, 167
per capita, 84
perceive, 114
per diem, 85
performance, 28
periscope, 177
permanent, 35
permission, 31
permit, 78
pernicious, 95
perpetual, 117
perquisite, 105
per se, 85
persecute, 99
persistent, 35
personal, 100
personnel, 100, 174

perspective, 105
Ph.D., 122
Philadelphia, 83
philatelist, 153
philharmonic, 140
Philippines, 83
philosophize, 38
Phoenix, 119
photogenic, 148
photographer, 41
photography, 153
physician, 150
physics, 143
physiology, 143
pica, 161
picket, 174
picture, 69
pier, 114
pierce, 114
Pierre, 120
pirouette, 139
Pittsburgh, 121
plagiarize, 138
plaid, 167
plaintiff, 102
plaintive, 102
planet, 132
plankton, 135
platform, 130
plausible, 106
playwright, 148
pleasant, 35
plurality, 105
plutonium, 133
pneumonia, 70
podiatrist, 150
poetry, 137
pointillism, 139
polar, 34
policy, 171
politician, 31
polo, 154
polygamy, 25
polytheism, 25

popular, 34
porous, 96
portfolio, 170
possession, 31
possessor, 29
practicable, 100
practical, 100
pragmatism, 96
Prague, 83
prairie, 166
precarious, 96
precaution, 26
precede, 26, 100
precedence, 26, 100
precinct, 129
preclude, 94
precocious, 26
preconception, 26
predecessor, 26
preeminent, 26
prejudice, 75
premises, 172
premium, 171
preparatory, 36
prerequisite, 105, 142
prerogative, 130
prescription, 75
present, 78
presidential, 129
prettier, 41
priest, 114
prior, 117
proceed, 100
produce, 77
productivity, 174
professor, 144
program, 134
programmer, 134, 164
project, 78
promissory, 36
promotion, 175
promptly, 40
pronunciation, 158
proof, 161

propaganda, 128
propellant, 132
propeller, 176
prophecy, 99
prophesy, 99
proprietor, 29, 165
propulsion, 177
prosecute, 99
prospective, 105
prospectus, 161
protector, 29
protégé, 85
pro tempore, 85
protocol, 128
proton, 133
Providence, 120
proxy, 130
pseudonym, 75
P.S.T., 122
psychiatrist, 150
psychologist, 150
psychology, 143
ptomaine, 150
Pulitzer, Joseph, 82
pun, 138
punched card, 134
punishment, 30
purchaser, 41
purser, 156

Q

quantity, 69
quarrelsome, 94
quarterback, 154
quartet, 140
questionnaire, 158
quicken, 39
quicker, 41
quiet, 100, 115
quietly, 40
quitclaim, 172
quite, 100
quorum, 129
quote, 104

R

racquet, 155
radar, 176
radiator, 29
radioactivity, 133
radiogram, 158
ragout, 149
rain, 91
raison d'être, 84
Raleigh, 120
raspberry, 75
rayon, 167
R.&D., 122
reactionary, 36
realism, 139
real-time, 134
realtor, 164, 172
rebel, 80
recall, 130
receipt, 114
receivable, 165
recess, 78
reciprocity, 130
recital, 140
recognize, 38
recollection, 31
recommend, 116
reconcile, 21
recondite, 93
record, 80
recover, 21
redeem, 21
redemption, 170
reduction, 31
reelect, 21
re entry, 132
referee, 154
referendum, 130
refinement, 30
reform, 21
registrar, 144
regulatory, 36
rehearsal, 139
reign, 91

reins, 115
reinstate, 21
release, 160
relieve, 114
remembrance, 73
remind, 21
reminder, 41
remunerate, 106
rendezvous, 85
repetition, 31
replacement, 21
reply, 105
representative, 128
reprint, 77
reproduce, 21
republic, 128
reputation, 107
rescind, 75, 96
residence, 28
resident, 35
respectable, 33
respectfully, 100
respectively, 100
restful, 106
restive, 106
restrain, 93
restriction, 31
résumé, 84
retaliate, 39
retailer, 175
retrieve, 94
reunion, 21
revenue, 170
reverence, 28
revive, 94
revolutionary, 36
revue, 148
reward, 93
rhapsody, 140
rhetoric, 143
Rhode Island, 120
rhythm, 117
Richmond, 120
rider, 171
Rio de Janeiro, 83

rite, 89
Roanoke Island, 83
Roosevelt,
	Franklin D., 82
rough, 69
royalty, 161
ruinous, 95
R.S.V.P., 122

S

Sacramento, 119
sacred, 73
sacrilegious, 75
saga, 137
Saigon, 83
St. Paul, 119
Salem, 120
salesman, 164
Salk, Jonas, 82
salmon, 75
Salt Lake City, 120
San Francisco, 121
sanitary, 36
sans, 85
Santa Fe, 120
sarcasm, 95
satellite, 132
satin, 167
satire, 138
sauerkraut, 149
sauté, 149
savoir faire, 85
scarcely, 107
scenario, 148
scenery, 36
Schenectady, 121
scholarship, 144
Schweitzer, Albert, 82
science, 143
scintillate, 70
scoop, 160
scrimmage, 154
script, 159
scriptures, 145

scuba, 135
sculpture, 153
secular, 34
security, 170
sedentary, 36
seed, 91
seersucker, 167
semantics, 158
semester, 142
semiannual, 25
semicircle, 25
semidetached, 25
seminar, 144
semiprecious, 25
senator, 29, 129
separate, 39, 80
sequel, 138
Sequoia National Pk., 83
serge, 89, 167
serial, 89
sermon, 145
session, 89
sextant, 156
Shakespeare, Wm., 82
shareholder, 170
shot-put, 155
shriek, 114
sidewise, 40
siege, 114
sight, 90
signature, 161
silence, 28
similar, 34
simile, 138
simpler, 41
sin, 104
singular, 34
site, 90
skeet, 153
skiing, 153
skillfully, 40
skin diving, 155
slalom, 154
slander, 127
sleigh, 115

slower, 41
smoother, 41
smorgasbord, 149
snobbery, 36
snorkel, 155
soccer, 154
society, 115
sociology, 143
Socrates, 82
software, 134
solder, 70
soliloquy, 138
solvency, 170
sonar, 135
sonnet, 137
sooner, 41
soufflé, 149
South Carolina, 120
South Dakota, 120
spaghetti, 149
specie, 169
species, 114
Spokane, 121
sponsor, 159
Springfield, 119
stadium, 154
staging, 132
stair, 89
stake, 89
Stalin, Josef, 82
standardize, 38
stare, 89
stationary, 90
stationery, 90
statistics, 143
stature, 106
status quo, 84
statute, 106
steak, 89
steerage, 156
stereophonic, 159
stern, 156
stet, 161
steward, 156
stewardess, 176

stockholder, 165
stole, 151
storage, 134
strength, 74
strengthen, 39
stupor, 94
subcommittee, 24
subdivision, 172
subdued, 24
subject, 80
subjugate, 24
sublet, 172
submarine, 24
submerge, 24
submit, 24
subordinate, 24
subpoena, 127
subscribe, 24
subsequent, 117
subsidy, 166
subsoil, 24
subtle, 70, 75
subway, 24, 177
suede, 151
sufficient, 115
summarize, 38
supersonic, 177
surf-riding, 155
surge, 89
surprise, 105
survivor, 171
susceptible, 33
suture, 135
sword, 69
syllabus, 142
symmetry, 116
sympathy, 93
symphony, 140
synagogue, 145
synchronize, 38

T

table d'hôte, 149
taciturn, 96

Tacoma, 121
taffeta, 167
Tallahassee, 119
technical, 142
technician, 31, 164
technicolor, 148
Tel Aviv, 83
telecast, 159
telegenic, 159
telegram, 158
telephone, 158
teleplay, 159
temerity, 96
tempera, 139
temperament, 74
temperature, 74
temperance, 28
temperate, 93
temporary, 36
temporize, 38
Tennessee, 120
tennis, 155
Terre Haute, 121
testimony, 107
tête-à tête, 84
Texas, 120
Thant, U, 82
theater, 148
theology, 145
theory, 74
thesis, 142
thief, 114
thrust, 132
tighten, 39
tonnage, 177
topcoat, 151
Topeka, 119
torte, 149
tourist, 156
tournament, 155
towards, 69
tracer, 133
trademark, 175
tragedy, 148
transaction, 175

transfer, 77
transient, 117
transistor, 159
transmitter, 159
transoceanic, 156
treatise, 137
Trenton, 120
triangle, 25
triennial, 25
trilogy, 138
tripod, 25
trisect, 25
trivial, 96
trophy, 154
trousseau, 151
truckage, 177
trust, 170
tuition, 144
turnpike, 177
tuxedo, 151
typographical, 161

U

ultimately, 117
umbrella, 73
umpire, 154
U.N., 122
unaffected, 24
unanimous, 128
unavoidable, 24
uncertain, 24
unclaimed, 24
unconscious, 24
underwriter, 164, 171
undivided, 24
uneventful, 24
unfavorable, 24
university, 144
unlike, 24
unnecessary, 24
unusually, 40
upper case, 161
upward, 40
uranium, 133

urban, 130
U.S.S.R., 122
usurious, 169
Utah, 120

V

vacation, 174
vacillate, 39
valedictorian, 142
valuable, 33
variegate, 74
variety, 115
vault, 169
vegetable, 74
vehicle, 75
vehicular, 34
vein, 115
velocity, 177
velvet, 167
vendor, 175
venerable, 33
verifier, 134
Vermont, 120
via, 177

vice versa, 84
vicissitude, 117
video, 159
Virginia, 120
virtuoso, 139
visa, 156
visibility, 177
visitor, 29
visualize, 38
vitalize, 38
vocabulary, 158
vocation, 174
vocational, 142
volleyball, 155
vs., 122
vulgar, 34

W

waive, 91
waiver, 171
warrant, 127
Washington, 120
Washington, D.C., 120
wave, 91

waybill, 177
weaken, 39
weather, 102
weaving, 153
Wednesday, 75
weigh, 115
West Virginia, 120
whether, 102
wholesale, 175
wield, 114
Wisconsin, 120
worsted, 151
wrench, 70
wrestling, 153
wright, 99
wring, 70
Wyoming, 120

Y

yield, 114
Yosemite, 83

Z

ZIP Code, 158